INVESTMENT INCENTIVES AND PERFORMANCE REQUIREMENTS

Patterns of International Trade, Production, and Investment

Stephen E. Guisinger and Associates

PRAEGER SPECIAL STUDIES • PRAEGER SCIENTIFIC

New York • Philadelphia • Eastbourne, UK
Toronto • Hong Kong • Tokyo • Sydney

Library of Congress Cataloging in Publication Data

Guisinger, Stephen E.
Investment incentives and performance requirements.

Includes index.
1. Investments, Foreign—Addresses, essays, lectures.
2. Investments, Foreign—Government policy—Addresses,
essays, lectures. 3. International business enterprises
—Addresses, essays, lectures. I. Title.
HG4538.G755 1985 332.6'73 84-26374
ISBN 0-03-002443-9 (alk. paper)

The World Bank does not accept responsibility for the views expressed
herein, which are those of the authors and should not be attributed
to the World Bank or to its affiliated organizations. The findings, inter-
pretations, and conclusions are the results of research supported by
the Bank; they do not necessarily represent official policy of the Bank.

Published and Distributed by the
Praeger Publishers Division
(ISBN Prefix 0-275)
of Greenwood Press, Inc.,
Westport, Connecticut

Published in 1985 by Praeger Publishers
CBS Educational and Professional Publishing
a Division of CBS Inc.
521 Fifth Avenue, New York, NY 10175 USA

© 1985 by The International Bank for Reconstruction
and Development/The World Bank

56789 052 987654321

Printed in the United States of America
on acid-free paper

Preface

This study of direct foreign investment incentives and performance requirements was authorized by the Board of Executive Directors of the World Bank in September 1981. The authorization called for a team of consultants, under the supervision of the International Finance Corporation (IFC), to examine the policies of governments and companies toward direct foreign investment in both developed and developing countries. The Development Department of IFC was designated to organize and supervise the study.

The study team, led by Stephen Guisinger of the University of Texas at Dallas, began work in February 1982 and carried out field work between June and October 1982. Neil Hood and Stephen Young of the University of Strathclyde, Glasgow, studied the automobile industry. Robert R. Miller of the University of Houston studied the computer industry. R. Hal Mason of the University of California at Los Angeles studied the food products industry. H. Peter Gray of Rutgers University and Ingo Walter of New York University studied the petrochemical industry. Michel Amsalem of Columbia University and Dennis Encarnation and Louis T. Wells, Jr., of Harvard University conducted the country studies. Eric W. Bond of Pennsylvania State University prepared a methodological study.

An advisory board, consisting of representatives of the governments of India, Peru, the Philippines, Switzerland, the United Kingdom, and the United States, offered suggestions on the scope and methodology of the study and helped establish guidelines for the study team to use in interviewing company and government representatives.

Development Department staff gathered some data on foreign investment policies for the study team, helped team members contact appropriate government officials, and provided valuable comments and advice. Raymond Vernon of Harvard University, Donald T. Lessard of Massachusetts Institute of Technology (MIT), and Joseph Grieco of Duke University also provided valuable counsel.

The study would not have been possible without the candor, patience, and interest of the government officials and corporate executives who consented to be interviewed.

v

Introduction

OBJECTIVES AND ORGANIZATION OF THE STUDY

Scope

The principal aim of this study is to assess the intensity of competition among countries for foreign direct investment and to determine the effectiveness of incentives and performance requirements in altering the investment and operational decisions of foreign investors. The foreign investment policies of host countries and the foreign investment decision-making processes of corporations are complex subjects. Competition is only one of many influences that shape host country policies, and incentives are but one set of factors among many that investors weigh in their decisions. To measure the role of competition and incentives in the decisions of countries and corporations, it is necessary to examine the processes by which governments formulate and implement investment policies — their objectives, resources, and policy options — and to determine the relative importance of policy and other factors in corporate investment decisions.

Few issues of importance to both developed and developing countries are as hard to analyze as foreign investment. Governments have a wide and extremely diverse set of concerns that must be weighed in setting foreign investment policies. Governments want to maximize their benefits from direct foreign investment and to minimize their costs. Determining the net benefit accruing from foreign investment is almost impossible because benefits and costs are numerous and diverse and occur unevenly across different social and income classes, imposing uncomfortable political choices on governments. Moreover, judgments about costs and benefits tend to be subjective and hence hard to measure. Compounding these difficulties are the facts that there are a limited number of foreign investment projects and that they are internationally mobile. Foreign investors can, to some extent, choose from among a number of alternative host country locations. In effect, host countries compete for a share in the "market" for foreign investment projects.

Corporations, too, weigh diverse concerns in their decisions involving foreign investments. Firms compare the returns on foreign investments with the risks, which often appear greater than for home country investments and which are always hard to quantify. The benefits from overseas operations arise from the financial, production, and marketing advantages provided by the market size, location, and economic resources of host countries. Against these benefits, however, must be weighed a number of costs, among them the managerial problems of coordinating affiliates in several countries. As with country policies, corporate investment strategies are made in a competitive and interdependent environment. The investment decisions of one competitor can set off a series of investment moves by rivals, adding a game theoretic dimension to an already complicated process of netting benefits against costs. Thus, the analyst must weigh the importance of host country policies, such as incentives, against an array of economic and strategic factors.

Analytical Approach

To simplify and interpret the data collected during the course of the study, this report draws, in part, on recent work in corporate strategy. The application of concepts of competitive strategy to the analysis of corporate international investment decisions is not new: a sizeable body of research suggests that corporations undertake investments not only on the basis of the financial merits of proposed projects, but also after a thorough analysis of the likely moves and countermoves of competitors if the project is undertaken.

Some of the concepts and theories derived from research on corporate strategy can be applied to the analysis of national foreign investment policies. Just as corporations use pricing, advertising, and other devices to achieve maximum advantage in the markets in which they operate, countries use incentives and other inducements to increase their share of new foreign investment projects.

But there are important differences between corporate and country strategies. Strategy is the most important contributor to the profitability of most corporations — indeed, to their survival. For a country, however, strategy is not the only, or even the most important, determinant of its ability to attract foreign investors. Investments are made on the basis of natural, geographic, political, and other considerations, and incentives may only marginally affect the share of foreign investments attracted to the country. For some countries, variations in strategy will have little influence on the volume or type of investments attracted; for others, variations can have significant influence. This study aimed to discover how much influence the variations in strategy have had and to assess how governments have adapted strategies to factors, such as size of population, location, and stage of industrial development which lie outside their immediate control.

This study makes no attempt to judge the appropriateness or to weigh the welfare implications of the strategies of individual countries. The study compares and contrasts strategies, using the features of strategies common to all countries as the major points of comparison.

ORGANIZATION OF THE STUDY

The study team gathered information on foreign investment policies of countries and foreign investment decisions of companies from interviews with corporate executives and government officials. The four industries that were intensively analyzed — automobiles, computers, food products, and petrochemicals — were chosen because they offered a diverse set of characteristics from the point of view of technology, scale requirements, and raw material dependency. The team selected the major firms in each industry and conducted interviews in the home offices of companies agreeing to participate in the study.

The company interviews produced information on a sample of recent foreign investment decisions. The study team collected information on a broad range of issues affecting each decision. For each investment project selected, team members asked corporate executives about alternative sites considered and the importance of host country policy variables in the decision to locate in a specific country. The team compiled a list of incentives and disincentives affecting each investment case. In all, more than 30 companies were interviewed, from which more than 70 investment decisions spread over 20 host countries were selected.

In choosing countries for intensive review, the team attempted to ensure the greatest possible overlap between the countries acting as hosts for the investment projects identified in the industry studies and the countries selected for the country studies. At the same time, it was important that countries of different sizes, income levels, and geographical regions be adequately represented. Limitations of time and resources available to the study precluded larger industry and country samples. Included in the sample were developed and developing countries from Europe, Africa, South Asia, and Latin America.

To ensure the comparability of data collected by different members of the study team, all team members used a common interview guide for collecting information on investment policies in the selected countries. In each country, team members interviewed government officials from agencies involved in the formulation and implementation of foreign investment policy. To determine how government policies affected plant operations, team members also held meetings with managers of foreign subsidiaries operating in the host countries, including a number of affiliates of firms included in the industry studies.

This book contains the summary report and the four industry studies. The summary report, Chapter 1, synthesizes the findings of the industry studies concerning the effectiveness of investment incentives and performance requirements and also examines the nature of national strategies to attract and control foreign investment. The industry studies, Chapters 2-5, review in detail the impact of investment incentives and performance requirements on corporate investment decisions, using the survey of multinational executives as their primary data base. A short summary of the primary conclusions is found in Chapter 6.

Foreign investment normally encompasses both portfolio and direct investment. Because this study focuses exclusively on direct investment, the term foreign investment in this book excludes portfolio investment. In addition, because the study did not examine the motivation or locational preferences of public-sector foreign investors, foreign investment is understood to refer only to private foreign investment. Finally, policy interventions can serve to attract investors (incentives) or discourage them (disincentives). Only the rather awkward term *distortions* groups incentives and disincentives together. This study occasionally uses *incentives* in a broad sense that includes disincentives as what they truly are, negative incentives.

Contents

1

A Comparative Study of Country Policies

Stephen E. Guisinger

INCENTIVES AND DISINCENTIVES TO FOREIGN INVESTMENT

The first step in examining the intensity of competition for investment and the effectiveness of incentives is to describe the policy instruments that governments use to attract and control foreign investors. If governments used only a small number of incentives and disincentives, it would be relatively easy to examine the degree of competition among countries and the effectiveness of government policy. The list of incentive and disincentive instruments, however, is very long, and estimating the net impact of all of these instruments on the profitability of foreign investments is hard, especially because the costs of some of the instruments to government and the benefits to investors are difficult to calculate.

Table 1-1 organizes incentives and disincentives according to their effects on a firm's income statement. The study team encountered most of these incentives and disincentives during the field research; some instruments used in countries not covered in the sample were included to show the range of government instruments applied to foreign investment projects. In this classification, instruments are categorized by whether they affect the revenues of the firm (category I), its input costs (category II), or the components of its value-added (category III). An instrument in any one of these categories will affect the after-tax return to owners' equity. For example, in category I, tariffs on competing imports that increase

1

TABLE 1-1
Classification of Incentives and Disincentives

Incentives/Disincentives	Effect on After-Tax Return on Owner's Equity
Affecting Revenues	
Tariffs	+
Differential sales/excise taxes	+ or −
Export taxes/subsidies (including income tax credits)	+ or −
Quotas	+
Export minimums	−
Price controls (or relief from)	+ or −
Multiple exchange rates	+ or −
General overvaluation of currency	−
Government procurement preference	+
Production/capacity controls	+
Guarantees against government competition	+
Prior import deposits	+
Transfer price administration	−
Affecting Inputs	
Tariffs	−
Differential sales taxes (and exemptions therefrom)	+ or −
Export taxes/subsidies (including utilities)	+ or −
Quotas	−
Price controls	+
Multiple exchange rates	+ or −
Subsidy or tax for public-sector suppliers	+ or −
Domestic-content requirements (including R & D)	−
Prior import deposits	−
Transfer price administration	−
Limits on royalties, fees	−
Multiple deductions for tax purposes	+
Cash or in-kind grants for R & D	+
Affecting Components of Value-added	
Capital	
Direct subsidy	
Cash grant	+
Tax credits/investment allowances — Specify if reduces book value:	+
Subsidized leasing — taxable or not	+

Continued

Table 1-1, continued

Incentives/Disincentives	Effect on After-Tax Return on Owner's Equity
Affecting Components of Value added, continued	
Cost of capital goods	
Tariff/sales tax exemption on imported/ domestic equipment	+
Prior import deposits	−
Local-content requirement for capital equipment	−
Limits on use of used equipment	−
Subsidized buildings	+
Subsidized cost of transportation	+
Cost of debt	
Subsidized loans	+
Loan guarantees	+
Covering of foreign exchange risks on foreign loans	+
Priority of access (including limitations on foreign firms)	+ or −
Cost of equity	
Subsidized equity through public investment agencies	+
Exemption from capital gains taxes/registration taxes	+
Dividend tax/waiver	+ or −
Guarantee against expropriation or differential treatment	+
Limitations on debt/equity ratio	−
Controls/taxes on remitted dividends	−
Minimum financial/in-kind ratio	−
Corporate tax	
Tax holiday/reductions	+
Accelerated depreciation	+
Special deductions and valuation practices (inflation adjustment; multiple plant consolidation)	+
Tax sparing and double-taxation agreements	+
Loss-carry-forward provision	+ or −
Contractual stabilization of rates	+
Labor	
Wage subsidies (including indirect, i.e., multiple deductions of wages for tax computations/reduction of taxes on labor)	+

Continued

Table 1-1, continued

Incentives/Disincentives	Effect on After-Tax Return on Owner's Equity
Affecting Components of Value-added, continued	
Training grants	+
Minimum wage	−
Relaxation of industrial relations laws	+
Local labor requirements	−
Land	
Cash subsidy for purchase/rental	+
Exemption/rebate of taxes on land	+
Not Classified	
Limitations on foreign ownership	
Free-trade zones	
General preinvestment assistance	
Countertrade requirements	
Foreign exchange balancing requirements	

Source: Study team interviews.

revenues will raise the rate of return. In category II, a quota on an imported input will tend to raise the price of inputs and, therefore, reduce the rate of return, assuming that the firm is not granted the quota and must pay the market price. And a tax holiday in category III will increase after-tax returns by the amount of the taxes saved. The direction of the effect of the policy on the after-tax return to owners' equity is indicated by a plus or a minus. Some instruments included in Table 1-1 — loan guarantees, for example — do not actually affect expected returns but instead reduce risk (the variance of returns). For simplicity, the value of the risk reduction created by these instruments is treated as an increase to a project's expected return.

The list of incentives observed in the sample countries is shown in Table 1-2. This list includes policies that these countries have employed at some point during the past five years and thus represents the portfolio of available incentives and disincentives that a country can draw on to attract and control foreign investments. There are a number of similarities and dissimilarities among the

TABLE 1-2
Incentives and Disincentives of Countries Surveyed

Incentives/Disincentives	Country									
	A	B	C	D	E	F	G	H	I	J
Affecting Revenues										
Tariffs	x	x	x	x	x		x	x	x	x
Differential sales/excise taxes										
Export taxes/subsidies (including income tax credits)	x	x	x	x	x	x				x
Quotas	x	x	x	x	x					x
Export minimums	x	x	x	x			x			
Price controls (or relief from)	x	x	x	x	x			x		x
Multiple exchange rates										
General overvaluation of currency	x	x					x		x	x
Government procurement preference		x								
Production/capacity controls	x		x				x			x
Guarantees against government competition										
Prior import deposits										
Transfer price administration	x	x		x		x	x	x	x	x
Affecting Inputs										
Tariffs	x	x					x	x	x	x
Differential sales taxes (and exemptions therefrom)										
Export taxes/subsidies	x	x								x
Quotas	x	x								x

Continued

5

Table 1-2, continued

	Country									
Incentives/Disincentives	*A*	*B*	*C*	*D*	*E*	*F*	*G*	*H*	*I*	*J*
Affecting Inputs, continued										
Price controls	x	x								x
Multiple exchange rates/overvaluation	x	x								
Subsidy or tax for public sector-suppliers	x	x	x	x						
Domestic-content requirements (including R & D)	x	x	x	x	x					x
Prior import deposits										
Transfer price administration	x	x	x	x	x	x				x
Limits on royalties, fees	x	x	x	x	x					x
Multiple deductions for tax purpose										
Cash or in-kind grants for R & D			x	x	x	x	x	x	x	
Affecting Components of Value-added										
Capital										
Direct subsidy										
Cash grant										
Tax credits/investment allowances	x		x	x		x	x	x		x
Subsidized leasing		x				x	x	x	x	
Cost of capital goods										
Tariff/sales tax exemption on imported/domestic equipment	x				x	x	x	x	x	
Prior import deposits	x	x								
Local-content requirement for capital equipment	x	x								x

Limits on use of used equipment	x	x							
Subsidized buildings	x	x				x		x	
Subsidized cost of transportation							x	x	x
Cost of debt									
Subsidized loans	x		x	x	x	x	x	x	x
Loan guarantees								x	
Covering of foreign exchange risks on foreign loans				x		x	x	x	x
Priority of access (including limitations on foreign firms)		x							x
Cost of equity									
Subsidized equity through public investment agencies		x		x	x	x	x	x	x
Exemption from capital gains taxes/registration taxes		x					x		x
Dividend tax/waiver			x				x		
Guarantee against expropriation or differential treatment				x					
Limitations on debt/equity ratio	x	x		x		x	x	x	x
Controls/taxes on remitted dividends		x							x
Minimum financial/in-kind ratio									
Corporate tax									
Tax holiday/reductions	x	x	x		x	x	x	x	x
Accelerated depreciation	x	x				x	x	x	x
Special deductions and valuation practices (inflation)									x
Tax sparing and double-taxation agreements									x
Loss-carry-forward provision	x	x			x	x	x	x	x
Contractual stabilization of rates									

Continued

Table 1-2, continued

Incentives/Disincentives	Country									
	A	B	C	D	E	F	G	H	I	J
Affecting Components of Value-added, continued										
Labor										
Wage subsidies										
Training grants	x	x				x	x		x	x
Minimum wage	x	x	x		x	x				x
Relaxation of industrial relations laws										
Local labor requirements	x	x	x	x	x					
Land										
Cash subsidy to purchase/rental										
Exemption/rebate of taxes on land								x	x	x
Not Classified										
Limitations on foreign ownership	x	x	x	x	x					x
Free-trade zones	x	x							x	
General preinvestment assistance										
Countertrade requirements									x	x
Foreign exchange balancing requirements	x									x

Source: Study team interviews.

country portfolios; the following section examines the factors that influence each country's mix of incentive instruments. A number of areas of concern made apparent by the country portfolios in Table 1-2 are discussed further in subsequent sections and only outlined briefly here.

Variety of Instruments

One area of concern is the diverse array of instruments countries use to attract and control foreign investments. Governments often have multiple objectives for foreign investment projects related to regional priorities, balance of payments, employment, ownership, and the like. Because the number of instruments appears far greater than the number of objectives sought, however, these questions arise: does the competitive process itself stimulate the wide variety of instruments, and to what extent do instruments substitute for one another? If, for example, a subsidized loan and a tariff have the same effect on the project's rate of return, are the two instruments substitutes in the eyes of investors?

Commodity and Factor Protection

The choice between commodity and factor forms of protection is another area of concern. Traditionally, *protection* has been used to refer to tariffs and quotas that raise project profitability by restricting imports. But direct subsidies can have the same effect on project returns as tariffs and quotas. Protection, in its broadest sense, simply means providing relative advantage through government intervention. Government intervention can alter the prices of goods and services purchased or sold by a firm, or can alter the prices of the factors of production — land, labor, and capital — employed by the firm. This book refers to incentives in the first category as *instruments of commodity protection* and to incentives in the second category as *instruments of factor protection*.

There is some substitution between these two broad categories, but it is not perfect. Some examples of factor protection, such as tax holidays and accelerated depreciation, depend for their effectiveness on a positive rate of profitability, whereas commodity protection can generate profitability independently. Yet, over a broad range of incentive instruments, governments have a choice between commodity and factor forms of protection with quite different implications for the distribution of costs and benefits among various groups in society.

Administration

Another area of concern suggested by the policy portfolios is management. Some of the countries surveyed have as many as 30 incentives and disincentives that affect the profitability of foreign investments. Can these be coordinated to ensure that the proper net incentive is provided to foreign investment? And what is the appropriate organizational structure to achieve efficiency in implementing foreign investment strategies? In some of the countries surveyed, administration of incentives is centralized and closely coordinated; in others, administration is decentralized and only loosely coordinated.

Linkages

Still another concern is the degree to which incentives are linked to performance and other requirements. For example, one country in the sample provides investment credits only to petrochemical investors willing to locate in certain regions of the country and willing to export a minimum of 30 percent of output for a period of three years. Some countries accomplish linking indirectly. One of the countries surveyed has no formal export requirements but awards incentives on a discretionary basis; a pattern of preference for export-oriented projects is apparent in the levels of incentives granted to different firms.

The study team found that the intensity of competition among countries for foreign investment was an important determinant of policy choices in each of these areas of concern. It was hard to explain a country's foreign investment strategy without taking into account the type of competitors it faced and the strategies that competitor countries deployed.

COMPETITION FOR FOREIGN INVESTMENT

This section examines two important questions about competition among countries for foreign investment: first, does competition exist; second, if it exists, how intense is it? In brief the study team found that competition varies with the market.

Existence of Competition

Competition among countries to attract foreign investment can be compared with competition among producers for market shares. Competition for foreign investment consists of the independent actions of countries to attract a socially profitable volume of foreign investment in the face of offers from other countries with similar attributes. That this competition exists at least among some countries of the world seems beyond dispute. The study uncovered many instances of countries seeking to attract foreign investors through generous incentive packages. Not only did some of these countries act independently of one other, but some bidding for certain projects took place as governments raised their incentives in response to competitive bids from other countries. To avoid the appearance of head-on competition, governments generally conduct low-key and indirect bidding, but the evidence gathered from the interviews with government officials clearly indicates that many countries view themselves in competition with other countries for foreign investments.

Many of the actions of government officials, apart from bidding on specific projects, also appeared consistent with competitive behavior. Some countries regularly collect data about the incentives rival countries offer. Interviews with officials of countries in the Economic Communities (EC) revealed considerable knowledge of incentive packages offered for specific projects by other members. Furthermore, some countries adopted incentive instruments designed more with an eye to the policies of other countries than to needs of the firms to be attracted. One officer of an industrial promotion agency stated that the main purpose of his country's cash grant program was to put the country in a position to meet competitive offers from other countries. In addition, there appears to be a "follow-the-leader" pattern in the introduction of new incentives and means of promoting new foreign investments. It would be hard to argue that the diversity of incentive instruments maintained by many of the surveyed countries (see Table 1-2) stemmed solely from their desire to meet the needs of investors and were designed and adopted without stimulus from the adoption of similar instruments by rival countries. In sum, evidence that at least some countries compete at least some of the time is abundant and beyond reasonable doubt. Existence of competition, of course, begs the second question: how intense — and extensive — is it?

Determinants of Competitive Intensity

The intensity of competition in any market arises from the structure of the market: the number, strength, and objectives of competitors, and the alternatives available to achieve the objectives. Although no formal "market" for foreign investments exists, countries competing to attract foreign investors act, in many ways, as if there were one. It is useful to draw an analogy between product markets, in which producers compete for market shares of consumer expenditures, and investment "markets," in which countries compete for market shares of new foreign investment ventures.

For the countries included in the survey, the market analogy can be further refined by asserting that, in fact, three separate "markets" for foreign investments exist: one for investments oriented toward the domestic market of a single host country, one for investments oriented toward countries within a common market, and finally one for investments to produce for the worldwide export market. Because the structure of each market differs substantially from the structure of others, the intensity of competition in each market varies widely. Table 1-3 shows that distribution of investment projects in the sample survey among these three markets.

The market for domestically oriented investments is a bilateral market between capital-exporting and capital-importing countries; almost one-half the projects included in the study fell into this first category. The projects in this category are designed solely or principally to serve the internal markets of their host countries; host countries face no direct competition from other host countries for these investments. The second market consists of investments created to serve common market area, combining production for

TABLE 1-3
Distribution of Sample Projects by Industry and Market Orientation

Market Orientation	Automobiles	Petro-chemicals	Food Products	Computers	Total
Domestic	7	8	11	10	36
Common Market	5	3	4	14	26
Worldwide Export	0	4	1	7	12
Totals	12	15	16	31	74

Source: Industry studies.

host country consumption with production for export to other member countries. Roughly one-third of the projects studied fell into this category, but these were divided between two separate common markets that differed considerably in the extent to which true free trade was realized within the common market area. The third market is for investments designed to compete in world export trade, often associated with "export platforms" in developing countries but found in many countries around the world. Countries in the sample tended to operate predominantly in one of the three markets, but several operated in two simultaneously.

Firms seeking a plant location abroad can be characterized to some extent as "buyers," while countries that are possible sites for the investments can be characterized as "sellers." In a narrow sense, the "product" is the specific plant site offered by countries, but firms rarely evaluate a prospective foreign investment only, or even principally, in terms of the attributes of the plant site and its immediate surroundings. Of more fundamental concern to the firm are the general economic and political conditions and the current and anticipated policies of the host country.

Given the broad definition of products in the market for foreign investment, it is evident that countries have considered latitude to modify their product to capture whatever share they seek of the total supply of foreign investment projects available. Countries can "market" their product through advertisements and through "sales" offices abroad. They can modify the attributes of the product in both narrow and general senses. Industrial parks can be built with necessary services. Economic policies — exchange rates and tax and business laws — can be altered to make the host country more attractive to investors. Countries can also "price" their product by offering cash grants, tax rebates, and other inducements specifically to individual projects in association with the general incentives provided to all producers through trade, monetary, and fiscal policies. Governments can even practice price discrimination if they can discern the buyers' degree of interest and their alternatives. When competition is fierce, countries are likely to try all methods of product modification and pricing to achieve their objectives.

According to Michael Porter, five broad forces determine the intensity of competition in an industry.[1] Porter's analysis is limited to the market for products, but his analysis can be extended to encompass the market for foreign investment. The five forces arise from these sources: conditions among suppliers of inputs to the industry; the nature of the industry's customers — the buyers; potential entrants into the industry; substitutes for the industry's project; and the behavior of the firm's competitors already sharing the market. In the market for foreign investment, the most important is the last of these, the behavior of existing competitors.

Existing Competitors

Porter argues that seven characteristics of rivals and the structure of the market in which rivals interact determine the degree of competitive intensity. The following subsection examines how each of these characteristics describes behavior in the market for direct foreign investment. It is impossible to provide quantitative profiles for each of these characteristics, but Table 1-4 summarizes the qualitative evidence gathered from interviews in the countries in the sample. The results point to quite important differences in the level of competition experienced in each market.

Number and Balance of Competitors

The larger the number of competing countries and the more similar rival countries are in resources, objectives, and policy instruments, the more likely countries are to engage in close competition. Dissimilar countries are likely to be complementary rather than

TABLE 1-4
Factors Contributing to the Intensity of Competition, by Market Orientation

Characteristics Contributing to High Level of Market Competition	Presence in Market for Foreign Investment		
	Domestic	Common Market	Worldwide Export
1. Numerous and equally balanced competitors	No, bilateral	Yes, equally balanced	Yes, numerous
2. Slow growth in demand for product	No, moderate growth	Yes, few greenfield investments	No, moderate growth
3. High pressure for capacity utilization	Yes	Yes	Yes
4. Lack of product differentiation	No	Yes	No
5. Low switching costs for buyer	No, no alternative way for firms to serve market	Yes	Moderate
6. High exit barriers	No (depends on country size)	Yes	
7. High stakes	No, moderate	Yes	Moderate
Total impact on competition (Sum of effects of seven characteristics)	Low	High	Moderate

Source: Study team assessments based on published data and interviews with government officials.

competitive, seeking quite different types of foreign investment projects. A small number of competitors in an industry is normally associated with stability and only moderate forms of open competition. This characteristic was, by definition, not relevant for the countries in the sample that operated in the market for domestically oriented investments. But, the characteristic was very much present for the countries surveyed in the EC, in which members are numerous (approaching ten) and relatively well balanced in comparison with countries outside the EC. Those countries in the survey that participated in the worldwide export market faced numerous, but imbalanced competitors.

Slow Growth in Demand for Industry's Output

When the number and value of foreign investment projects rapidly expand, competition declines because governments are content with existing market shares. In contrast, when the flow of investment projects dries up, competition intensifies as each country strives to maintain the level of investment inflow by increasing its market share. Between 1977 and 1980, most of the countries competing in all three markets experienced a deceleration in the flow of new foreign direct investment, but this deceleration varied substantially between markets and countries. Information on numbers of new foreign investment projects is incomplete, but Department of Commerce data suggest a drop in "greenfield" investments (that is, new plants) by U.S. firms inside the EC over the period. EC countries in the survey generally expressed greater concern over the apparent decline in aggregate numbers of new foreign ventures than in other countries.

Pressure for Capacity Utilization

Firms have the option of running their plants at less than full capacity, but countries are committed to maintaining high levels of employment — that is, running the national "plant" at full capacity. Lacking the option of slack capacity, governments vie even more fervently for market share, especially in times of economic recession, in order to maintain full employment. Governments everywhere now face severe cyclical unemployment and have vowed to use public means to create new jobs.

Lack of Differentiation

Close similarities in products generate intense competition because buyers have few reasons other than price on which to base purchase decisions. For this reason, contiguous countries are more likely to be in competition than widely separated countries. Countries that have similar resources and markets attempt to differentiate their policies, as will be discussed later. Again, lack of differentiation does not apply to countries in the sample that attract primarily inward-oriented investments, but corporate investors regarded the EC countries surveyed as relatively homogeneous in the sense that alternative sites could be found in several EC countries. Within the EC, government officials tended to identify contiguous countries or regions as their most important competitors.

Low Switching Costs

If buyers in a market can switch easily from one seller to another, competition to retain customers will be intense. The lack of differentiation noted earlier contributes to low switching costs, but other factors are involved. One example of a high switching cost noted by several respondents during the industry interviews was a preference of U.S. firms to locate in the English-speaking regions of the EC. Yet, this preference was not true of U.S. firms in general, and corporations considered switching costs to be generally low in common markets because the market of any one member country can be served from all other member countries. Moreover, operations in different countries within the EC can be managed through one regional headquarters. In contrast, managers perceive countries that operate principally in the market for worldwide export investments to present higher costs of switching because they are so widely scattered around the globe and so varied in their economic environments.

High Exit Barriers

In the market for foreign investment, exit barriers are measured by the costs of not seeking foreign investments. Size and stage of development of the individual country appeared to be the two principal determinants of officials' views on the costs of exiting the market for foreign investment. Officials in small developed countries deemed the cost of not seeking foreign investment to be unacceptably high, whereas officials in large developing countries hosting inward-oriented investments had mixed views. Few denied the net economic gain, but some saw only a small net gain when domestic political costs of permitting multinational firms to operate in their countries were taken into consideration.

The values assigned in Table 1-4 to each characteristic for the three markets and the weights used to arrive at an overall assessment of competitive intensity for each market are very subjective. They are intended only to suggest that the structures of the three markets are very different and that the level of competition each country experiences is likely to vary by market type. Data collected by the study team support the conclusion that the highest degree of competition is found in common markets and the lowest degree in the market for domestically oriented investments.

Agencies responsible for foreign investment policy in countries engaged principally in the market for inward-directed foreign investments did not perceive their country to be in competition with agencies from other host countries. They also seldom had representatives abroad who actively solicited foreign investments, and they tended to regard negotiations with foreign investors as essentially a bilateral process. In contrast, officials from common market countries, especially the EC, frankly recognized that they were participating in a competitive process. These officials acknowledged that whereas investment incentives were designed primarily to channel domestic savings into priority areas, investment policies, at least at the margin, were influenced by competitor country policies. All EC countries have official representatives in major capital-exporting countries to identify prospective investors and provide information about their countries. Officials from countries participating in worldwide export also tended to perceive their countries to be in competition for foreign investment, but not to the same degree as officials from EC countries.

Governments' perceptions about competitive intensity were mirrored in the attitudes of the corporate officers surveyed. Firms planning investments oriented to a host country market did not expect competitive bids, whereas firms locating plants within the EC expected competitive bids as a matter of course. None of the company respondents mentioned solicitations from the inward-market-oriented countries, whereas personal calls from government representatives and mailings of marketing literature from investment promotion agencies of EC countries were commonplace.

Summary

All countries compete for foreign investment to some degree. Foreign investments are generally oriented toward one of three markets: the domestic market of a single host country, a common market, or one for investments to produce for the worldwide export market. The intensity of competition differs among these markets for the countries surveyed by the study team. Evidence for this difference in the intensity of competition was found in the perceptions of government officials interviewed, the levels of incentives offered, the numbers of competitive offers that projects received, and the forms in which incentives were extended.

The next section describes in greater detail the ways in which the intensity of competition that countries face shapes their strategies for attracting and controlling foreign investment.

NATIONAL FOREIGN INVESTMENT STRATEGIES

Competition limits and helps shape a country's strategy toward foreign investment. Just as corporations formulate and implement strategies designed to gain a relative advantage over competitors, governments select instruments to attract and control foreign investors with an eye to what competitor countries are doing. This section describes the ways in which countries have adapted competitive strategies to their objectives and resources.

Countries in the sample that faced little competition generally had a relatively small number of incentive instruments; preferred passive forms of incentives — for example, commodity protection — over more aggressive forms of factor protection, such as cash grants; and linked incentives with explicit performance requirements. In contrast, countries facing intense competition used multiple incentive instruments; made extensive use of factor incentives, especially

loans and grants; and imposed few explicit performance requirements. Some countries operated in two foreign investment markets
simultaneously; because competition in the two markets differed,
the countries offered different packages of incentives to investors in
each market.

Examination of country strategies revealed evidence of the
effects of competition with respect to every important aspect of host
country foreign investment policies. Competition naturally has a
greater influence in countries that depend on the inflow of foreign
capital for a substantial portion of domestic industrial investment.
For many countries, however, foreign investment plays only a minor
role in total capital formation in manufacturing; thus, investment
policies are designed primarily to increase and focus domestic investment. Yet, the effects of competition can be seen even in these
countries, although in a far less pronounced way than elsewhere.

Ten Elements of a Country's Competitive
Strategy toward Foreign Investment

The surveys of country policies found that ten principal elements
generally constitute a country's foreign investment strategy. Each
of these elements represents a particular aspect of investment policy.
Most of these elements can be quantified, if only in approximate
terms, and thus it is possible to assess the degree to which each
element is present for a particular country. For example, all the
countries in the sample provided incentives to foreign investors, but
in varying degrees. Thus, the incentive element in a country's investment policy can be described along a continuum from "low" to
"high." The profile made by variations in the degree to which each
of these ten elements is present defines each country's foreign
investment strategy. No two countries in the sample had identical
profiles. Yet, one can observe certain patterns that clarify the nature
of competition for foreign investment. The ten elements are:

1. Type of incentive offered: Commodity or factor protection
2. Price: Total net incentive offered
3. Explicit or implicit policies
4. Linking of incentives with disincentives
5. Variety of incentives

6. Selectivity: Industrial priorities
7. Discrimination among firms
8. Degree of promotion
9. Service: Provision of infrastructure to investors
10. Centralization of government authority

Table 1-5 indicates how each of these elements varied between large and small countries in the sample and between the three different market orientations for investment strategies. The discussion that follows explains the rationales of countries with respect to each of the strategic elements and to the influence of competitors' strategies on policy selection. The assessments of each element reported in Table 1-5 represent an average for countries in the study. These averages hide some of the variations between individual country policies. The successful strategies of individual countries probably do not conform to the average. Yet, by distilling foreign investment strategies into these ten elements and grouping countries according to size and market orientation, it is possible to discern important differences that have a bearing on the intensity of competition for foreign investment. Each of the elements is described in some detail in the next ten subsections. Then some of the structural determinants of country strategies are examined.

Type of Incentive Offered: Commodity or Factor Protection

Countries can vary the mix of policies used to provide incentives to foreign investors by emphasizing commodity or factor protection. Most countries use both, but the mix of these policies varies substantially among countries and within countries across the three different markets for foreign investment in which a country participates. For example, in one large developing country that operated predominantly in the inward-oriented foreign investment market, commodity protection accounted for more than 80 percent of the total incentive provided (commodity plus factor protection). By comparison, one small developed country in the survey operating principally in the market for common market investments provided only 40 percent of its total protection through distortions in the prices of commodities. In general, a country chooses a mix of commodity and factor protection based on the effectiveness of incentives (which varies with their level and timing); international agreements

TABLE 1-5
Strategy Profiles by Size of Country and Market Orientation

Size of Country	Domestic[a]	Common Market	Worldwide Export
Small (1-10 million population)			
Commodity or factor protection		Factor	Factor
Price: Total net incentive		High	High
Explicit or implicit policies		Explicit	Explicit
Linking of incentives with disincentives		Limited	Very low
Variety of incentives		Very high	Very high
Selectivity: Industrial priorities		High	High
Discrimination among firms		High	High
Degree of promotion		High	High
Service: Provision of infrastructure		High	High
Centralization of government authority		High	High
Large (50+ million population)			
Commodity or factor protection	Commodity	Factor	Commodity and Factor
Price: Total net incentive	High	Moderate	Moderate
Explicit or implicit policies	Explicit	Implicit	Explicit
Linking of incentives with disincentives	High	Moderate	Moderate/Low
Variety of incentives	Low	Moderate	Moderate
Selectivity: Industrial priorities	Moderate	Moderate	Moderate
Discrimination among firms	High (with linking)	Moderate	Low
Degree of promotion	Low	Moderate	Moderate

Service: Provision of infrastructure	Low	Moderate	Moderate
Centralization of government authority	Low, but exceptions	Moderate	High

[a]Too few observations were available in small countries to form judgments about strength of various components for domestically oriented investments.

Source: Study team assessments based on surveys of government policies.

limiting commodity protection; and distribution of costs and benefits of the two types of protection.

Effectiveness of Incentives. Factor protection provides a much wider
range of choices in the time distribution of incentive benefits over
the life of the investment than do the various forms of commodity
protection. For example, officials of a number of companies mentioned that cash grants were attractive from several points of view.
Some countries offered nontaxable cash grants amounting to as
much as 60 percent of the proposed fixed investment. The availability of cash grants in the initial years not only reduced total
investment costs but also reduced cash injections from the parent
company – an important consideration for new, rapidly growing
firms that lack liquidity. Also, cash grants at the "front end" of an
investment are certain, whereas the benefits of commodity protection must be realized through profitable operations over a period of
years. Officials of several firms in the computer industry mentioned
that very little cash outlay was needed to launch a new investment
in the EC, largely because of generous front-end factor incentives.
In one case, only $500,000 of parent company funds was needed to
build and equip a $50 million facility, a feature the cash-strapped
parent company found very attractive.

Commodity protection was the principal instrument used by host
countries to attract investors to produce for the internal market.
For the worldwide export market, however, factor protection was
the principal means of providing incentives; with the sole exception of raw material price subsidies (typically on petroleum), commodity protection was totally absent from projects surveyed in the
market to produce for worldwide export.

International Agreements Limiting Commodity Protection. Where
agreements at the international or regional level limiting the use
of commodity protection exist, countries can often use factor
protection to maintain competitiveness without violating these
agreements. For example, developed countries found that factor
protection affords them the only opportunity to raise the level of
profitability of new investments in certain sectors of the economy
without violating the General Agreement on Tariffs and Trade
(GATT). Factor subsidies aimed directly at promoting exports
come under GATT's purview, but a number of more general factor

protection devices that raise the profitability of all industries, including those producing for export, are not specifically precluded by GATT agreements. Some of these general factor subsidies, however, do come under restrictions established by regional trading groups, such as the EC, and ceilings have been placed on the level of factor incentives that can be granted to new investments. The ceilings vary according to the development level of the subnational region, the highest ceilings applying to the least developed areas. All the countries studied participated in agreements that limited their use of commodity protection devices.

Distribution of the Costs and Benefits of the Two Forms of Protection. When provided by tariffs, commodity protection transfers income from consumers to government and producers — both existing producers and new investors entering the industry. In contrast, factor protection typically transfers income from taxpayers, who may not be consumers of the industry's products, to new investors, bypassing existing producers. These distinctions are not trivial. Officials of countries with cash grant programs emphasized that cash grants reduce redundancy by giving new investors only what is necessary to attract them. In contrast, tariff protection benefits the "free riders," those firms that would have produced with lower protection. But the benefits of discrimination among beneficiaries are gained at the cost of having to raise revenues through taxes, whereas the principal transfer produced by commodity protection occurs indirectly, outside the formal tax system. Because of the high visibility of cash grants, one of the countries surveyed recently experienced a lively public debate over the benefits and costs of its cash grant program. The issues were far more sharply defined than they would have been if the debate had been over the benefits and costs of tariff protection. These benefits and costs are harder for the average citizen to comprehend.

Price

In the market for foreign investments, the analogue of price in product markets is the net incentive that governments are willing to offer for new projects. This net incentive should include both commodity and factor forms of protection and be truly net — that is, the total incentive reduced by the value of all disincentives. Because of the variety of incentive and disincentive instruments, it is impossible to calculate a meaningful average net incentive for each country studied in the survey. Some of the EC countries surveyed had calculated the net cash equivalent of some of the incentives they offer, and these data show a slight upward trend during 1970-80. Some countries in the sample had clearly adopted an aggressive price strategy, stating frankly their intention to meet any competitive offer for a socially desirable project. These countries invariably practiced price discrimination, giving different net incentives to different firms. Other countries pursued a much more passive pricing role, offering incentives that, although sometimes relatively high, were automatic and relatively unvarying over time. The study team encountered one cash-grant-equivalent offer in the automobile industry that amounted to more than $75,000 per job created.

The use of pricing in foreign investment markets is obviously limited. First, the higher the price paid, the lower the social returns from any particular foreign investment project; in the extreme, negative social returns are possible. This possibility is increased when price policy is implemented through front-end factor protection, granted to investors at the beginning of the project. These incentives are hard to recoup if the project does not succeed. Back-end incentives may never need to be paid to unsuccessful projects.

A second limitation on the use of aggressive pricing policy is that it may ignite price competition. If all countries raise their prices in the same proportion, each will experience lower welfare (and foreign investors higher profitability) without a change in market share. A higher price in all countries may induce a higher aggregate level of investment from which all countries gain in proportion to their market shares, but no country gains relative to others. In the course of the study, officials of several governments reported that they analyzed social benefits and costs, including incentives, for at least major investment projects, but these analyses were not made available to the study team. It was, therefore, hard to determine whether competition had, in fact, driven the social return down to marginally acceptable, or to less than acceptable, levels. Certainly, the government officials interviewed were aware of the dangers of price wars.

Explicit or Implicit Policies

Most government incentives and disincentives to foreign investment take the form of explicit policies, but the study team found that some countries used implicit means of providing both incentives and disincentives. Implicit policies operate through the powers that host countries possess but do not always use. Sometimes the potential, rather than the actual, exercise of power affects the location decisions of investors. For example, the government of one country made it known to one of the computer companies surveyed that the government would find it much easier to purchase the company's products under public procurement if the company established a local plant. The company chose this country over several others because of the potential advantages of government sales.

Implicit policies are sometimes more generalized. Several of the location decisions in the automobile industry were strongly influenced by the host country's capacity to close off important markets to the companies. These companies believed that, from a long-term strategic point of view, they would be better off manufacturing in these countries even though current cost and demand conditions did not fully warrant an investment and the governments had not made any threats about limiting imports.

Linking of Incentives and Disincentives

Countries vary in the extent to which they link incentives to performance and other requirements that act as disincentives. Linking generally takes place through an investment agreement stating the incentives received by the investor and the conditions that must be met. But linking can take place implicitly when governments grant incentives to projects that are likely to meet certain performance goals – exports, use of domestic inputs, and so on – even though these firms are under no explicit obligation to achieve these goals. With implicit linking, firms have more discretion in their management decisions, but the result – in terms of the government's objectives – may be the same.

All countries in the sample practiced linking to some degree. The countries least likely to link, either implicitly or explicitly, were small countries oriented to the worldwide export market. The countries in which linking was widely practiced were the large developing countries. One of these, for example, provided tariff protection and investment tax credits to petrochemical firms that would agree to export at least 30 percent of installed capacity for three years. Large countries are able to use the attraction of their large internal markets as a bargaining chip in extracting commitments from investors to meet various requirements. Developing countries without large internal markets have no monopoly power with which to impose conditions on prospective investors.

Variety of Incentive Instruments

All the countries surveyed maintained at least three alternative means of providing incentives to foreign investment projects; one country offered eight forms of factor protection. Table 1-2 described the range of incentive instruments used in each country. Officials in countries engaged in intense competition for foreign investment view a variety of incentive instruments as essential. An industrial promotion agency official in a country experiencing stiff competition justified the introduction of a new incentive instrument on the grounds that it "effectively differentiated [his country] from its competitors." A number of the companies interviewed in the official's country mentioned the variety of incentives as one of the attractive features of the country's incentive system. Not only does a variety of incentive instruments permit countries to vary the mix to meet the different needs of corporations, but also the number of instruments itself indicates that the country is willing to extend itself to attract investors. The variety is a signal of the country's commitment to attracting investors and maintaining their goodwill.

The government officials interviewed did not stress this point, but a diversity of incentives increases the opaqueness of incentive systems. Because of the problems of equating the benefits of each instrument to a common denominator, variety also reduces the visibility of incentives to competitors, to international bodies charged with monitoring incentive levels, and to taxpayers.

Selectivity: Industrial Priorities

All the countries surveyed had established industrial priorities, and incentive levels tended to correspond to these priorities. In most countries, priorities were established explicitly; in a few, priorities seemed to arise more from the actual practice of granting incentives than from a predetermined plan. In almost all the sample countries, governments had assigned priority to three of the four industries covered in the industry studies (automobiles, computers, and petrochemicals). One important aspect of selectivity is the different emphasis given to industries oriented toward domestic markets and those oriented toward exports. Countries included in the study had trade policies that ranged from strong discrimination in favor of the local market to neutrality between import substitution and export promotion.

Discrimination among Firms

All the countries surveyed had the administrative capacity to vary the levels of incentives not only between industries but also among firms in the same industry. Some countries actively discriminated among firms; other countries preferred more automatic and uniform incentive packages among firms. The interest in discrimination among firms arose from four considerations:

As noted, discrimination, if properly exercised, minimizes redundancy and reduces the fiscal cost of achieving a given level of foreign investment.

When performance requirements are applied to an industry, the incentive level can be altered to compensate each firm in proportion to the burden imposed on it by the performance requirement. In one country, the government signed separate contracts with each firm that specified the export and domestic-content requirements and the incentives to be received. No two contracts were alike.

Discrimination among firms adds to the opaqueness of a country's incentive system, a feature that officials of some countries criticized in the incentive systems of other countries but seemed to seek for their own countries.

The fact that a company believes that it is being given special treatment provides the country with a marketing advantage. One of the countries in the study emphasized to prospective investors, in its marketing literature and more emphatically during visits of its representatives abroad, that foreign investors would be given special treatment. Some of the corporate officials who were interviewed expressed the view that governments with made-to-measure incentives were more likely to be cooperative in the future than were countries that offered uniform and seemingly rigid incentives.

Degree of Promotion

More than half the countries surveyed actively market their country abroad to prospective investors. Five of the countries surveyed maintain representative offices in major capital-exporting countries. These offices enable countries to establish close and continuing contacts with officials of firms considering a move abroad. Countries that are active promoters also use magazine advertisements, brochures, seminars, and similar means to generate interest in and provide information about their countries. The remaining countries in the sample respond to requests for information but do not actively pursue foreign investors, even in industries that are regarded as essential or highly desirable for the country.

Service: Provision of Infrastructure to Investors

The sample countries differed notably in the degree to which they were willing to spend public funds on infrastructure useful to foreign investors. Some of the countries surveyed were well organized to respond to investors' requests for improved infrastructure — roads, telecommunications, ports, for example. Other countries were poorly organized to provide needed infrastructure, and investors often had to incorporate the cost of these infrastructure investments in their own project cost calculations.

Centralization of Government Authority

Each of the preceding elements is significantly affected by the way in which governments are organized to deal with foreign investors. The ability to vary the net incentive, to discriminate among firms in giving incentives, to offer a variety of commodity and factor incentive instruments, and to link incentives and disincentives depends on the administrative structure and control exercised by governments. Organization is perhaps not so much a separate component of strategy as the framework in which strategy is formulated and implemented. Yet organizational forms, independent of other dimensions of strategy, play a major role in the effectiveness of countries to attract and control foreign investors.

The importance of organization to competitive strategy arises from the costs incurred by prospective foreign investors in securing government approvals. Many branches of government — departments of finance, labor, and commerce, and public-sector corporations — see their interests affected by foreign investments and insist on a role in formulating foreign investment policies and in negotiating individual entry agreements when their agency's interests are at stake. But government attempts to involve each branch in the entry process can discourage foreign investors. Some countries have minimized investor costs by reducing the number of government agencies involved in the approval process.

The study team identified three broad approaches to government organization in the countries surveyed: decentralization (diffusion), coordination, and delegation (concentration). Each approach reflects a different degree of centralization of power. Each approach has advantages that must be weighed against disadvantages. The degree of centralization is not tied to a particular attitude toward foreign investment: countries that wish to promote and attract foreign investors as well as those that wish to emphasize control may both prefer to concentrate authority over foreign investment in one agency. Countries that wish to maintain a passive attitude toward foreign investment and, at the other extreme, countries that wish to ban foreign investment altogether may both adopt a decentralized approach.

Decentralization is the standard approach adopted by governments that are not actively promoting foreign investment, but this approach is also employed in countries that wish to encourage foreign investment yet give each affected agency of government an opportunity to negotiate with investors. Decentralization is thus compatible with either automatic policies or discretionary policies in which high priority is given to the independent judgment and negotiating skills of different branches. In the case of discretionary policies, the advantages and disadvantages of decentralization are clear. Decentralization ensures maximum application of the technical skills of concerned agencies, but it sometimes imposes high costs on investors who must secure approvals from each concerned agency. Moreover, with decentralization, there is no assurance that the independent negotiations of each government department necessarily secure the greatest social gain from each investment project approved or promote the appropriate level of total foreign investment. Two of the countries in the sample concentrated power to negotiate foreign investor entry in a single agency. The other countries pursued a mixture of either coordination or decentralization.

Coordination represents government's desire to reduce the confusion and costs of decentralization while permitting affected branches to have a voice in negotiations with foreign investors. The move to a coordinating agency form of organization has often been an evolutionary stage in the development of a country's strategy toward foreign investment, following a learning experience with uncoordinated negotiations. Coordination can take place through permanent boards or ad hoc committees. Permanent boards may oversee negotiations covering a wide range of industries, or several specialized boards may simultaneously have responsibility for individual industries. Ad hoc committees are normally established only for specific industries.

The power of coordinating agency and the political power of board members can vary greatly. A coordinating body may serve only as a clearinghouse for information while the real power rests with individual departments. Or a board may have final decision-making authority and truly serve as a one-stop agency, at least for the major negotiating issues. Coordinating boards may be dominated by one or a few members, or power may be diffused among all members. Whatever the specific span of control and authority of a coordinating agency, the existence of such an agency in a country indicates that the government is attempting to emphasize foreign investment issues whether the government's interest lies in attracting or in controlling foreign investors.

At the far end of the spectrum of control are centralized organizations, which often take the form of delegated authority — a concentration of effective control over the major foreign investment issues in the hands of one agency. Concentrated authority over all foreign investment negotiations is sometimes found in small countries, where powerful, independent, permanent bodies are established to promote foreign investment through incentives and disincentives. Such wide-ranging autonomous bodies are rare elsewhere, but designated agencies (for example, state-owned enterprises) with authority over specific industries or regions are more common.

One important form of delegated authority is the one-stop agency that some governments have established to help foreign investors in their encounters with government bureaucracy. Investor-oriented agencies were found in two of the sample countries that were experiencing moderate or severe competition. The goal of the one-stop agency is to minimize the cost to investors of securing permits and licenses and of obtaining access to public services (for example, water and electricity). Although neither of the two countries has created a truly one-stop service, both have been able to simplify procedures. Some one-stop agencies have even interceded on the side of the investor in negotiations with other branches of government when conflicts have arisen; others that are nominally one-stop agencies offer little more than a directory of contact points in relevant agencies.

This characterization of the governments' organizational forms falling into a single continuum from decentralized to centralized oversimplifies in a number of ways:

Governments may adopt different organizational forms for different industries. For example, in one of the sample countries, a public-sector corporation handles negotiations with foreign investors in the energy sector, whereas a coordinating board handles negotiations for low-priority sectors such as footwear and cosmetics. In one of the countries studied, responsibility for export-oriented investments, especially those in free-trade zones, are concentrated in one agency, whereas domestically oriented investments fall under another administrative arrangement.

Organizational form and decision-making power are not always linked: sometimes agencies in which responsibility has been concentrated do not have true authority, and sometimes coordinating agencies attempt vainly to achieve consensus among independent functional agencies.

Organizational structures are inherently transitional; in all the countries in the survey, responsibility and power among various branches of government have continued to shift over time. Organization is as much a dynamic process as a static form.

Structural Determinants of Country Strategies

Strategy implies an element of choice. The ten elements just described define the choices over which governments exercise control. However, all strategies are constrained to some degree by factors outside the strategist's control; these constraints are imposed by forces that do not change at all or change only slowly. A country's legal system, cultural heritage, and traditional ways of conducting the business of government, political ideologies, availability of skilled technicians and managers needed to evaluate and implement foreign investment policies — all are examples of influences external to the policymaker's realm of control that bear on a country's foreign investment strategies. The following paragraphs address three other constraints: cooperative international agreements, limited economic development, and small population.

International Cooperative Agreements

Unlike companies, which are generally forbidden to enter into cooperative ventures with competitors, governments find significant mutual advantage in international agreements that restrict the policy choices available. The GATT is an example of a restrictive cooperative agreement — that limits participants' rights to raise tariffs or impose quotas. Another example of a cooperative agreement is the Treaty of Rome, in which governments agreed to limit certain types of investment incentives. In addition, in EC countries, ceilings for subnational regions vary with the region's level of development. To achieve their countries' objectives, policymakers may seek international agreements that restrict the range of policy choices in the ten areas already described.

Limited Economic Development

A country's level of income and degree of industrialization affect strategy in a number of ways. Poor countries lack tax revenues to finance factor protection policies, such as cash grants, or to undertake aggressive price incentives. The scope for commodity protection is necessarily limited to those sectors for which a large internal market is available, such as consumer goods; high rates of effective protection are self-defeating when domestic prices are pushed above affordable levels.

Poor countries often face shortages of technical, managerial, and professional staff to formulate, negotiate, and implement effective foreign investment policies; these countries are especially ill equipped to manage complex incentive programs that require differentiation between industries and between firms in the same industry. Because these countries lack both attractive domestic markets and funds for factor protection, their ability to link performance requirements to incentives is severely limited. Hence, limited development does not remove the element of choice among the various strategic elements; but the stage of development does limit the latitude with which choices can be made.

Small Population

Most small countries, even those with high per capita incomes, lack internal markets to support plants of minimum scale for efficient production of many industrial goods, so their governments must give priority to industries that offer export opportunities and to those that permit efficient import substitution.

Large countries, in contrast, control access to markets that manufacturers find profitable for import-substitution investments. The rents associated with tariff protection in these internal markets can be channeled to investors who agree to meet other objectives of the host country, such as promotion of exports, regional balance, or growth of domestic supplier industries. Large countries also are more likely to be able to employ credible implicit policies, such as threatening to close off important markets for multinational firms. At the same time, however, many large countries are federations of states that possess important tax, expenditure, and regulatory powers; so the problem of orchestration of federal government branches is compounded by the need to incorporate subnational governmental units as well. In addition, active promotion of foreign investment often requires a country to help the manufacturer find a site within the host country; when a country has regions defined by language or ethnic distinctions, it may be politically difficult to recommend one region over another.

Profiles of Country Strategies

Even though the profiles of foreign investment strategies contained in Table 1-5 are highly abstracted, they suggest that strategies are adapted both to a country's population and to competitive conditions in the market for foreign investment. Strategies employed by members of common markets to attract investment produce the most intense competition, both in terms of price and nonprice competition. Large and small member countries engage in competition for the same investment projects but use a different mix of the ten elements just described. Smaller member countries are more prone to employ aggressive incentive pricing tactics, displaying a willingness to match or exceed competing offers. Because they can centralize negotiating authority within one agency, small member countries are more able to be selective among industries, to discriminate among firms and to coordinate a variety of incentives.

Large member countries are unwilling to delegate price setting to one agency or to a tightly coordinated set of agencies. Instead, large countries compete through implicit policies, threatening, for example, to withhold government procurement contracts from companies not agreeing to establish a local plant. It is obviously hard to measure the importance of implicit policies of this type, but interviews with company officials made it clear that they attach significance to government statements about the importance of local sourcing for public purchases.

Larger countries also are more successful than small countries in linking performance requirements to incentives because of government control over access to substantial national market. The absence of a centralized authority usually implies less selectivity among industries and less discrimination among firms. The variety of incentives, however, is often as great as that in small countries because of the number of institutions empowered to grant incentives — regional development agencies, states, even municipalities.

The absence of intense competition is apparent from the strategies adopted by large countries seeking investments oriented to the home market. Because of the absence of competition, no need exists to centralize authority. Although the total net incentive may be as high as in other markets, pricing is rarely aggressive. Governments in these countries make few efforts to promote foreign investment and have greater success in linking incentives with disincentives, such as requirements for minimum exports, domestic content, and local ownership.

In sum, all countries compete to some extent for foreign investment, but the intensity of competition experienced and the strategies pursued vary among countries. Small countries may appear to be more intensely competitive because their strategies call for centralized authority and aggressive incentive pricing, both highly visible. But larger countries are capable of exerting as much competitive pressure as smaller countries to attract foreign investors although the mix of ten strategic elements differs. The degree of competition for foreign investment faced by any country cannot be measured along a single dimension but can only be understood by examining each of these elements in detail.

EFFECTIVENESS OF INCENTIVES AND DISINCENTIVES

It is clear that countries devote considerable effort to designing, implementing, and modifying strategies to influence the location and operation of foreign investment projects. Do strategies actually work?

Our research indicates that incentive components of strategies do, in fact, influence the location decisions of foreign investors. Evidence presented later in this chapter suggests that in two-thirds of the cases studied the policies of host country governments influenced the location decision. This finding appears to run counter to some other research on the subject, but there are important differences between our measure of effectiveness and the measures used in previous studies. Because of this finding, it is important to scrutinize some of the standard explanations given for the insignificant effects of investment incentives.

It is often argued that investment incentives are generally insignificant compared to important determinants of investment location, such as production costs and market size. In addition, one country's incentives are often matched by those of competitors. Competitive responses of one country to a change in incentive policy by another are consistent with the rationale for country strategies already described. But, the analysis of country strategies provided earlier in this chapter emphasized that pricing is only one element among many from which governments could choose. Yet, increasing the incentives is often the most effective, and certainly the most expeditious, way to counter a competitor's threat to market share.

Competitive price responses in a zero-sum game situation produce the well-known "prisoner's dilemma." The prisoner's dilemma takes its name from a situation in which an agreement (for example, an agreement that neither would confess to the crime) between two persons jointly accused of a crime would make both better off, but the rewards from successful cheating on the agreement lead each person to choose a course of action that results in both being made worse off. More generally, the term is used to refer to situations in which cooperation rather than competition is needed to produce a mutually desired result but in which it is hard to establish an enforceable contract among the cooperating parties.

In the market for foreign investment, a prisoner's dilemma arises among countries when one country's increase in incentives is matched by increased incentives from a competitor. A point will be reached when the incentive levels stabilize and no country will be better off: unchanged relative incentives will produce the same market share as before. Indeed, both countries may be worse off because income is transferred to firms with no gain in market share. Only if incentives stimulate an increase in the total supply of investment sufficient to compensate for the loss of revenue can incentive matching increase the welfare of host countries.

On this last point – the elasticity of supply of foreign investment with respect to a change in the general level of incentive – this report has little to say. The case study approach we pursued does not permit generalizations about the responsiveness of aggregate flows of foreign investment to changes in incentives. It seems likely that the value of the elasticity of supply of foreign investment will remain moot until economists can accurately estimate the elasticity of domestic investment in response to government incentives.

The prisoner's dilemma aspect of incentive policies in many parts of the world complicates analysis of the effectiveness of incentives. On the one hand, if incentives of various countries offset one another, or even only nearly offset one another, investors will state, quite correctly, that the presence of incentives in a country does not seriously influence location decision or that it does not influence them at all. This statement does not mean, however, that the absence of incentives would not affect investment location decisions. If one country were to eliminate its incentives while others maintained theirs, the country's share of foreign investment projects might decline substantially. Because the study team did not examine the performance of incentive systems in the sample countries over a period of time, it was impossible to estimate the effects of changes in relative incentive levels on foreign investment.

Interviews with officials from countries operating in the most intensely competitive markets led to the following conjecture: increases in incentives are more likely to be matched by other countries than are decreases. If this conjecture is correct, general statements about the effectiveness of incentives can only be judged by attempting to determine how the location of investment would be affected by different policy scenarios that cannot actually be observed.

On the other hand − and this is the other part of the dilemma − if existing incentives alone cannot be used to infer effectiveness, what alternative assumptions should be made about incentives? If one country were to eliminate incentives altogether, would other countries maintain existing incentives, eliminate incentives, or choose an intermediate course between the two choices? And would all countries respond the same way? Once the relatively safe, but inadequate, body of data on actual incentive levels and investment patterns is abandoned, the permutations and combinations of alternative assumptions about country incentives produce a perplexing array of information from which a variety of conclusions can be drawn.

We have resolved this dilemma by asking the following question: would a foreign investment project have located in a particular country if that country had eliminated its incentives and disincentives while other countries maintained incentive policies at existing levels? This assumption will yield a measure of the maximum effectiveness of incentives. For countries that participate in competitive markets with no opportunity for cooperative agreements limiting incentive policies, this assumption may be very relevant.

Determinants of the Location of Foreign Investment

Many considerations bear on the location decision of foreign investors, but they can be classified into two broad categories: factors other than incentives and incentive policies.

Factors Other Than Incentives

This category refers to all considerations other than government incentive policy that an investor would apply to a location decision. The category is obviously very broad, including all the advantages of production, marketing, and transportation that a country naturally provides in the absence of incentives. For example, manufacturers of food products locate plants in the foreign markets they serve because for many types of foods, weight-to-value ratios make transportation over long distances prohibitive. The natural advantages of foreign production are sufficient to attract many multinational food products manufacturers; hence, incentives are not required. This category also encompasses factors such as exchange rate and price stability; the quality of public management of monetary, fiscal, and social policy; and political and social stability.

These factors could be further subdivided into various classifications, but this would not further the objective of this study, which is to determine the effectiveness of incentives in relation to all the other factors included in the investment decision. One type of nonincentive factor, however, deserves special attention. Each firm may evaluate a country's attractiveness as a possible investment site according to criteria specific to that firm. For example, an existing plant may have underutilized managerial capacity; this plant could be expanded (to take advantage of savings in management overhead) with a rate of return greater than a greenfield investment of identical capacity would produce in any other country. As a result, the firm would prefer one country (where the existing plant is located) over all other countries. Other firms in the industry may have no such preference.

Another firm-specific reason relates to corporate strategy. Companies in oligopolistic industries often find it advantageous to match competitors' moves internationally to avoid loss of market share, producing a follow-the-leader pattern in foreign investments. A firm may find itself drawn into investment in a foreign market because of a concern for strategic balance that has little to do with general economic factors or incentives.

Incentives and Disincentives

The other category of factors comprises all government incentives and disincentives that affect foreign investment, whether applied only to foreign investments or to investments in general. These policy measures, and especially the distinction between commodity and factor protection, were described earlier in this chapter. Incentives and disincentives also can be divided into explicit and implicit policies. Implicit policies refer to changes in either commodity or factor protection that governments can make but, for a number of reasons, have not made. If policy changes occur, existing investors may benefit and firms that have not invested may suffer. Implicit policies may, therefore, induce some firms to invest even though economic factors and explicit incentives are inadequate. Many implicit policies are implemented on a discriminatory basis among firms; often governments and firms bargain over these policies, and the outcome is always uncertain. As a result, in the analysis that follows, implicit policies have been characterized as "government-strategic," to emphasize the interactive bargaining framework in which implicit policies operate.

Investment Location Decisions in Four Industries

To explore the importance of incentives in foreign investment decisions, the team studied four industries: automobiles, computers, petrochemicals, and food products. Before we discuss the results of the surveys of specific investment decisions, it is important to put these findings in perspective by reviewing some characteristics of the firms in these industries and the market forces that affect their investment strategies.

Automobiles

The worldwide automobile industry is characterized by a relatively small number of large producers. The eight firms interviewed for this study account for the majority of wordwide sales of automobiles and trucks. With the exception of the Japanese, the major automobile manufacturers have had overseas production facilities for many years — the U.S. firms began producing in Europe over a half-century ago. Even the smaller firms began manufacturing abroad long ago.

There is a pervasive belief among automobile manufacturers that, as one manufacturer said, "It makes sense to produce automobiles where they are sold, provided you have sufficient volume." Thus the country screening that normally takes place at the beginning of the investment decision process is limited to countries where automobile sales volume is high. In regional markets unified by a common tariff, such as the EC, the national sales volume of prospective host countries is a less important criterion than in other markets. But, this volume is still important because manufacturers are convinced that local firms are likely to receive preferential treatment over firms that serve the local market through imported vehicles.

Compared with many other industries, the automobile industry is technologically footloose: the raw materials, infrastructure, and factors needed for production are found in many countries. Automobile firms do not have particular difficulty in meeting environmental standards for plant operations. Automobile plants must be located near rail and port facilities, which most countries can easily provide, and they must have a reasonably large labor pool in the immediate area to draw upon because the average size of an automobile facility is relatively large. Differences in labor costs do not play an important part in manufacturers' calculations of the relative advantages of alternative sites. The median employment level in the investment projects selected for this study exceeded 1,500 workers.

Because of the mobility of production facilities, automobile companies are prime targets for host country investment promotion efforts, often involving incentive packages that are among the most attractive offered to foreign investors in any industry. Several of the investment cases studied were offered cash grant equivalents that exceeded $50,000 per worker.

Host countries expect a number of advantages from automobile investments, not the least of which is a large, direct employment effect. A major advantage is the opportunity for local firms to become suppliers. Historically, automobiles have been assembled from components supplied both from affiliated companies and from independent suppliers. To ensure that the process of backward integration to local suppliers proceeds rapidly, many host countries have adopted domestic-content requirements. Another advantage governments perceive is the prestige conferred by the industry itself: automobile production is a measure of industrial maturity, a highly visible sign of the strides a country has taken to reduce imports, and a symbol of national economic independence.

With the exception of the Japanese companies, automobile manufacturers have located plants abroad principally on the basis of estimated sales in one of two markets: a single host country's market or the common market region of which a prospective host country is a member. Few projects have been located abroad solely for production that would enter the worldwide export market. For investments oriented toward the domestic market, negotiations have occurred principally over the degree of commodity protection; the main issue has been the amount of tariff protection required to overcome the disincentives of domestic content. Recently, some host countries have enlarged the concept of domestic exports. To meet this requirement, firms that import more than they export can reduce imports through local production or through purchases from local suppliers; alternatively, firms can increase exports directly or, in some cases, indirectly through sales to companies that, in turn, export finished products.

For new plants in a common market, such as the EC, automobile manufacturers have only to indicate their interest in building a new plant to be inundated with offers. At an early stage in the investment decision, manufacturers develop a short list of countries and then negotiate over incentives and performance requirements. These negotiations are often conducted at the highest levels of government. Incentive packages frequently contain an array of benefits that go beyond standard cash and tax concessions to include special agreements on the local market shares the firm can claim and even limitations on the entry of competitors into the local market.

Computers

The computer industry has three characteristics that distinguish it from other industries in the sample:

1. It is a relatively new industry, and experience with overseas investment for most firms has been limited to the last decade.
2. It is characterized by a much wider size distribution of firms — sales range from several hundred million to several billion.
3. U.S. firms dominate all but the Japanese market.

Unlike the automobile industry, in which foreign investments are principally market driven, computer manufacturers undertake investment abroad for one of two reasons: to reduce costs or to serve markets. Many investments to reduce costs occur in the newly industrializing countries of the Far East — Singapore, Malaysia, Korea, and Taiwan — where wage costs and labor skills provide a considerable competitive edge to firms in the production of labor-intensive components. For investments designed to serve a market in developed areas, cost and other production-related considerations do enter into site selection and, within a common market, into country location. Among these considerations are access to an efficient communications system and proximity to major universities, airports, and pools of professional and skilled labor.

Investment decisions tend to fall fairly clearly into the two categories described, and investment incentives are unlikely to draw cost-reducing investments from low-wage countries to high-wage countries that have the markets. Yet, incentives can influence a company's choices among low-wage countries in the production-oriented investments and among countries in the market-oriented cases, especially among members of the EC. But even this conclusion drawn from the experience of the past decade may not be applicable to the future. In this rapidly changing industry, labor-intensive production may be replaced by capital-intensive production resulting from new products and automation.

Most governments welcome the computer industry. Whereas automobile manufacturing symbolizes a country's industrial coming of age, computer manufacturing attests to membership in the technologically advanced era. The response of governments to the challenge of building a domestic computer industry varied considerably. Some have gone out of their way to attract computer manufacturers, placing few, if any, performance requirements on manufacturers and offering generous incentives. Other governments, however, have been cautious in their approach to major international computer companies, establishing public-sector corporations and special coordinating bodies to ensure that their national interests are safeguarded.

Governments are important purchasers of computers — for defense, education, and research, as well as for general government operations. The power of public procurement is used to influence location decisions as well as the character of the investment, including ownership, export levels, and use of local inputs.

U.S. and Japanese computer firms have quite different foreign investment strategies. Until now, U.S. producers have engaged in follow-the-leader behavior in their foreign investment decisions. Whether U.S. companies follow their competitors abroad to prevent preemption of overseas markets or merely to use a competitor's investment as a source of market or production cost information is not known. The Japanese, in contrast, have made only a few international investments, and most of these have been limited to semiconductor products in which the Japanese have technological and market dominance. However, the Japanese now feel pressure from governments to manufacture "where the markets are," and have planned for a network of strategically placed investments to forestall public criticism and protectionist reactions.

Food Products

The food products industry differs from the other industries in this study in a number of important respects:

Food production is, for the most part, a technologically mature industry, and companies are distinguished less by their possession of proprietary technology than by brand names and managerial styles.

Production is seldom integrated worldwide, but rather takes the form of relatively small-scale, import-substituting investments in host countries, often making extensive use of local raw materials.

In developing countries, governments take special efforts, including controls and subsidies, to ensure that food prices are kept low.

Because food manufacturing is technologically relatively unsophisticated and food pricing is politically sensitive, governments have ambiguous, fluctuating, and even sometimes, contradictory policies toward multinational food producers. The benefits that governments perceive from foreign investments in this industry relate principally to rapid growth from import substitution that requires little technological mastery, only simple skills, and backward linkages to agriculture. Few governments wish to retard the growth of food production, and foreign investments offer proven technologies and superior managerial skills, especially in marketing and distribution. However, governments also perceive significant costs. Foreign presence, and, worse, foreign dominance, in a vital sector such as food is, to many governments, politically unpalatable. Moreover, the simplicity of the technology and the ease with which it may be diffused to local producers create a constant tension and pressure for increased domestic equity participation and, ultimately, control. The lack of export potential in many food-sector investments only underscores the perceived foreign exchange drain created by foreign equity participation.

In terms of the number and nationality of multinationals, the food industry is much more diverse than any of the other three industries addressed in this study. U.S. firms account for an important share of overseas investment, but that share remains well below the shares held by U.S. firms in automobiles and computers. Perhaps because of the relatively simple technology or the relatively small scale of the food industry, multinational firms from developing countries account for a greater share of foreign investments in this industry than in any of the other three industries.

Petrochemicals

The petrochemical industry spans a multitude of manufacturing steps that begin with the breakdown of basic raw materials — oil and gas — and conclude with production of end products that range from fertilizers, detergents, and pharmaceuticals to fibers, films, and fabrics. Crude oil is the basic feedstock of Western European petrochemical companies, whereas natural gas is the preferred raw material for North American producers. Feedstocks are converted into approximately 20 primary petrochemical products, which are transformed into more than 100 major intermediate products. These, in turn, are processed into thousands of petrochemical products that may be used for final consumption, such as fertilizers, or may be further transformed — for example, synthetic fibers may be woven into cloth, and cloth, fashioned into garments.

The petrochemical industry is distinctive among the industries included in this study in several respects:

To a far greater extent than in any of the other industries, the home countries for multinational firms in the petrochemical industry also serve as host countries for foreign investments. Japan is the notable exception. The crisscrossing nature of foreign investment in this industry is rooted largely in each company's perception that the best method for exploiting the value of its proprietary process technology is through foreign production.

Petrochemical companies are extensively involved in all three markets for foreign investment. Primary production of petrochemicals is often oriented toward the world export market because many plants are located in regions, such as the Middle East, that offer feedstock supply but only a limited market for primary products. Intermediate products and, especially, final products are more home-market oriented, so plants tend to be located near sources of demand — either in the EC or in major developing countries.

One important trend in the investment pattern of the petrochemical industry is the shift in the location of plants, especially for primary products such as ethylene, from developed to oil-exporting developing countries. Petroleum-exporting countries in the developing world accounted for only 2 percent of the world's ethylene capacity in 1979, but 25 percent of all new ethylene plants under, or scheduled for, construction are located in these countries. A number of problems in developing countries reduce their attractiveness to investors. These problems include the high costs of plant construction, shortages of skilled and managerial labor, and high transportation costs due in part to inadequate infrastructure. Yet the major petrochemical companies believe that joint ventures with the oil-exporting countries are important for strategic reasons. And the oil-exporting nations, in turn, see strategic benefits from partnerships with major multinational petrochemical firms; these partnerships not only provide access to technology but also serve as insurance against the rising protectionism in developed countries. The effective level of protection in countries belonging to the Organization for Economic Cooperation and Development (OECD) has traditionally been high because of the cumulative nature of nominal tariffs between the feedstock, primary, intermediate, and end-product stages. Commodity protection has traditionally been a major stimulant to petrochemical foreign investments. A return to stringent import quotas and higher tariffs in developed countries could render export-oriented production facilities in developing countries unprofitable.

Results of the Industry Surveys

Officials of more than 30 corporations in these four industries were questioned about factors influencing the location of

74 investment projects. The results of this survey are shown in Table 1-6.

Incentives

In one-third of the investment cases studied, factors other than incentives dominated the location decision. Even if all incentives from the host country had been removed beforehand and if the attractive incentive packages in other countries had remained, these investments would have located in the same host country. Because of the small number of projects involved, it is hard to tell whether this share varies significantly among the three markets for investment — the domestic market for a single host country, a common market, and one aimed toward production for worldwide export.

In the remaining two-thirds of the cases, incentives of one sort or another were the decisive factor — that is, in the absence of incentives, a foreign investment would not have been made, or it would have been located in another country. Of these cases, about 10 percent were influenced by implicit (government-strategic) incentives. These cases included, for example, automobile companies that wanted to establish a production presence in major markets even though the markets could be supplied offshore as cheaply and current incentives were insufficient to justify the investment.

In about one-third of the cases, commodity protection influenced country location, but there are sharp variations among the three markets. Tariffs may persuade investors to locate inside a common market area, but by the definition of a common market, they cannot be used to influence choices among member countries. Some other kinds of commodity protection, such as government procurement and subsidized inputs from public corporations, are permitted, or at least tolerated, in the EC. For worldwide export projects, commodity protection was used in only one of the 12 cases, and this involved subsidized petroleum for a petrochemical complex.

The removal of import protection from foreign investment strategies of common market countries has had two effects. First, there has been substitution of factor protection for commodity protection. Table 1-6 does not show protection levels, but that more than 40 percent of the projects chose a particular country because of factor protection is strong evidence that factor incentives have to some extent replaced commodity incentives as an instrument

TABLE 1-6
Dominant Factor in Location Decision by Industry and Market Orientation

Number of Investment Cases Studied	Influences on Investment Decision				
	Factors Unrelated to Incentives	Implicit Incentives*	Explicit Incentives		
			Commodity	Factor	Total
Market					
Domestic					
Autos	1	1	5		7
Petrochemicals	1		6	1	8
Food products	5		6		11
Computers	1	2	6	1	10
Common					
Autos	1	2		2	5
Petrochemicals	1			2	3
Food products	3			1	4
Computers	4	4		6	14
Worldwide export					
Autos					0
Petrochemicals	2			2	4
Food products	1				1
Computers	4		1	2	7
All Industries					
Domestic	8	3	23	2	36
Common	9	6	0	11	26
Worldwide export	7	0	1	4	12
Total	24	9	24	17	74

*Government-strategic

Source: Study team assessments based on company surveys and industry studies.

to influence the location of foreign investments within common markets. Second, explicit policies have been replaced with implicit policies. Nine projects were located in host countries on strategic grounds: either anticipation of benefits from favorable future treatment by host countries because of the corporation's investment commitment or avoidance of future unfavorable treatment, usually associated with import restraints or loss of government contracts. In all cases of strategic investment decisions, it is noteworthy that each corporation believed that future government actions would benefit only the corporation itself and not the industry in general. Investment decisions were generally undertaken only after extensive negotiations with host countries.

In the market for domestically oriented investments, factor incentives play an insignificant role: in only two cases did firms state that the principal determinant of the investment decision was factor, rather than commodity, protection. In every instance in which commodity protection was the principal reason for the investment decision, some form of factor protection was provided. Often, factor protection was granted to encourage firms to locate in certain regions. The results of the survey, not reported here, suggest that these incentives were effective in altering the subnational choice of investment sites. For many projects, however, factor protection was offered without regional or other requirements; for at least some investments, therefore, factor protection may be redundant.

Comparison of these findings with previous research is complicated by two factors. First, the measure of effectiveness employed in this study is a judgment about events that would have occurred without incentives. Second, the definition of incentives is broad, incorporating explicit and implicit incentives and comprising effective protection and incentives to factor use. Previous studies have used a narrower definition of incentives and have analyzed effectiveness only on the basis of observed incentive policies. For example, using a narrow definition of investment incentives, Reuber and associates concluded from a review of previously published studies that "incentives provided, while of some consequence, in stimulating the inflow of foreign inventment [to developing countries] were relatively ineffective."[2] In contrast, the Business and Industry Advisory Committee (BIAC) Committee on International Investment and Multinational Enterprises found that "once a decision is made to invest in Europe, the selection of a particular site from a group of similar locations may hinge on the incentives given."[3]

Performance Requirements

Of the 74 investment cases examined in the survey, 38 were subject to performance requirements, usually in the form of specified levels of domestic content for exports. A variation of the explicit performance requirement established at the time of entry is a requirement that firms offset their imports with a comparable value of exports. In effect, this obligation is a floating performance requirement: the lower the level of exports achieved, the higher must be the domestic content. The experiences of firms that have been subjected to performance requirements have varied. In some cases, company officials told the study team their companies would have eventually achieved the desired levels of exports or domestic content. Thus, the performance requirements were not always binding, or, at best, the requirements accelerated the firms' plans to develop local suppliers and enter export markets. In other cases, however, performance requirements altered investor decisions, either the initial decision to invest or a decision regarding the degree of local content and exports.

Performance requirements enter into foreign investment decisions in ways that are extremely difficult to measure empirically. Even the limitation adopted in this study — examining only trade-related performance requirements — does not overcome all the problems of measurement. The survey did not include cases of decision *not* to invest because of unacceptable performance requirements imposed by host countries, although some firms surveyed, especially in the computer industry, indicated that they had chosen not to invest in certain countries because of performance requirements. In addition, a number of countries grant incentives on a discriminatory basis that effectively accomplishes the same objectives as performance requirements without the requirements ever being made explicit in the entry agreement. Finally, performance requirements are only part of a country's portfolio of policy instruments. In some countries surveyed, it is obvious that if performance requirements had not been available, some other policy instrument aimed at the same objective — increasing exports or reducing imports — would have been substituted.

In the absence of information on what substitutions would occur, the effectiveness of performance requirements can be judged only on the assumption that they are removed and no substitution occurs. Within these limitations and qualifications, some conclusions about the effects of performance requirements can still be drawn. These fall into two categories: the effects of performance requirements on the location of foreign investment and the effects of performance requirements on the pattern of imports and exports in foreign investment projects.

Effects on Location

In four of the 74 investment decisions studies, performance requirements determined the country in which the investment was located. (All four cases involved automobile firms.) In two of the cases, the investing companies already had substantial production in the host countries imposing the performance requirements, and the investments were undertaken to comply with new regulations requiring companies to balance imports with exports. This requirement necessitated new investments in export-oriented capacity, as opportunities for import substitution were limited. These investments were of a defensive nature, designed to preserve the company's access to the domestic market, which the host country threatened to close off unless imports were balanced with exports. In effect, the addition of the balancing requirements reduced overall protection but implicitly subsidized exports: the increased profitability of exports to the company could be measured as the difference between the opportunity cost of losing access to the exporting. Similarly, the balancing requirement also implicitly subsidized import-substituting investments in inputs that were previously imported by the company.

In the other two cases, firms agreed to invest and to meet performance requirements in order to maintain market shares that had previously been gained through exports to the host country. In each of the cases, the firms accepted performance requirements in order to maintain access to a large domestic market.

Effects on Imports and Exports

Of the 74 projects in the study, 38 were subject either to domestic-content or export requirements or to some form of foreign exchange balancing. And, as already noted, an unknown number were subject to indirect performance requirements: governments purposefully discriminated among alternative projects, scaling incentives to the net foreign exchange balance provided by the investment.

The industry surveys clearly revealed that performance requirements have sometimes substantially altered a firm's export and import plans, but the incidence of performance requirements varies across industries. In the computer industry, performance requirements did not significantly affect the operations of investment projects actually established. In the petrochemical and food products industries, the effects were significant but relatively minor. Most food industry projects are naturally oriented to the host country's market and to the use of local raw material, so export minimums are impractical and domestic-content requirements unnecessary.

In the automobile industry, however, performance requirements appeared to significantly affect the import and export decisions in the cases studied. The automobile industry seems especially susceptible to performance requirements; nine of the 12 cases studied were subject to them, a far greater percentage than in the other industries. Automobiles may be more susceptible to performance requirements because, unlike computers and petrochemicals, the technology appears to governments as only moderately sophisticated; as a result, local content appears to be an attainable objective. Also, host countries may see export minimums as a necessary incentive for multinationals to open up their worldwide marketing and distribution systems to new sources of supply. In the petrochemical and food industries, in contrast, price incentives — export subsidies, for example — appear sufficient because the overseas markets for these goods are more competitive. These are only conjectures; inter-industry and intercountry variations in performance requirements could not be studied in sufficient detail to provide better insights into these issues.

The enforcement of performance requirements by countries also appears to differ among industries. One government levied a fine on an automobile manufacturer for failing to achieve performance requirements. In other industries, firms easily met performance requirements or, when they failed to meet them, were allowed to effectively renegotiate more favorable requirements.

Overall, performance requirements appear to be more prevalent and more rigorously enforced in the automobile industry than in others. Moreover, performance requirements in all four industries are concentrated on inward-oriented foreign investments rather than on investments oriented toward a common market or the worldwide export market. Also, large countries with attractive internal markets are more likely to impose performance requirements than are small countries. Thus, the cases in this study that involve automobile investments oriented to the home markets in large countries clearly indicate that performance requirements affect trade patterns. In other regions and industries, explicit performance requirements were less prevalent. No case was found, for example, of a computer investment in a common market country that had significant trade-related performance requirements.

NOTES

1. Michael Porter, *Competitive Strategy* (New York: The Free Press, 1980), p. 4.
2. G. Reuber, H. Crookell, M. Emerson, and G. Gallais-Hamonno, *Private Foreign Investment in Development* (Oxford: Clarendon Press, 1973), p. 131.
3. Business and Industry Advisory Committee (BIAC), "Relationship of Incentives and Disincentives to International Investment Decisions" (New York: BIAC, April 1981), p. 25.

APPENDIX
PAPERS PRODUCED BY THE STUDY OF INVESTMENT INCENTIVES AND PERFORMANCE REQUIREMENTS

Main Report

Guisinger, Stephen. "Investment Incentives and Performance Requirements: A Comparative Analysis of Country Foreign Investment Strategies." July 1983.

Industry Studies

Gray, H. Peter, and Ingo Walter. "Investment Incentives and Performance Requirements and Patterns of International Trade, Production, and Investment: The Case of the Petrochemical Industry." December 1982.

Hood, Neil, and Stephen Young. "Investment Incentives and Performance Requirements on the Patterns of Trade and Investment in the International Economy: The Case of the Automobile Industry." January 1983.

Mason, R. Hal. "Investment Incentives and Performance Requirements in the International Food Processing Industry." March 1983.

Miller, Robert R. "Investment Incentives and Performance Requirements and Patterns of International Trade, Production, and Investment: The Case of Computers." March 1983.

Other Studies

Bond, Eric W. "International Differences in the Rental Cost of Capital: Evidence from the Philippines, U.K., Canada, and Mexico." December 1982.

Bond, Eric W., and Stephen Guisinger. "The Measurement of Investment Incentives Using the Rental Cost of Capital Model." June 1982.

Encarnation, Dennis J., and Louis T. Wells, Jr. "Government Negotiation with Foreign Investors: Organizational Patterns in South and Southeast Asia." January 1983.

2

The International Food Processing Industry

R. Hal Mason

INTRODUCTION

This chapter presents the results of interviews with several leading multinational firms in the food processing industry. It is evident from those interviews that countries have several objectives with respect to investment incentives and performance requirements in this industry. Of key importance is the desire to develop the capability to export to other markets — especially the markets of already developed countries. Exportation to these markets requires that production quality must meet the standards of the international marketplace. A second important objective is that of stimulating industrial employment. Also of importance, in conjunction with the employment objective, is the contribution to regional development in most countries. Such development has to do with expansion of the industrial base in depressed areas or movement of expansion away from congested urban areas or both. Finally, agricultural development figures into the countries' objectives. Because some of the multinational food firms do have expertise in the development of contract and other relationships at the farm level, their presence is valued as a source of know-how with respect to field culture, new varieties of crops, and logistical support in developing cash crops or other agricultural inputs.

In most instances, multinational corporations (MNCs) do not receive investment incentives (hereafter referred to simply as incentives) that are not also available to local firms, that is, foreign investors are not treated systematically any differently than other investors. These firms, however, have, on occasion, negotiated special deals with host governments — deals that fall outside the published guidelines some way. Such situations appear to be exceptional.

Technology *per se* does not seem to be a primary driving force in this industry insofar as the countries' incentive systems are concerned. No particular subsectors appear to receive preferential treatment, although in some countries there does seem to be preferential treatment for projects that will contribute to development of basic agriculture — the introduction of new crops, new animal varieties, or new methods and field culture that allow for the production of higher quality outputs or varieties more suitable for products aimed at international markets. Also, some countries have sought to increase export capability through coproduction agreements and attraction of so-called high-technology installations.

While virtually all the firms interviewed — eight headquarters groups and two foreign subsidiaries — have received subsidies of some kind, these incentives have not weighed heavily in decisions about where and whether to invest. The common practice in calculating feasibility of an investment is to examine for feasibility without including incentives other than cash grants in the calculations. If a project is not feasible without continuing incentives, firms tend to avoid investment simply because there is little faith that incentives are a permanent and reliable source of cost reduction. Incentives may play a role in marginal investments or in keeping an existing investment from shutting down permanently. Thus, it seldom appears that a firm would invest in one country instead of another simply because of overt incentives such as cash grants, tax holidays, and similar fiscal inducements. Only two specific instances were encountered in which firms indicated that they had invested in one country rather than another, or were considering doing so, because of such incentives. However, tariff protection and other limits on imports of final products are widespread. Without such protection, a sizeable proportion of existing investments likely would not have taken place, and markets would have been served from either the home or another country.

Manufacturing plants in this industry tend to be relatively small, aim at serving the domestic market, employ relatively few people, often compete with local firms, and, accordingly, are not as heavily subsidized as firms in many other industries where the impact on employment and exportation is potentially much greater. Also, the industry is not perceived as being a high-technology industry capable of making major contributions to industrial transformation. This is a rather limited view in the sense that the processing, storage, and distribution of food is a complex business. Particularly for export markets, the know-how involved is not widely dispersed. Nor is there wide dispersion of the know-how required to bring many small farmers into a reliable network of supply contracts to produce raw materials of consistently high quality on schedules required by modern food processing plants. The mastery of these complex processes seems to be the know-how that makes attractive the presence of multinational firms in this industry.

PROFILE OF THE WORLD FOOD PROCESSING INDUSTRY

Introduction

The food processing industry is, in fact, an agglomeration of industries that are independent from one another in some respects and overlapping with one another in other respects. Most plants in the industry tend to be relatively small and specialized. For example, a meat processing plant does not also process dairy products or fruit and vegetable products. Among the firms comprising the industry, many are small specialized firms that process one or a few raw materials into a small number of final products. Superimposed are several larger diversified firms that process numerous raw materials and intermediate ingredients into literally hundreds of final products. However, each of these large firms does contain a core business that constitutes the bulk of the processing activities. These large diversified firms consist of numerous plants that are specialized around raw materials and/or the mixing of selected ingredients.

Plants can usually be classified by the types of processes involved. A canned food plant seldom becomes involved in dehydration or freezing processes. Generally, firms are classified not so much by the processes used as they are by the final products manufactured.

Processing generally has more than a single objective. Processing is aimed not only at making ingredients edible and flavorful but also at preserving the food against spoilage. The degree to which a food must be preserved depends on the nature of the raw material, its ability to withstand bacterial and other agents that bring about spoilage, its availability over time, consumption patterns, and the need for further processing over time. Preservation is also important in providing a means for inventory adjustment during cyclical disparities between output and final consumption. For example, fluid milk can be consumed immediately as milk and cream. A large part of total consumption is in fluid form in households. However, milk can also be fermented to form cheese. Milk can also be used in sterile condensed or dehydrated forms as an ingredient in a host of other products such as puddings, soups, dips, dressings, ice cream, and many other products. Milk in evaporated or dehydrated form or converted forms such as cheese can be stored for a much longer period than can raw or pasteurized milk. Thus, cyclical instability between raw milk production and consumption of final milk-based products can be smoothed by inventorying more stable products such as cheese and dehydrated milk.

Food Processes

The origin of some food processing techniques is lost in antiquity. Such methods as drying (dehydration), curing, fermentation and pickling, cooling, grinding, and milling were used in biblical times. Some forms of food preservation and conversion of raw materials are as old as organized society. However, vast improvements have been achieved in the ability to convert raw materials, recombine materials, and preserve raw materials, intermediate products, and final products. As noted, above, the object has been not only to extend the period of availability but also to make foods more palatable and free of toxic and undesirable microbiological by-products.

Most foods spoil because of natural enzymatic processes within the food material itself, activity of microbiological organisms and infestation by insects, rodents, birds, and other animals. Food processing, preservation, and storage are designed to curtail or eliminate these problems over varying time periods. Various methods of doing so include: dehydration, curing and pickling, fermentation, sterilization and pasteurization, refrigeration and freezing, fumigation, distillation and refining, milling and separation, and mixing and recombination.

Within each of these broad processing categories there are several distinctly different processes that are specialized either by raw material or by final product. Some processes are interchangeable within limited ranges of performance to produce the same or similar output.

Final Products

To a major degree, perhaps more than in any other industry, food manufacturing subsectors are an agglomeration of classes based on combinations of raw material inputs, processes, and final goods. For example, distilling of spirits has more to do with process than raw material — a process is used to convert various raw materials into a variety of final products. By comparison, the manufactured milk products subsector uses a variety of process (flash heating, condensation, fermentation, canning, freezing, and dehydration) to convert milk and ancillary materials into a wide variety of final products. With these caveats in mind, the subsectors in Table 2-1 are included in the food manufacturing industry (ISIC-31).

The firms included in the sample span the entire gamut of this classification. Among the eight firms in the sample, at least one is represented in each of the processing classifications listed.

Size of the Food Processing Industry

There are no reliable estimates of the value added or other measures of output for the food processing industry on a worldwide basis.[1] An estimate of the worldwide value added was made for the year 1975 by the U.N. Centre on Transnational Corporations as reported in Table 2-2.

As can be seen, the large bulk of food processing takes place in the industrialized countries. Only about 13 percent of the total occurs in developing countries. Table 2-3 provides perspective on the relative importance of various countries in terms of industry size.

Only five countries among those with free-market economies had a total value added in food processing exceeding $5 billion in 1975. The United States was by far the largest followed by France, West Germany, Japan, and the United Kingdom. The ratio of total sales to value added is approximately 3.5 times on a worldwide basis. Thus, sales of processed foods amounts to about $695 billion

TABLE 2-1
Four-Digit ISIC for Food Manufacturing

ISIC	Subsector
3111	Slaughtering, preparing, and preserving of meat
3112	Manufactured dairy products
3113	Canning and preserving of fruits and vegetables
3114	Canning, preserving, and processing of fish
3115	Manufactured vegetable and animal oils and fats
3116	Grain mill products
3117	Manufacture of baked products
3118	Sugar factories and refineries
3119	Manufacture of cocoa, chocolate, and sugar confections
3121	Manufacture of food products n.e.c.
3122	Manufacture of prepared animal feeds
3131	Distilling, rectifying, and blending of spirits
3132	Wines and alcoholic drinks other than malt
3133	Malt liquors and malt
3134	Soft drinks and carbonated beverages

TABLE 2-2
Value-added in the Food and Beverage Industry
   (Excludes centrally planned economies in Asia)

Region	Billions of 1975 U.S. Dollars	Percentage
Total	196.0	100.0
Western Europe	51.5	26.2
North America	39.6	20.2
Japan	11.0	5.6
Other (includes Australia, Greece, Israel, Malta, New Zealand, Portugal, South Africa, Spain, and Yugoslavia)	10.3	5.3
Centrally planned	57.6	29.4
European economies	26.0	13.3

Source: Adapted from Table 1, U.N. Centre on Transnational Corporations, *Transnational Corporations in Food and Beverage Processing* (New York: United Nations, 1981), p. 5.

TABLE 2-3
Value-added by Country in 1975
(Billions of U.S. Dollars)

Country	Value-added
West Germany	12.7
United Kingdom	6.0
Italy	4.7
France	13.4
Netherlands	3.1
Belgium	2.7
Switzerland	2.2
U.S.A.	35.6
Canada	4.0
Japan	11.0
Spain	2.7
South Africa	1.0
Australia	2.9

Source: U.N. Centre on Transnational Corporations, *Transnational Corporations in Food and Beverage Processing* (New York: United Nations, 1981), p. 147.

TABLE 2-4
Firm Size and Foreign Operations

Size of Firm Sales	Percent of Sales from Foreign Operations	Number of Firms
$3 billion and greater	80.3 ⎫	2 ⎫
$1-$3 billion	38.8 ⎬ 38	2 ⎬ 43
$.5-$1 billion	32.8 ⎭	11 ⎭
$.3-$.5 billion	26.4	28
Less than $.3 billion	13.9	91

Source: Derived from tables in U.N. Centre on Transnational Corporations, *Transnational Corporations in Food and Beverage Processing* (New York: United Nations, 1981), p. 12.

worldwide excluding the centrally planned economies of Asia. Some 189 firms account for 27 percent of these worldwide sales with about 22 percent coming from foreign operations. As Table 2-4 indicates, the proportion of foreign sales increases with firm size.

In the survey conducted by the Centre on Transnational Corporations, there were only 43 firms that had worldwide food processing revenues exceeding $300 million in 1976. An average of 38 percent of these firms' total revenues came from overseas food processing operations.

Sectoral Distribution of Overseas Operations by Multinational Food Processing Firms

Whereas the Centre on Transnational Corporations identified 279 firms that have sizeable food processing operations, only 134 of these have overseas operations of any consequence. Moreover, not all large food processing firms have significant overseas operations. Of the 61 firms that have revenues of over $1 billion in food processing, only 37 have a sizeable proportion of their assets invested abroad. Those food processing firms that are both the largest and most diversified are listed in Table 2-5.

Further information of interest is the degree of foreign involvement on a sectoral basis. Table 2-6 provides information on the overseas operations of the food processing industry on a sector by sector basis. As can be seen, a relatively few firms are involved internationally in each subsector. Total estimated sales worldwide by international food processing firms in the subsectors above were nearly $160 billion in 1976 with some $40 billion, or more than 25 percent, in foreign locations.

These sales figures are not indicative entirely of the degree to which foreign manufacturing subsidiaries of multinational food firms export to other countries. Evidence on this issue can be but suggestive because we have data only for U.S.-based multinationals.

Domestic Market Orientation of Multinational Food Processing Firms

An examination of data on the overseas operations of U.S.-based food manufacturing firms indicates that in 1977 these generated

TABLE 2-5
Size and Diversification among the 25 Largest Food Processing Firms

Firm	Country	Participating in Number of Subsectors*	1976 Food Processing Revenues†
Unilever	Neth./U.K.	9	7.9
Nestle	Switzerland	6	6.2
Kraft Foods	U.S.A.	5	4.8
General Foods	U.S.A.	5	4.4
Esmark, Inc.	U.S.A.	3	4.0
Beatrice Foods	U.S.A.	7	3.9
Coca-Cola	U.S.A.	5	2.9
Ralston-Purina	U.S.A.	3	2.4
Borden	U.S.A.	7	2.3
United Brands	U.S.A.	5	2.1
Imperial Group, Ltd.	U.K.	5	2.1
Pepsico, Inc.	U.S.A.	5	2.1
Associated British Foods	U.K.	2	2.1
Carnation	U.S.A.	3	2.0
CPC International	U.S.A.	5	2.0
Heinz	U.S.A.	3	1.9
Ranks, Hovis, McDougall, Ltd.	U.K.	3	1.8
Procter and Gamble	U.S.A.	4	1.8
Nabisco	U.S.A.	4	1.8
General Mills	U.S.A.	4	1.7
Unigate	U.K.	3	1.6
Campbell's Soup	U.S.A.	3	1.6
Cadbury-Schweppes	U.K.	4	1.5
Mars, Inc.	U.S.A.	4	1.5
BSN-Gervais	France	3	1.4

*The nine subsectors included are meat products, dairy products, fish, fruits and vegetables, cereal products, oils and fats, sugar and related products, alcoholic beverages, and tropical beverages.

†In billions of U.S. dollars.

Source: Adapted from Table V-3, U.N. Centre on Transnational Corporations, *Transnational Corporations in Food and Beverage Processing* (New York: United Nations, 1981), pp. 183-89.

TABLE 2-6

Overseas Operations by Industry Subsector in Food Processing (1976)

Product Line	Firms with Foreign Operations	Total Sales	Foreign Sales	Percent Foreign	Total Affiliates
Meat processing	42	$28.6	$3.1	10.8	118
Dairy products	28	12.5	4.8	22.3	205
Wheat flour industries	17	7.1	1.6	22.5	84
Corn milling	8	3.0	0.9	30.0	71
Animal feeds	27	6.0	0.2	3.3	124
Crackers and biscuits	21	3.7	1.4	37.8	105
Breakfast cereals	14	2.9	1.0	34.5	77
Bakery industry	28	5.9	1.0	16.9	80
Vegetable oil processing	24	6.8	2.3	33.8	74
Margarine and table oils	17	8.3	3.8	45.7	91
Fruit and vegetable industries	43	14.3	4.5	31.5	302
Sugar and related products					
Sugar milling	10	6.0	1.0	16.7	20
Soft drink concentrates	17	3.5	1.3	37.1	108
Confectionery	35	5.9	2.4	40.7	130
Alcoholic beverages					
Beer	19	12.8	2.1	16.4	97
Wines and brandy	11	2.3	0.5	21.7	31
Distilled spirits	11	5.1	1.7	33.3	48
Tropical beverages					
Coffee industries	16	4.9	2.4	49.0	92
Cocoa industries	19	4.0	2.0	50.0	111
Tea	9	2.3	1.2	52.2	59
Fish products	26	3.3	1.3	39.4	123
Total		157.9	40.5	25.6	2150

Source: Compiled from Tables V-5 through V-27, U.N. Centre on Transnational Corporations, *Transnational Corporations in Food and Beverage Processing* (New York: United Nations, 1981), pp. 193-222.

$21.8 billion in sales of which $18.5 billion, about 85 percent, was in the domestic markets of host countries. Only 2.5 percent was exported back to the United States whereas 12.3 percent was exported to countries other than the United States.

Among the 16 manufacturing sectors reported separately, food manufacturing ranks fourth behind transport equipment, chemicals and nonelectrical machinery in terms of sales by overseas affiliates of U.S. firms.[2] However, it ranks last in terms of its proportion of export sales by overseas affiliates (see Table 2-7). Some 31 percent of sales by foreign manufacturing affiliates go to countries outside the host. In the food subsector only 15 percent of such sales go to nonhost countries. If the experience of parent firms worldwide is

TABLE 2-7
Sectoral Sales by U.S. Owned Foreign Affiliates and Percent of Sales Exported

Manufacturing Sector	Sales (Billions of U.S. Dollars)	Percent Exported
Total	194.2	31
Food and kindred products	21.8	15
Chemicals and allied products	32.4	26
Primary and fabricated metals	11.6	27
Nonelectrical machinery	28.4	37
Electric and electronic equipment	18.7	34
Transportation equipment	48.7	39
Tobacco manufacturers	1.8	24
Textile products and apparel	3.1	35
Lumber and wood products	1.7	39
Paper and allied products	5.1	37
Printing and publishing	1.3	19
Rubber products	5.8	18
Misc. plastic products	1.2	28
Glass products	1.3	30
Stone, clay, cement, and concrete	2.4	26
Instruments and related products	6.3	32
Other	2.6	27

Source: Compiled from Table III.H-2, U.S. Bureau of Economic Analysis, *U.S. Direct Investment Abroad, 1977* (Washington, D.C.: U.S. Department of Commerce, April, 1981), p. 319.

similar to that of U.S.-based parents, it could be concluded that the food processing industry is domestically oriented in foreign affiliate sales within host countries.

Summary

The food processing industry is, in fact, an agglomeration of different industries, each based upon several primary inputs and perhaps utilizing several processes to produce a variety of final products. Processing has the objective of making food more palatable and increasing its availability over time.

Products may be used either for final consumption or as intermediate goods in the creation of other final products. An estimate of total food processing value added among countries outside socialist Asia indicates that the industry generated some $196 billion in 1975. Only about 13 percent of this occurred in developing market economies. Only five countries had a value added exceeding $5 billion in the industry. To generate the $196 billion of value added required sales of about $695 billion.

Food processing is strongly influenced by large multinational firms. About 27 percent of worldwide food sales was contributed by 189 firms. Of these firms, 168 are headquartered in either the United States or the United Kingdom. Subsectors within the industry differ widely regarding the proportion of revenues generated by overseas operations.

When compared with other manufacturing industries, food processing is much more oriented to domestic markets when measured by the proportion of foreign affiliate sales exported.

ANALYSIS OF CASE STUDIES

Introduction

As noted earlier, interviews were undertaken with corporate level executives in eight large multinational, food processing firms. Two additional interviews were conducted with operating subsidiaries. All of the firms included in the study are headquartered either in Europe or the United States. From information provided in the industry profile above, it is evident that there are few firms from Canada, Australia, Japan, and elsewhere that have major investments abroad. The eight firms selected for study are among the most prominent in the industry. All have had extensive and lengthy experience with international investment. All produce a diversity of products in both advanced and developing countries.

From the interviews, some 28 different subsidiaries were identified as possibilities for detailed study. For 16 of the 28 subsidiaries, reasonably complete information was obtained on the incentives received, disincentives imposed, and age and size of the investment. Three of the investments were still under negotiation; that is, no plant had yet been started in these cases. The subsidiaries examined are located in the following countries: Australia, Belgium, Brazil, Canada, East Asia, France, Greece, India, East Africa, Mexico, Peru, Philippines, Portugal, Spain, Thailand, Turkey, United Kingdom, and Venezuela.

The products manufactured by this group of subsidiaries includes processed dairy products, vegetable oils and margarine, pet foods, grain mill products and baked goods, instant coffee and other drinks, canned fruits, vegetables and tomato products, and snack foods and other highly prepared foods.

Results of the Comprehensive Checklist on Incentives

In the questionnaire, two checklists were used to examine the degree of importance firms place on the presence of investment incentives and performance requirements of various types. A six-point scale (one being high and six being low) was used to measure the relative importance of investment incentives. Results were as follows:

Incentive	*Score*
Tax exemptions	
Income tax	4.33
Corporate tax	5.33
Capital gains tax	5.00
Property tax	2.50
Customs tax remission	
Capital goods	2.30
Materials/components	2.30

Incentive	Score
Tax credits	2.25
Dividend tax waiver	3.00
Subsidies	
Free or subsidized land	5.00
Cash grants	1.30
Low-interest loans	2.30
Leasehold subsidies	4.00
Export subsidies	5.00
Training subsidies	6.00
Other	
Rebates on ingredients	1.00

In addition to the items above, other factors were examined that could be considered forms of inducements to invest, although they are more a matter of actual business practice than of direct incentives. Included are the following, as measured on a seven-point scale.

Other Inducements	Score
Freedom to adjust product prices	1.80
Government supplied low-cost materials	4.50
Timeliness of government dealings with firm	4.00
Willingness to honor technical service fees	1.00
Freedom to remit dividends	1.00
Equal treatment of foreign and local firms	1.00

As can be seen from the above, firms in the food industry are quite concerned about the removal or counterbalancing of tariffs on imported capital goods, materials, and components; receipt of cash grants; subsidized interest payments on loans; removal of price controls; ability to remit technical service fees and dividends; and not being discriminated against when compared with local firms. Property tax subsidies may be important to some firms: however, the property tax subsidy does not seem to be used by many countries as an incentive.

Results of the Comprehensive Checklist on Performance Requirements and Disincentives

Whereas the performance requirements involved in individual investments are discussed below, there is a composite view developed from the checklist used during the interviews. The results were as follows using a six-point scale to measure the relative degree of importance.

Performance Requirement or Disincentive	*Score*
Local content on capital goods	3.7
Local content on materials	4.0
Import restrictions (nonlocal content)	3.3
Foreign exchange deposits on	
Material imports	3.0
Capital imports	3.0
Capital and dividend repatriation	2.7
Debt to equity limits	4.3
Limits on imported used equipment	5.0
Limits on use of expatriates	4.3
Indigenization of workforce	3.5
Joint venture requirements	3.5
Equity spin-offs	2.7
Export requirements	3.0
Price controls	2.5
Controls on remittances	1.0
Restrictions on transfer prices	4.0
Import/export offsets	4.5
Coproduction requirements	4.0
Lifetime employment	4.0
Severance pay requirements	3.7
Extra months pay with no work	5.0
Locals on the board of directors	5.0
R & D requirements	4.0
Technology transfer requirements	3.5
Job creation requirements	1.0
Limits on service fee payments	1.0

The scoring indicates that firms are most concerned by restrictions on the movement of capital, price controls, job creation, export requirements, and limits on fees paid for services provided by the parent to the subsidiary. Of lesser importance are such restrictions as local content, severance pay, workforce indigenization, and life-time employment. It appears from this analysis that firms are least concerned about those aspects of doing business that are most closely tied to the local environment and most concerned with those that impinge upon their ability to conduct business internationally. Only the job creation requirement, among the local environmentally related variables, is of great concern. But this, when linked with the export requirement, also affects the ability to be competitive in international markets.

By its nature, the food industry must rely heavily upon local supplies of ingredients. Thus, the local content requirement is not of major concern in most segments of the industry — certainly in dairy products, fruits and vegetables, and even in some grain milling opera-tions. Also, severance pay requirements and 13 months' pay for 12 months' work are common around the globe — differing only in degree among countries. Accordingly these are not major issues.

The issues of the number of expatriates in residence and of having local members on the board of directors seem to be moot points. Virtually all the firms interviewed follow a policy of indigen-ization at the earliest time possible with the result that there are few expatriates in these firms' overseas operations. All the firms include nationals on the boards of most of their subsidiaries. These nationals are there because they occupy key management posts. While the firms tend to insist upon majority ownership positions, they also have subsidiaries that involve local partners. The rather low impor-tance attached to some of these variables seems to be a natural out-growth of the industry's long experience with foreign operations.

Nature of Investment Decision Making in the Sample of Food Manufacturing Firms

Food manufacturing firms have been operating abroad for many years. In 23 of the 28 subsidiaries studied, there had been a recent investment. Of these, only eight involved plants built *de novo*. The other 15 were expansions to existing plants, and two involved no new investment but did involve performance requirements or incentives not connected to new investments. Only one new plant involved expenditures in excess of $40 million. The others averaged less than $10 million each. Among the expansion programs only two exceeded $40 million each. The others averaged less than $10 million each. By comparison with other industries, food manufacturing involves relatively small investments. In the petrochemical industry, for example, investments typically exceed $250 million. The same is true of the automotive industry.

Incentive packages available to multinational firms in the food industry are generally no different from those offered to local firms. Only when the investment has some unique facet, such as new technology, development of basic agriculture, or special ability to export, might there be extraordinary treatment involving an agreement that falls outside standard investment guidelines. In only four of the subsidiaries among the 28 in the study was there special treatment, and, in one of these cases, the negotiations are not yet complete. It is questionable in that case whether the subsidiary will obtain the tariff concessions needed to make the investment attractive.

Firms do not exhaustively search the environment when considering foreign investments. The screening procedure and the method of locating investment sites tend to focus on individual country markets rather than on making comparisons among countries. For most food products, it is less costly to serve markets locally than by exports from another location once market size is great enough to accommodate a manufacturing plant. Thus, intercountry comparisons in site selection occur only in situations such as the EC where distances between markets are relatively small. Even there, opportunities to exploit economies of scale may be limited simply because of differences in local tastes. Where formulations must be adapted to local preferences, a wide variety of products must be produced. Production runs are consequently small, and, accordingly, the benefits of large plants often are negated. Hence, the tendency among the firms interviewed is to install small specialized plants to serve each national market. Also because of the tendency among countries to protect agriculture and to insist on the use of local ingredients, the industry is circumscribed from being able to install large specialized plants to serve several national markets. Finally, many food products do not have long shelf lives. Thus, plant location near points of final consumption can be important even in the absence of incentives and performance requirements.

The main considerations in making investment decisions are: the need for capacity to serve the local market, the projected profitability of the investment, and the attractiveness of the investment climate regarding economic and political stability and freedom to repatriate dividends and service fees. It appears that performance requirements and disincentives are of more concern than incentives. Firms tend to eschew situations in which there are specific employment targets, export requirements, and limits on transfer of funds insofar as new investments are concerned. Of course, usually investments are not really new, but rather are expansions or modernizations of already existing plants. This clouds the issue of investment location and the degree to which incentives and performance requirements can or do influence the decision.

The host countries' desire to export and the insistence to do so are probably the most persuasive reasons for not investing. Repeatedly, the interviewees suggested that exportation is noneconomic except where the country clearly has a comparative advantage as some countries do in tropical fruits, tea, coffee, grain, and meat. However, whether there is a comparative advantage in producing and exporting final products rather than the raw materials is not always clear. Canning of pineapple in the Philippines for export to Japan clearly is an instance of exportation on the basis of comparative advantage. It is not clear, however, whether the dehydration of coffee for export from Brazil is an instance of trading on comparative advantage because dehydrated coffee is a blend of coffees coming from several countries including Brazil. It may be more economic to ship the beans to central locations for roasting, grinding, blending, extraction, and dehydration than produce the final product within the country where raw coffee is grown. Much the same can be said for grain mill products and processed meat products.

Because of the industry's local orientation, access to domestic markets is the major stimulus to invest in food manufacturing. If given their choice, most firms would give up incentives if they could also escape performance requirements and still have market access. From their point of view, it is the performance requirements that make necessary the incentives as a counterbalance. At the same time, it should be noted that two-thirds of the plants in place hide behind some form of tariff protection or import quotas on final products. At least eight of the 25 investments would not be located in the host country had protection been nonexistent.

Incentives other than commodity protection do impinge upon the location of investments within countries. But again, the incentives are needed either to offset some imposed performance requirement or to compensate for the undesirable features of the subsidized site. For example, firms normally would not locate within depressed areas if it were not for incentives. At the same time they often are not allowed to expand operations unless they do locate in depressed areas. Indeed, without incentives they likely would not locate in the country at all. Again, this primarily is a matter of gaining access to the local markets while receiving an incentive in exchange for locating in a depressed area.

The process of deciding on an investment almost always involves a proposal to the host country government. The firm may propose a package that falls outside the guidelines. For example, a firm may give up incentives if a performance requirement is removed. This does occur but appears to be rare. Because most of the firms' subsidiaries have been in place for several years, renegotiations of existing contracts are more common than negotiation of contracts for new investments. However, the focus is similar in the two situations. The firm attempts to avoid or gain removal of as many performance requirements and disincentives as possible while obtaining or keeping intact as many incentives as possible. The countries, of course, take just the opposite tack. Firms do attempt trade-offs among incentives and performance requirements. They may, for example, give up an incentive such as preferred location to avoid having to take on a local partner. Or one performance requirement may be traded off against another such as accepting an employment creation target and infusion of additional capital in exchange for removal of an export requirement or elimination of a requirement to locate in a depressed area.

Country and Site Selection

Among 25 existing investments (three of the 28 examined were in process of negotiation), in only one had an incentive other than commodity protection or factor subsidies shifted the location of the investment from one country to another. In one other instance, the incentive package increased the size of the plant and altered its location within the country. However, without the incentives, the firm still would have installed a plant, albeit a smaller one, within the country. Thus, its location between countries would have been affected in the sense that part of the capacity would have been relocated to one or more other countries in order to achieve the required total capacity in the EC.

Of the 25 projects already in place, nine were located in advanced countries and 16 were in developing countries. A total of 18 countries were involved, that is, seven advanced and 11 developing. There were no instances of a plant being shifted from a developing country to an advanced country or vice versa. In the two shifts noted above, one involved the EC and the other involved an African and a Southeast Asian country. This review suggests that incentives, other than commodity protection, seem to have little bearing on site selection across countries. Of course, this cannot be said with equanimity because it is not possible to place a precise value on the benefits of incentives (including protection) and the costs of the disincentives as represented by performance requirements and other factors.

Among the 25 projects, only six had received regional (within country) incentives. In only three of these did the incentives actually influence the locational decision; that is, in three cases the firms were going to locate where they did by expanding an existing plant regardless of incentives. In these cases, the incentives (depressed area grants) were "icing on the cake."

In one instance, a performance requirement (pressure from the host country government) induced investment in a research and development facility that otherwise well might have gone elsewhere.

When tariffs and other protection are ignored, other incentives and performance requirements seem to have had only marginal effects on plant sitings across countries. In summary, it appears that nine subsidiaries would not have entered the countries they did and one would have been partially relocated to another country had there not been tariff protection and other incentives. Within countries, regional incentives induced shifts in plant location for half of those subsidiaries receiving regional incentives.

Incidence of Incentives and Performance Requirements

It is evident that incentives in one form or another are quite widespread. Of the 25 projects in place, 19 or 76 percent had received incentives. This same percentage, approximately, applied to projects in both advanced and developing countries.[3] Table 2-8 provides a general tabulation of the number of projects receiving incentives and confronting performance requirements *qua* disincentives. The proportion of firms being subjected to performance requirements is lower than the proportion receiving incentives, that is, 76 percent versus 64 percent. However, performance requirements are more prevalent in developing countries than in advanced countries where the percentages are 88 percent and 22 percent respectively. There also are inducements to invest that are not exactly part of a negotiated investment proposal, for example,

TABLE 2-8
Incidence of Incentives and Performance Requirements among Sample Firms

	Total	*Adv. Countries*	*Dev. Countries*
Number of projects in place	25 = 100%	9 = 100%	16 = 100%
Projects receiving incentives	19 = 76%	7 = 78%	12 = 75%
Projects subject to other inducements to invest	19 = 76%	7 = 78%	12 = 75%
Projects subject to performance requirements	16 = 64%	2 = 22%	14 = 88%
Projects subject to other conditions or disincentives	19 = 76%	4 = 44%	15 = 94%
Total projects receiving incentives and subject to other inducements including protection	23 = 92%	8 = 89%	15 = 94%
Total projects subject to performance requirements and other conditions or disincentives	19 = 76%	4 = 44%	15 = 94%

Source: Compiled by author.

general tariffs. The same proportion of firms have been subject to these inducements as the proportion receiving explicit incentives.

In the case of other conditions, not included under the performance requirements, again 76 percent of the sample had been subjected to one or more of these, but they are more common in developing than in advanced countries. Some 94 percent of the projects in developing countries were faced with such conditions.

In terms of the incidence of specific incentives, other inducements, performance requirements, and other conditions imposed, Tables 2-9 and 2-10 provide detailed information on the occurrence of these among the projects examined. As can be seen, the most prevalent incentive is some form of export subsidy followed by regional development grants and investment tax credits. Accelerated depreciation, beyond that normally offered, and low-cost financing were mentioned in only four instances each. Other incentives are of lesser importance. In the case of the export subsidies, five of nine instances take the form of low-interest (subsidized) financing of working capital and four involve direct cash rebates, tax credits, or favorable exchange rates.

Fiscal incentives (direct cash grants, tax forgiveness and tax credits, direct rebates and subsidies, and accelerated depreciation) are more in evidence than monetary incentives (low-interest financing, for example). It also appears that inducements other than direct incentives may be at least, if not more, important than the incentives. For example, tariff protection is involved in nearly two-thirds of the projects (16 of 25). Other inducements seem not to figure prominently in the activities of these subsidiaries. Even though majority control is mentioned, this is only of concern in countries having a requirement, such as Mexico's, to accept local equity control unless one is prepared to export or locate in an economically depressed area.

As has been noted, performance requirements are encountered in 16 of 25 completed projects. Export and local content requirements are mentioned most often. The local content requirement tends to be imposed simultaneously with the export requirement. Local content requirements are not always explicit or formally stated. In some instances, local content comes about because of food formulation requirements that essentially prohibit the use of foreign procured ingredients.

Even though only three projects had an explicit employment target, this requirement is one about which some firms will not

TABLE 2-9
Occurrence of Incentives and Inducements by Types

Type	Number
Projects Actually Receiving Incentives	19
Incentives received	
Regional/depressed area grants	6
Income tax forgiveness (holiday)	3
Property tax forgiveness	1
Investment tax credit	6
Accelerated depreciation	4
Export subsidies	9
Low-cost financing (not part of export package)	4
Duty free import of capital goods	2
Rebate (subsidy) on ingredients	2
Subsidized land lease	1
Projects Subject to Other Inducements	23
Other inducements encountered	
Tariff protection	16
Removal of expansion constraint	1
Country opened access to foreign investment to serve domestic market	1
Majority control allowed	2
Technical service allowed	1
Necessary raw materials become available locally making possible a new plant	1
Governmental pressure (host)	2
Total number of projects	28
Projects still in process	3
No incentives received (completed projects)	6

Source: Compiled by author.

78

TABLE 2-10
Occurrence of Performance Requirements by Type

Type	Number
Projects Subject to Performance Requirements	16
Type of requirement	
Exportation of specified proportion of output	12
Creation of specified number of jobs	3
Local content (implicit or explicit)	12
Local ownership participation	2
Debt/equity limits	2
Projects Subject to Other Conditions (Disincentives)	19
Other conditions	
Price controls	3
Foreign exchange deposits	1
Assist in development of contract farming	3
Import controls on ingredients and/or capital goods	19
Dividend limits	7
Limits on licensing and service fees	7
Limit on use of expatriates	1
Total number of projects	25

Source: Compiled by author.

negotiate; that is, if there is a specified employment level to be achieved, they will not invest. There appear to be few other performance requirements affecting these firms. Among other conditions that apply, import controls appear to be most prominent. Of the 25 projects, 19 are affected by explicit or implicit import controls where implicit refers to government pressure rather than formal requirements. Limits on the repatriation of dividends and service fees are the next most important forms of constraint or condition involved in gaining market access.

Price controls were distinctly mentioned in only three projects, but it is likely that they figure into a larger proportion of projects because, in general discussions of disincentives, price controls were mentioned prominently among conditions considered undesirable by these firms. Countries in the sample that have had price controls on food ingredients or final food products are Mexico, Brazil, Philippines, India, Australia, and the European Common Market countries. Firms consider price controls to be onerous. Their influence on investment decisions is unclear. They may well deter firms from expanding operations or locating new plants in countries that have them. However, countries sometimes use price controls to reduce the cost of food to consumers. Firms in turn are compensated through rebates on basic ingredients but not on other ingredients. The desired outcome is a reduction in the cost of basic foods, such as bread and milk, while reducing the production of food products that are considered luxury items. The effect on the firm depends on its mix of products and the importance of subsidies on ingredients in relation to price controls on final products. One firm in the sample closed a plant because of price controls. Another is gradually reducing its presence in India because of controls including price controls.

The large majority of firms receives incentives and encounters performance requirements and other disincentives. The most often encountered performance requirement is the export requirement. And, in turn, perhaps it is not surprising that the most frequently offered incentive is the export subsidy. For most countries, exportation of processed foods would not take place even in the face of export requirements unless there were export incentives. Lack of comparative advantage makes necessary the use of subsidies to generate exports. Local content requirements, associated import controls, and employment targets also work against comparative advantage and may require subsidies as offsets.

Experience with Incentives, Disincentives, and Performance Requirements

The effects of incentives, disincentives, and performance requirements are difficult to identify because of the subtleties involved. Incentives or subsidies may merely be a means of offsetting the effects of performance requirements. Also, where there is an already existing plant subject to performance requirements, firms may be able to use an expansion program as a device to renegotiate with the government to obtain removal or alteration of an existing performance requirement in exchange for additional investment. For example, one firm in Mexico was able to avoid Mexicanization of an existing subsidiary by installing a new plant whose output was destined for the export market. Such trade-offs, however, seem to be the exception in this industry.

Another form of trade-off is expansion via nonfood products. Most of the firms interviewed have nonfood activities in one or more of the following areas: chemicals, soaps and detergents, cosmetics, fertilizers, animal feeds, pharmaceuticals, and industrial ingredients. Often these nonfood products are considered more desirable areas for investment than food manufacturing. Countries can and do pressure firms to invest in nonfood products if they are to either maintain or expand their existing food manufacturing activities. For example, one firm's Indian subsidiary was forced to invest in nonfoods to avoid losing its majority ownership position.

Requirements and/or controls sometimes result in bizarre behavior. For example, the Belgian government imposes price controls on dairy products. However, firms can renegotiate prices whenever they make a new investment that will generate new jobs. Because of this, firms have adopted a strategy of stepwise investment, that is, dividing a major investment program into small, discrete packages so that prices can be renegotiated more often. For this reason, each new investment as proposed may involve creation of no more than five to ten new jobs even though the firm's ultimate plan is for several times that many jobs.

In terms of individual treatment, firms believe that foreign investors receive equal treatment: that is, there is little in the way of playing favorites among foreign firms. However, in some instances firms have negotiated separate agreements, particularly where exports are involved. Generally, these were few and were based upon the peculiar expertise of the firms involved.

Interviewees also thought that the treatment received after agreements were negotiated was as expected. Moreover, the monitoring systems on performance requirements (local content, employment, import controls, and export performance, for example) seldom allow for any major deviation from agreed levels. The countries are more likely to fail to meet their side of the bargain. This occurs during times of economic stress. For example, one firm had a project that had to be renegotiated. This was caused by a change in economic conditions that foreclosed the possibility of achieving projected levels of output. In this instance, the host government was amenable to a renegotiation that reduced the level of employment specified while also lowering the level of the subsidy initially agreed upon.

Firms also were asked whether performance requirements had been imposed even though no incentive other than tariff protection was being offered. Over 80 percent of them had encountered such situations. Countries where this had occurred included Brazil, Philippines, Mexico, Nicaragua, the Andean Compact Group, and India. Some forms also either gave up incentives to avoid imposition of a performance requirement or accepted one performance requirement to avoid imposition of another. For example, one firm was offered an incentive by the government to relocate outside a congested urban area. The firm chose not to move, that is, did not accept the incentive of a cash grant to meet the performance requirement of moving to a depressed area. The firm felt a need to be close to the market. In two countries, other firms accepted export performance requirements in order to avoid local majority ownership.

In some instances a larger incentive could have been received in exchange for tighter performance requirements. This occurred among the Andean Compact Countries and in Mexico, Brazil, and the EC countries on exportation and low-cost financing.

Renegotiation of agreements is quite common. It appears that renegotiations are more likely to be initiated by the country than by the firm and involve performance requirements rather than incentives. Among the firms interviewed, the following types of renegotiations were encountered.

Type of Renegotiation	*Initiated By*
Increase in firm's equity share in exchange for an increase in invested capital where the guideline had been aiming toward reduction in foreign ownership share	Firm
Decrease in employment level to accommodate changed economic conditions	Firm
Reduction in royalties or services fees	Country
Removal of expansion constraint	Local Partner
Extension of tax holiday	Firm
Reduction in foreign equity share	Country
Firm forced to export final goods to obtain foreign exchange required to purchase imports	Country

The most common renegotiation subjects appear to be: (1) the level of imports and exports, (2) the level of service fees paid for use of parent's technology by its subsidiary, and (3) the number of jobs to be created or maintained. Generally, from the firm's point of view, these renegotiations seldom leave it in a better position than it held before.

Effect of Incentives and Performance Requirements

There is no precise way to measure the effect of incentives, performance requirements, and disincentives. However, performance requirements and disincentives seem to weigh into decisions more heavily than do incentives. Together, though, they do influence decisions regarding plant designs and location within countries. Firms in the food industry tend to look at individual countries as localized markets rather than as parts of a large integrated international market. As has been noted, for several reasons the food industry is more fragmented in its approach to the international market than any other industry because plants are oriented primarily to national or subnational markets. Trading off one country against another in response to competitive incentive/performance requirement packages offered appears not to occur very often. Totally new investments are the exception. Hence, there are few opportunities for comparison shopping because there are few *de novo* investments. Moreover, with the industry being largely domestic market oriented because of tariff protection and local content requirements, most expansion programs are seldom designed to serve export markets. Again, the consequence is that there are few opportunities to bargain across countries in search of the most enticing package. Only in the European Common Market does there appear to be comparison shopping. The reasons for this are obvious. In Europe there are more opportunities to treat the market as largely integrated both in terms of availability of ingredients and accessibility of consumers.

Effects on Plant Design

As was noted above, with exception to import barriers on final products, incentives and performance requirements have affected the investment decisions of firms primarily in terms of the siting of plants within countries. In addition to the potential effects on plant location, firms could be influenced in other ways by incentives and performance requirements. For example, these could affect plant size, level or degree of plant integration, labor content of output (or degree of mechanization), breadth of product line, and timing of entry. Firms were asked about these aspects of their decisions. Largely, the response was that market size is the overriding variable that determines the nature of plant design. However, in a few instances plant design was influenced. One firm, which accepted a specified employment level, indicated that the plant was more labor intensive than it otherwise would have been. Also, the timing of entry was altered by the incentive package; the firm entered earlier than it otherwise would have. Some other effects involve plant characteristics. It appears that in these terms, performance requirements have a greater impact than do incentives. Yet it is difficult to disentangle the relative effects because, even though incentives sometimes are unaccompanied by performance requirements, they often come together as a package. Table 2-11 illustrates some of the effects of incentives and performance requirements on plant design, location, and selected other characteristics for six firms in the sample. None of these firms shared identical experiences; therefore, it is not possible to make direct comparisons of perceptions and behavior.

One firm (number 2 in Table 2-11) chose not to invest further because of performance requirements imposed in India, Brazil, Mexico, and Spain. These led to reduced profitability. Another firm (number 1) invested in response to incentives but was required to export and create a specified number of jobs. It now admits that its decision was a mistake because locating in another country in the EC would have been more profitable. A third firm (number 3) expanded in response to removal of a performance requirement that had foreclosed modernization of a plant in Peru. The modernization reduced the labor content, increased the level of mechanization, and moved the level of plant efficiency toward that of plants in the home country.

Effects on Efficiency

All six firms indicated that the efficiency level of plants subject to performance requirements is lower than that of plants in the

TABLE 2-11
Effects of Incentives and Performance Requirements or Characteristic of Plant Design in Food Manufacturing

	Firm 1	Firm 2	Firm 3	Firm 4	Firm 5	Firm 6
Incentives	Cash grant, tax relief	None. Chose not to invest further	Tax credit, accelerated depreciation	Export incentive	None	Tariff protection, tax relief
Performance requirement	Job creation, export	Exports and various others depending on country	Actually involved removal of employment requirement and altered worker ownership share	Export requirement relative to imports, use of local equipment	Export required, removal of expansion constraint	Export large proportion of output
Countries involved	Belgium	India, Mexico, Brazil, Spain	Peru	Mexico, Brazil	Turkey	Southeast Asian country
Plant scale	Larger	Chose not to expand	Expanded	No effect	Shifted capacity to export, no effect	Standard design
Degree of integration of processes	No effect	No effect	Increased	No effect	No effect	No effect
Diversity of product line	Broadened	No effect	Broadened	No effect	No effect	No effect
Labor content	Higher	No effect	Reduced	No effect	No effect	No effect
Export level	Higher	No effect	No effect	Increased	Increased	Higher
Level of imported products	No effect	No effect	No effect	Decreased	Decreased	No effect
Degree of mechanization	Lower	No effect	Increased	Lower than otherwise, had to use local equipment	Lower, had to avoid import of foreign equipment	No effect
Timing of investment	Earlier	No effect	Later, because of previous requirement	No effect	No effect	No effect

Continued

Table 2-11, continued

	Firm 1	Firm 2	Firm 3	Firm 4	Firm 5	Firm 6
Site location in the country	Changed	No effect	No effect	Changed	No effect	Located where it would be easy to export
Profitability	Lower	Performance required a lower return	Improved	No difference	Export commitment, lower profitability	Without incentives would not have built plant
Efficiency relative to plants in home country	Lower	Lower	Moved toward that level but still lower	Lower	Lower	Lower
Comments	New plant, comparison is with hypothetical situation of no incentives and no performance requirements		Expansion, comparison is with operation before removal of performance requirement and subsequent expansion	Expansion, comparison is with operation prior to imposition of performance requirements	Expansion, comparison is with operation before change in performance requirements	New plant, comparison is without incentives and performance requirement

firms' home countries. Relative profitability of these plants must then depend heavily upon the relationship between the performance requirements imposed and the incentives received. Where there was no investment by firm number two, there were performance requirements but no incentives. Where there were new plants by firms one and six, there were performance requirements that must have been perceived as being offset by incentives because both firms invested. Firm three expanded and modernized a plant based primarily upon removal of a performance requirement; that is, the level of employment and worker ownership participation were reduced. Firm four invested to expand in Mexico and Brazil even though there was a requirement to export. Export incentives accompanied this performance requirement. Firm five received no direct incentives but invested because a performance requirement (or constraint on expansion) was removed.

It should be noted in this context that the expansion programs of firms three, four, and five were involved with ongoing operations. But for this, these investments might not have been undertaken. The joint effects are important. For example, in the case of Mexico, one of these expansions, which made possible export activities, allowed the firm to avoid Mexicanization of its other subsidiary in Mexico. Several such instances were encountered during interviews whereby there were trade-offs between a new investment and already existing operations in terms of performance requirements in a country. Given that this does occur, it is difficult to determine where and to what extent expansion projects stand alone rather than constitute a part of a renegotiated package.

Hypothetical Effects of Absence or Removal of Incentives and Performance Requirements

On balance, firms indicated that incentive/performance requirement packages reduce efficiency and, hence, profitability. Particularly in the food industry, recent investments have tended to be expansions of existing facilities. Accordingly, it is nearly impossible to conduct a before-and-after comparison of expected efficiency and profitability with actual experience. Expansion projects are seldom established as a separate accounting center for purposes of before-and-after measurement. At any rate, no such comparisons could be unearthed at the corporate headquarters level of the firms interviewed. Thus, one must rely upon anecdotal evidence and the results as perceived by experienced executives. From this, the consensus view of executives is that incentive/performance requirement systems lead to inefficiency, fail to result in high levels of profitability, and frustrate firms in their attempts to develop investment programs, whether for new plants or plant expansions. Moreover, given that most countries have them, these incentive/performance requirement systems seldom induce firms to locate in one country rather than another. They also result in inefficiently small plants, bring about exportation not based on comparative advantage, and induce some firms to reduce their investments as compared with what would have happened otherwise.

If one took executives' comments at face value, one would conclude that incentive/performance requirement systems reduce total international investment in the food industry. Executives say that incentives do not induce investment shifts from one country to another, nor do they generally result in plants that are larger than they otherwise would have been. However, performance requirements tend to reduce investments whereas their removal tends to increase investment in those instances where we have evidence. This suggests that foreign investment in the food industry is lower than it would be in the absence of incentive/performance requirement systems. It appears that, at best, most incentives offer but a *quid pro quo* to offset the effects of performance requirements. For example, in nearly every instance explored in which firms were induced to locate in depressed areas as a result of incentives, the postinvestment conclusion was that the firm would have been better off to have located elsewhere while refusing the incentive. In a few instances the performance requirement would have made impossible an investment outside a depressed area. For example, in Mexico one either invested outside Mexico City or did not invest at all. The *quid pro quo* is an offsetting incentive such as a cash grant, tax holiday, low-cost financing, or some combination.

The firms were certainly not unanimous in their opinions about how incentive/performance requirement systems could or should be improved. Five of the eight headquarters responded to the question of how incentive/performance requirement systems could be redesigned to make them more effective. The answers can be summarized as follows:

Firm 1 Remove incentives and performance requirements. Have no restrictions.

Firm 2 Do not redesign these systems. Eliminate them. Advise governments to improve the investment atmosphere.

Firm 3 Incentives should consider the country's deficiencies. There is no sense in incentivating exports from an inefficient base. Don't give incentives and don't impose performance requirements. Maximum freedom to invest is the best incentive.

Firm 4 If there is any incentive at all make it an investment grant up front so that it can be brought into the calculation of feasibility. Get rid of performance requirements. They increase the level of uncertainty and make investments go sour.

Firm 5 Incentives, to be effective in attracting investments, should be permanent for the firm and for the country. Avoid incentives linked to peculiar situations, such as subsidies on raw materials or subsidies based on some time horizon. Investments attracted by such incentives lead to general noncompetitiveness for the country.

Those firms having plants with sizeable export commitments indicated that they could not survive without export incentives. They view export incentives not only as necessary but as a necessarily permanent fixture. However, as a broad generalization, firms appear to favor a system free of incentives and performance requirements. It appears that this industry increasingly is being squeezed by performance requirements. Stated differently, the performance requirements relative to the incentives offered are becoming more burdensome over time. Should this be true, then firms would tend to increase the level of their investments if the incentive/performance requirement systems were to disappear.

Other Issues Involving Incentives and Performance Requirements

Some issues connected to the negotiation of investment packages may or may not involve incentives and performance requirements. Among these are the degree to which subsectors within the industry may be treated differently, the effects on service fees, and the degree to which firms can make and countries will honor counterproposals in the negotiating process.

It appears that the subsectors that are most intimately involved with basic agriculture are those most favorably treated in terms of receiving incentives. Those subsectors that can bring in technology that improves agricultural productivity while being labor intensive are considered to be more favorably treated than are subsectors providing luxury items such as snack foods and beverages. Also, basic agriculture is highly protected in virtually all countries. Thus, direct users of agricultural outputs are likely to be given more favorable treatment than those who utilize intermediate goods and imported ingredients. Firms were unable to cite specific instances in which they or other firms had been treated more favorably than others. However, mention was made of instances in which firms were encouraged to enter and produce products that relied directly on basic agricultural inputs. Examples include animal feeds, broiler production, processed dairy products, improved tomato products, pineapple production, canned fruits and vegetables, and vegetable oil based products.

All of these are highly protected subsectors especially in developing countries. In those countries, the drive is for high protein foods for domestic consumption and for other products, such as canned tomato products and fruits, for export. The actual production of raw materials such as grain, fruits, vegetables, and milk are usually in the hands of local farmers, but multinational firms are encouraged to assist in the development of basic agriculture through contractual arrangements with farmers. This includes planting and harvesting schedules, use of fertilizers and pesticides, use of high yield varieties, and other modern methods to produce superior products for use in manufactured foods.

Use of Counterproposals

Because some firms can offer technical assistance, they can develop counterproposals. However, not all counterproposals involve technical assistance such as that noted in the preceding section. Seven of the eight firms interviewed had been involved in counterproposals.[4] Examples include:

1. A firm in an EC country proposed that a potential plant site be reclassified as being in a depressed area (even though it was not

depressed) so that the firm could receive incentives. The government agreed but set an employment target.

2. In a European country a firm proposed that an imported raw material be given preferential treatment so long as it was re-exported in a finished product. The government agreed and made the action firm specific; that is, the same conditions were not extended to other firms.

3. A subsidiary in Latin America would be forced to sell a majority of its equity to nationals if it did not export. However, the products manufactured were not suitable for export. The firm counterproposed to set up a second subsidiary for export only, but, as a condition, the existing subsidiary would remain wholly owned. The government accepted.

4. In a Latin American country, a firm was subject to price control. It counterproposed for relief from price controls in exchange for an increase in equity capital and increased investment. The government agreed.

5. In a Southeast Asian country, a firm proposed to include a new plant and an existing distribution company as a package and to apply both under a tax holiday incentive offered on new investments. The country rejected and removed the distribution company from the package. The firm invested anyhow.

6. A firm with a 20 percent locally owned subsidiary in an Asian country proposed to set up an experimental fish hatchery to develop new technology and products leading to new export markets for the country. The country set a guideline of an increase in local equity to 30 percent, no service fees, and no expatriates in residence. The company refused and is awaiting a response.

There are other types of counterproposals, such as the supply of technical know-how in a special package. For example, one firm entered three different countries to produce solely for export and to develop a reliable supply of agricultural inputs — in this case fruits and vegetables. Each project was negotiated outside the guidelines and involved generous incentive packages. The firm received virtually everything for which it asked. These examples demonstrate that there is flexibility in the negotiating process and the guidelines governing that process. The degree of rigidity depends on what the firm brings to the bargaining table in terms of know-how and existing investments in the country, the country's investment climate, and its past experience with the firm.

Payments for Service Fees and Technology

Service fees are of major concern. Of the six firms queried on this subject, five have licensing agreements and service contracts. These agreements become a part of the negotiations on investment proposals. Usually, licensing and service contracts are negotiated separately from the investment proposal, yet they become a part of the total package because countries are interested in the potential technology to be provided to and paid for by the project. The firms tend to see service fees as legitimate payments from subsidiaries to support continued research and development by the parent firm. Also, service fees may support the basic quality control infrastructure that involves use of expatriates either traveling to remote locations or being in residence. Controls that disallow or reduce payments for these activities are considered dysfunctional by investing firms.

There is another major reason why firms dislike not being able to collect service fees as they wish. The tax laws of most home countries have allowed the expensing of costs against service fees. This reduces the total taxes paid as compared with not having this avenue available. Also, some countries use various devices to limit the remission of dividends by foreign subsidiaries to their parents. Accordingly, service fees may serve another function, a substitute for dividends. On both counts, service fees are a more attractive method than dividend payments of developing and remitting income. However, if there were tax harmonization, no limits on dividend repatriation and no difference in tax treatment between dividends and service fees, there would be no incentive for firms to differentiate among methods of remitting income from host to home country.

According to the firms, there is pressure in some countries — especially in developing areas — to reduce the service fees remitted as the subsidiary ages. Service agreement contracts vary in duration but appear to call for renegotiation every five years or so. In some countries, not only the fee structure must be renegotiated but also the length of any follow-on contract. Seldom are service fee contracts made more liberal for the firms upon renegotiation.

Liberalization would occur only if the firm brought something new to the package, for example, in terms of technology or management. Also, occasionally agreements might be liberalized by a change in political regime, as was true in Chile. However, according to interviewees, the trend is toward less liberal terms over time. Service agreements usually must be approved by the Central Bank, a science agency, or some other authority both at the time of first negotiation and at any subsequent renegotiations. Change, if any, as a result of renegotiation, seldom leaves the firm better off than it was before. The type of agreement most likely to be attacked by the host government is the one that is general in nature, that is, a percentage of sales paid for the use of broadly specified technology, trademarks, and research results. However, even those service agreements that specify the individual services to be received by the subsidiary are also scrutinized, albeit more benignly.

SUMMARY AND CONCLUSIONS

Using the United States as a surrogate measure of overseas investment, the food manufacturing industry ranks fourth in size after transport equipment, chemicals, and nonelectrical machinery. However, in terms of the operations represented by that overseas investment, the food industry, among manufacturing industries, is least likely to export from host countries to other countries including the home country. Only about 15 percent of the sales generated by overseas subsidiaries go to markets outside the host country. The food industry, internationally, is well populated by firms with overseas investments. Yet only five countries harbor the vast bulk of parent firms.

To examine the effects of incentives, disincentives, and performance requirements, eight major firms were interviewed. The results of these interviews suggest that incentives and performance requirements do influence investment decisions. However, in the absence of protective tariffs, they seldom influence firms to invest in one country rather than another. There are some locational effects of incentives within countries. Incentives are viewed as being tentative and temporary. Indeed, incentives are usually not even included in feasibility studies. Incentives may be accompanied by various types of performance requirements that are considered undesirable.

The firms see access to domestic markets as the key incentive to invest. However, of the 25 projects examined, tariff protection was evident in about two-thirds of the cases. It is also true that performance requirements are in evidence and include local content and import controls that tend to isolate country markets from one another. Tariffs may be but an offset required to entice firms in or to keep them there once they have entered. These are not the only explanations for the food industry's tendency to be localized. National markets require special treatment because of differences in preferences. These coupled with administrative barriers (locally imposed formulations in some instances) result in short production runs that negate potential economies of scale. Accordingly, plants tend to be small and inefficient. Indeed, some firms have adopted a strategy of small plants for small markets. Firms make their investment decisions based on (1) the need for capacity in each market, (2) the projected profitability of the project, and (3) the attractiveness of the investment climate within the country.

Performance requirements appear to be of more concern than incentives. Firms tend to treat very gingerly those situations involving specific employment targets, export requirements, or limits on the transfer of funds. There are trade-offs between incentives and performance requirements and between one performance requirement and another. However, if given their preference, at least hypothetically, they would be willing to give up incentives in exchange for the removal of performance requirements.

On balance, it appears that incentive/performance requirement schemes have the primary effect of reducing international investment in the food industry rather than altering that investment across countries. Of course, in some broad sense, there must be some effect on the allocation of resources as between home and host countries and between broad groups of host countries, such as advanced countries where there tends to be incentives and few performance requirements and developing countries where there tends to be fewer incentives and more performance requirements.

NOTES

1. United Nations Centre on Transnational Corporations, *Transnational Corporations in Food and Beverage Processing* (New York: United Nations, 1981), p. 3.

2. International Investment Division, U.S. Department of Commerce, Bureau of Economic Analysis, *U.S. Direct Investment Abroad, 1977* (Washington, D.C.: U.S. Department of Commerce, April 1981), Table III.H2, p. 319.

3. Advanced countries: Australia, Belgium, Canada, England, France, Greece, and Spain. Developing countries: Brazil, India, Mexico, Peru, Philippines, Portugal, Turkey, Venezuela, and not named because of potential disclosure are an East African country, an East Asian country, and a Southeast Asian country.

4. The term counterproposal as used here refers to reaching an agreement that falls outside the investment guidelines as stipulated in the published government priorities for the food industry.

3

The Automobile Industry

Neil Hood and Stephen Young

THE BACKGROUND OF THE AUTOMOBILE INDUSTRY

This study takes place at a time when considerable research effort is being devoted to the automobile industry. Because of this, because of the oligopolistic nature of the industry and because of the visibility of the sector and its producers, more information is available concerning international trade, production, and investment in automobiles than in most other industries. Much of this work focuses on the future of the automobile industry, looking at policy options for countries and companies. It is not the intention of this initial section, therefore, to make a comprehensive review of the literature and debates, which are well summarized elsewhere,[1] but simply to point out a number of issues that are relevant to this present study concerning the influence of investment incentives and performance requirements in the auto industry.

Changing Patterns of Trade, Production, and Investment

The very rapid developments in international trade, production, and investment over the last two decades are of major significance. During the 1960s, exports of finished vehicles averaged about 20 percent of worldwide production, and there was little movement of parts and components internationally. These flows posed few threats to domestic industries, which operated in fairly isolated cells. By the end of the 1970s, the share of exports in world production had doubled, with sharply increasing price and quality competition across national boundaries. Moreover, trade in components, equipment, and technology had become of considerable significance, responding both to competitive pressures and to government regulations. The direction of international trade has also shifted with the emergence of Japan as the lowest cost world producer; by the end of the 1970s Japanese-produced vehicles accounted for over 30 percent of world-wide vehicle exports.

The development of the Japanese auto industry saw production and exports rise by 122 percent and 426 percent respectively between 1970 and 1980, while EC output remained virtually stable and exports fell by nearly 23 percent in terms of units.[2] The U.S. industry also suffered a mauling, mainly at the hands of the Japanese, who account for 80 percent of automobile imports into America. As a consequence, production in 1980 fell by almost 30 percent compared with the previous year alone; aggregate losses of the Big Three manufacturers totalled in excess of $4,500 million; and nearly one-fourth of the workforce in the auto sector was laid off. Alongside these changes among the traditional producing countries, new manufacturing nations increased their share of world production from 10.3 to 19.8 percent between 1970 and 1980. Of particular importance are three groups of countries: state-trading nations, countries that have applied for membership in the European Community (Spain and Portugal), and the newly industrializing states. Characteristics of the latter two groups include low motor vehicle density combined with high market growth, and underdeveloped automotive sectors, albeit with governmental commitments to develop the auto industry as a means of stimulating economic development and bringing about an improvement in the balance of trade.

These changes cannot be disassociated from the activities of multinational companies in the auto industry. The 22 largest auto corporations operating in the market economy countries accounted for 97 percent of worldwide production in 1980, with one-fifth of this output being undertaken in foreign locations.[3] Five firms had foreign production of 20 percent or more of total output, and three had foreign production of over 30 percent. For these major auto firms, the bulk of productive facilities are located near the main markets in developed countries, with technological innovation being very much of a home-based activity. Within this structure, there are important differences between the U.S. firms, which have been highly multinational in their activities; the Japanese companies, which have remained essentially home-based; and the European corporations, which have been in an intermediate situation. Nearly all authors are, however, of the view that the major producers, irrespective of nationality, will become increasingly multinational, if not by choice then by force of government intervention. The causes of foreign direct investment activity, and the associated growth in parts and components trade, are of major significance in the context of this project and, thus, form the basis for the discussion in the remainder of this section.

Foreign Sourcing and the World Car Concept

With the competitive pressures facing auto producers in Western Europe and the United States, much has been made of the development of the world car concept and with it the creation of a manufacturing base for the worldwide sourcing of components. Under the world car concept, "automobiles little differentiated in size and design among geographic areas are assembled from parts and components that are to a large extent standardized and interchangeable."[4] Major cost advantages accrue in research, development, and engineering expenditures, with integrated production in optimum-sized plants. This world car concept has been associated with the worldwide sourcing of components; and, as Table 3-1 shows, there has been a big upsurge in commitments by, for example, U.S. manufacturers to produce components at their subsidiaries abroad or to purchase parts and components from foreign companies. But this is rather misleading. The need for capital conservation partly explains the moves offshore to purchase selected components. In addition, a shortage of engine capacity for down-sized cars among a number of manufacturers simultaneously, at a time when government regulations were being changed in certain Latin American countries, created a large buildup in outsourcing. However, this seems to have been more coincidental than a big drive offshore.

Worldwide sourcing has also been seen as implying the large-scale shifting of production to low-wage countries. To date this has not happened, and auto manufacture and trade remain highly

TABLE 3-1
Foreign Sourcing — Recently Announced Commitments by U.S. Automobile Manufacturers to Purchase Foreign-Made Components for Use in Domestic Vehicles Production

Automobile Manufacturer	Description of Component	Intended Use	Manufacturing Source	Approximate Number of Components	Period
GM	2.8 lit V-6	Cars	GM Mexico	<400,000/year	1982-
	2.0 lit L-4 with transmission	Mini trucks	Isuzu (Japan)	100,000/year	1981-
	1.8 lit diesel L-4	Chevette	Isuzu (Japan)	small numbers	1982-
	1.8 lit L-4	J-car	GM Brazil	250,000/year	1979-
	THM 180 automatic transmission	Chevette	GM Strasbourg (France)	~250,000/year	1979-
Ford	2.2 lit L-4	Cars	Ford Mexico	<400,000/year	1983-
	Diesel L-4	Cars	Toyo Kogyo	150,000/year	1983-
	2.0 lit L-4	Mini trucks	Toyo Kogyo	<100,000/year	1982-
	2.3 lit L-4	Cars	Ford Brazil	~50,000/year	1979-
	Diesel 6 cyl.	Cars	BMW/Steyr	100,000/year	1983-
	Turbo-diesel/4 cyl.	Cars	BMW/Steyr	—	1985-
	Manual transaxles	Front disc cars	Toyo Kogyo	100,000/year	1980-
	Aluminum cylinder heads	1.6 lit L-4	Europe, Mexico	—	1980-
	Electronic engine control devices	Cars	Toshiba	100,000 +/year	1978-
	Ball joints	Cars	Musashi Seimibu	1 million/year	1980-84
Chrysler	L-6 and V-8 engines	Cars	Chrysler Mexico	<100,000/year	early 1970
	2.2 lit L-4	K-body	Chrysler Mexico	<270,000/year	1981
					Continued

Table 3-1, continued

Automobile Manufacturer	Description of Component	Intended Use	Manufacturing Source	Approximate Number of Components	Period
Chrysler	2.6 lit L-4	K-body	Mitsubishi	1 million	1981-85
	1.7 lit L-4	L-body (Omni)	Volkswagen	1.2 million	1978-82
	1.6 lit L-4	L-body	Talbot (Peugeot)	400,000 total	1982-84
	2.0 lit Diesel V-6	K-body	Peugeot	100,000/year	1982-
	1.4 lit L-4	A-body (Omni replacement)	Mitsubishi	300,000/year	1984-
	Aluminum cylinder heads	2.2 lit L-4	Fiat		
AMC	Car components and power train	AMC-Renault	Renault in France and Mexico	300,000/year	1982-
VW of America	Radiators, stampings	Rabbit	VW Mexico	250,000/year	1979-
	L-4 diesel and gas	Cars	VW Mexico	300,000 +/year	1982-

Source: Commission of the European Communities, *The European Automobile Industry: Commission Statement,* Bulletin of the European Communities, Supplement 2/81 (Brussels, 1981), Annex 5, p. 58.

concentrated in the industrialized nations. Lack of infrastructure, shortages of labor skills, low volume, and quality problems are some of the factors offsetting any wage advantage possessed by the nontraditional producing countries. Although such countries have not yet become integrated to any extent into the global production strategies of auto MNEs, output in a number is rising rapidly. This has led to considerable discussion concerning the applicability of the product cycle model to the industry.[5] The automobile industry is seen as a mature oligopoly in the United States and Western Europe. The production facilities that were set up abroad by the U.S. MNEs from the early years of this century and the growing internationalization of the European producers are regarded as evidence of this maturity, as companies attempt to reduce costs in the face of stable product and process technology.

Before accepting this thesis, however, it is necessary to consider the reasons for locating overseas. There is a strong tendency on the part of both developed and developing nations to stress the significance of an indigenous automobile industry. According to one author, "These developments are tending to convert the product-cycle hypothesis from an empirically testable descriptive proposition into a normative criterion of behaviour."[6] This implies the importance of government policies — both industrial policy and trade policy — in foreign direct investment decisions and the development of automobile industries. From its inception, the auto industry has certainly been affected very materially by govenment regulation. At the turn of the century, automobile output was greater in Europe than in the United States, and the United States developed its indigenous industry behind a 45 percent ad valorem tariff.[7] Some have gone so far as to argue that "throughout its entire history, almost all foreign direct investment decisions have been prompted by tariff barriers to exports."[8] This is oversimplistic, and whereas tariffs and other policy instruments may have affected the timing of investments, market demand, cost, and competitive factors have all played a part in the internationalization of the industry over time. Yet policy issues are important; witness the comment by one observer that protection in Europe so far has kept out around 500,000 cars a year from Japan — or the equivalent of two assembly plants and one engine plant of minimum efficient scale.[9]

Even if the product cycle has provided a partial explanation for internationalization, this is not to say that the same sequence will continue in the future. With an acceleration in the speed of product innovation, the industry may have been forced back to an earlier stage of its development cycle when close coordination is required between R & D, engineering, and marketing activities. In addition, the increasing capital intensity of assembly operations through the use of robotics, sophisticated transfer line equipment, and other advances to some extent offsets high labor costs in developed countries. The net result of these and other factors is that an overwhelmingly large proportion of planned investments will be located in the home countries of the multinationals concerned, with much of the remainder being accounted for by developed host countries and, thereafter, by the major Latin American countries, Brazil and Mexico. An analysis of the foreign investments of Ford over the period 1976-83 reveals about three-quarters of the dollar value being allocated to the United Kingdom and continental Europe, 16 percent to Latin and Central America, and the remainder to Australia and the Far East.[10] For GM, the equivalent figures were continental Europe and United Kingdom, 55 percent; Latin and Central America, 9 percent; Australia and Far East, 9 percent; and Canada, 27 percent. This study investigates a number of the specific investment decisions involved in these patterns, widening the analysis to take account of both European and Japanese auto producers.

CASE ANALYSIS

Introduction

This, the major section of the study, summarizes the results of the case analyses undertaken in the automobile industry. The individual projects are not identified to preserve confidentiality to the extent possible. In each case, the researchers undertook personal interviews with executives at corporate headquarters, and, in some instances, with appropriate personnel at regional headquarters. Clearly, company responses to requests for the type of, often very sensitive, information required varied considerably. Many firms, nevertheless, were very frank and helpful, on the understanding that specific company material would not be disclosed. This study relates to 12 investment decisions with a total value of approximately $5.2 billion. The basic details of the investment decisions are given in

Table 3-2. They cover eight manufacturers, three U.S.-, three European-, and two Japanese-based; nine host countries, four in Europe, two in Latin America, two in Asia, and one in North America; and a range of types of activity, albeit with an emphasis on engine manufacture and car assembly. Eight decisions were made in 1978 or later; three, in the years 1975-77; and one, in the period 1974-76.

Most of the major world producers have been included, and the host country orientation of the investment decisions is fairly representative of the balance of activity. Most companies have been involved in the establishment of minor assembly facilities in the smaller South American countries, in Africa, and in Asia, but these have represented only a small part of total investment activity and have largely been omitted. What is, nevertheless, important is the evolution of auto industries in developing countries, and some details on policy trends in Mexico are included on pages 135, 139, and 141. One potentially important host region is the Eastern Bloc, whose countries account for about 7 percent of world motor vehicle production, furthered by the transfer of technology mainly from Western Europe in the form of turnkey factories. Even though important, such investments have been considered as outside the scope of this project. More significant perhaps is the omission of any licensing arrangements, joint ventures, or collaborations between companies in the industrialized countries, mainly because these agreements have not involved investment incentives or performance requirements. To that extent, the focus on incentives and requirements means that the study does not pick up important emerging trends in international involvement in developed countries.

The investment projects to be included in this study were selected mostly by the present authors. Whereas the companies interviewed did not usually attempt to influence this selection, some firms did draw attention to other projects that they considered to be of interest, and a number of these are included as brief cases in the appendix to this section. It should be noted that virtually all the majors have undertaken or are planning new investments in Mexico and/or Brazil. Only a number of these have been included to avoid distorting the host country mix of projects, but comments on the similarities or differences in company responses to incentives and performance requirements are incorporated in the text.

Before reviewing the analysis of the investment decisions, it is worth stating the point that is implied above: considerable similarities

TABLE 3-2
Investment Decisions

	Location of Facility	Type of Activity	Ownership Involvement (Percent)	Period of Decision[a]	Period of Commencement of Manufacture	Size of Investment ($ million)	Extent of Former Manufacturing Involvement in Country
Case 1 U.S. MNE	EC	Car engine manufacture	100	1975-77	1978-80	250-499	Extensive since 1920s
Case 2 U.S. MNE	Non-EC Europe	Car assembly	100	1981-83[c]	1984-86	500-999	None
Case 3 U.S. MNE	Non-EC Europe	Stamping and car assembly	100	1972-74	1975-77	500-999	None
Case 4 U.S. MNE	Non-EC Europe (2 sites)	Car assembly and components	100	1978-80	1981-83	1,000 and over	None
Case 5 U.S. MNE	Non-EC Europe	Car engine and transmission manufacture[d]	100	1978-80	1981-83	500-999	None
Case 6 Eur. MNE	North America	Car assembly	100	1975-77	1978-80	100-249	None
Case 7 Japan MNE	North America	Car assembly	100	1978-80	1981-83	100-249	None in automobiles; exports commenced in 1970
Case 8 Eur. MNE	Latin America	Buses and trucks manufacture	40	1975-77	1978-80	100-249	None
Case 9 Eur. MNE	Latin America	Car engine manufacture[e]	40[f]	1978-80[g]	1984-86	250-499	Involvement since 1960s

Case 10 U.S. MNE	Latin America	Car engine manufacture	99	1978-80	1981-83	100-249	Extensive links – through Mexican-owned company initially
Case 11 Japan MNE	Asia	Stamping and car engines	42	1975-77, 1978-80[h]	1975-77, 1978-80	100-249	Involvement since 1968 on KD import and sales basis
Case 12 Japan MNE	Asia	Truck bodies and components	60	1978-80	1978-80	Under 100	Involvement since 1970 for import and sale of KD parts and CBUs

[a] Only periods given to avoid disclosure of confidential information.
[b] Only ranges given to avoid disclosure of confidential information.
[c] Decision not yet taken.
[d] The decision on adding a transmission unit was made some months after the engine plant announcement.
[e] Engine manufacture only one of a number of associated projects in which company involved at present. Others include assembly of a new compact car which in turn is related to a restructuring of the company's Mexican operations.
[f] A new wholly owned subsidiary has been formed to handle the engine project.
[g] But project considered to be uncertain for a further two years after the decision was taken.
[h] Two related projects.

Source: Compiled by the authors.

105

and clear interrelationships emerge regarding the major producers' international direct investment intentions. This applies most obviously to the surge of engine investments in Mexico but goes much further than this to include projects in Europe and elsewhere. In relation to the former, for instance, one U.S. manufacturer negotiated an arrangement with a non-EC country in Europe that was then accepted by another U.S. auto maker that was able to conclude a deal with the government concerned in two weeks. Again, one of the European companies in this study had been seeking to enter Brazil since 1962, when the firm was rejected in favor of three other major European producers.

The Nature of Investment Decision Making in the Sample Firms

As is well known, the decision to make a foreign direct investment involves a series of related steps, beginning with the investigation of overseas operations, working through the choice of the location of investment to the determination of the size of the investment, timing, and so on.[11] In the case of the auto industry, however, decisions to commence manufacturing internationally were made a good number of years ago by the major producers (excluding the Japanese), and most of these main manufacturers have a wide spread of international operations. Stress is placed upon the principle that "substantial production, investment and employment commitments be made in the major markets in which . . . (the company) has a significant volume of sales."[12] This principle emerged frequently in discussions with the sample firms, whether expressed in terms of "basically it makes sense to build vehicles where they are sold, provided you have sufficient volume" (U.S. manufacturer) or the concept of international manufacture as a means of building and enhancing the company's sales position in major international markets (European producer).[13] The meaning of such comments is not always easy to interpret. In part, the implication is that there are potential cost reductions in terms of freight, tariffs, and other expenses. But, chiefly, local manufacture is important from a demand perspective, enabling the company to compete effectively with domestic producers and to overcome nationalistic buying policies. Implicit in these remarks, in any event, was a rejection of global scanning for site selection. Even though environmental appraisal might be undertaken on a worldwide basis, decision making has tended to focus on the continent or region,[14] or indeed on particular countries — especially those with large market potential where the company does not have a manufacturing presence. In some developing countries in this category, corporations have been prepared to take a very long-term view of this investment, believing that the need to secure market share overrides short-run profitability. The view that a company will have an advantage as a domestic manufacturer also emerges commonly in investments in Europe and the United States and could have a strong influence on the investment decision. As one company commented in relation to its investment in non-EC Europe, "the profit from 70-80,000 incremental units a year far outweighs the influence of factors such as incentives." By this same principle of "participating in the markets in which you sell," countries like Italy and France would tend to emerge from investment appraisals undertaken by the U.S. auto firms in Europe, simply because their manufacturing presence is limited or nonexistent.

By the same token, investment decision making in the auto industry has not been influenced to any great extent by labor cost differentials internationally. One European enterprise argued that the company was convinced that if all the influencing variables, including longer-term trends in productivity, interest rates, exchange rates, and tariffs, were taken into consideration, it would not be possible to say that for reasons of labor costs alone an investment should be made in one location rather than another. In the case of a truck investment, for example, labor costs account for only 1 percent of the value of a vehicle. But a similar view emerged from other companies, typified by the opinion that "a country like Korea doesn't have the infrastructure or the labor skills, and labor rates alone don't cut anything."

The position is different with respect to the Japanese producers. In the first place, overseas assembly and manufacture are both more recent and less extensive, and, second, the focus of these operations is Southeast Asia and Oceania. Company views regarding overseas operations are also different. The philosophy expressed by one of the interviewed companies was that foreign activity was only undertaken by the "enforcement of individual governments." The company regarded Japan as having been (and remaining) the best place to manufacture cars, the output being cheaper and of a higher quality than it had ever attained elsewhere. So in its view no overseas production decisions had been made in "a free market." The apparently contrasting philosophy of the other Japanese company visited was that it needed to be acceptable in every country in which it trades.

Reflecting the comments above, in considering the background to the sample of investments, Table 3-3 indicates the importance of market supply factors in the investment decisions relating to Europe and the United States. In Latin America, market access was regarded as important in case 8 whereas defense of a market position was the underlying factor in cases 9-12. Most of these investments were adding capacity, although two companies were prepared to admit that the new factories were designed to replace existing facilities and thus lead to job losses in the latter. The engine plant in case 10 is particularly interesting in this regard and apparently was not the only investment in this category.

The procedures followed by the auto companies in the initial stages of investment screening seemed to be fairly similar. All appeared to undertake regular environmental evaluations on a worldwide basis. For one U.S. company, for instance, the purpose of this is to rank order countries into primary, secondary, and tertiary groups against two criteria: first, a place to do business and, second, an export source (recently). Mostly such studies would be followed up by more in-depth country analyses, undertaken by internal staff members. The procedure followed by another U.S. MNE in Europe was different in this regard, where a consultants' study was commissioned to look at possible country locations, ranking countries in terms of three groups of variables — nonrecurring factors, recurring factor costs, and intangibles — but the end result was still a number of more detailed internal evaluations. What is important in these evaluations, however, is that, because no negotiation with countries is involved, only the "standard package" of incentives/performance requirements can be taken into consideration.

For investments in Europe, a small number of countries might thereafter become the focus of further study and approaches to governments. The procedure as outlined by the companies seemed fairly similar, involving high-level approaches to governments — at prime ministerial level — indicating that the auto maker would like to be considered for a particular project and put in touch with the appropriate officials in commerce and development departments; the latter sketch out what is available; a package is put together; and

TABLE 3-3
Background to Investment and Steps in Investment Decision

Case 1 — U.S. MNE

Background: New generation of engines required for new small car to be launched in Europe

Investment Capacity: Replacement for engine built in EC country

Steps in Investment Decision:

Initial — Existing location was center of expertise for small engines in Europe — study of possibilities of introducing to this location

Subsequent (1) — Existing location unsatisfactory, company approached government in same country and was offered three alternative sites

Subsequent (2) — News of investment possibility leaked and approaches to company from six European countries

Subsequent (3) — "Quick and dirty" cost calculations indicated only alternatives as existing EC country and Ireland

Subsequent (4) — Greenfield plant in existing EC country selected

Case 2 — U.S. MNE

Background: Requirement for additional assembly capacity in Europe in 1982 identified in 1977 but pushed back four or five years because of recession

Investment Capacity: Largely additional

Steps in Investment Decision:

Initial — Investment appraisal procedures indicated expansion at existing sites or new build in France or Italy

Subsequent (1) — Italy rejected, package negotiated in France, but subsequently withdrawn by French government

Subsequent (2) — Austria investigated and deal negotiated but financially unattractive

Subsequent (3) — Investigation of fall-back position of expanding existing plants when approached by non-EC European country

Subsequent (4) — Non-EC European country selected

Case 3 — U.S. MNE

Background: Requirement for capacity for new small car, mainly for European market

Investment Capacity: Additional

Steps in Investment Decision:

Initial — Investment appraisal procedures indicated expansion at existing sites in EC or new build in non-EC Europe

Subsequent (1) — Detailed investigation of non-EC European country

Subsequent (2) — Negotiations with government — company entered

Continued

109

Table 3-3, continued

negotiations wanting to enter, provided viable to do so
Subsequent (3) — Non-EC European country selected

Case 4, Case 5 — U.S. MNE

Background: European expansion plans involving boosting capacity by 29 percent or 300,000 units annually by 1982/83. Both decisions emerged from these overall plans
Investment Capacity: Additional
Steps in Investment Decision:

Initial — Consultants' study on wide range of European countries. Analyzed nonrecurring factors (buildings and equipment, front-end incentives) — top ranked countries, U.K., Rep. of Ireland, Greece, Italy; recurring factors (labor, transport, etc.) — top ranked countries, U.K., Spain, Rep. of Ireland, Italy, France, Austria; and intangibles (work ethic, political stability, etc.) — top ranked countries, W. Germany and Austria
Subsequent (1) — Conclusions of consultants' study rejected: did not take market size or growth into account and included only generally available incentives
Subsequent (2) — Detailed study of France, but subsequently rejected, then non-EC countries — in one case after approaches from government
Subsequent (3) — Non-EC European countries (2) selected

Case 6 — Eur. MNE

Background: Rebuild significant market share lost during the 1970s; roots of decision go back to breaking of ties between the dollar and the gold standard
Investment Capacity: Additional
Steps in Investment Decision:

Initial — Several consulting studies commissioned in early 1970s to establish what the regional differentials within the United States would mean for company
Subsequent (1) — 200 offers of sites and facilities. Extensive appraisal reduced this list to 13 and then to 3
Subsequent (2) — Negotiations with governors' offices and several state departments
Subsequent (3) — N.E. United States selected

Case 7 — Japan MNE

Background: Shortage of capacity in Japan, protectionist threats in U.S., strong demand for company products in United States
Investment Capacity: Additional

Continued

Table 3-3, continued

Steps in Investment Decision:

    Initial — MITI advice to all Japanese producers to prepare for U.S. assembly. Unavailability of space for expansion in preferred location — Japan

    Subsequent (1) — Studies of U.S. market by two separate consulting firms. Both recommended same location

    Subsequent (2) — Negotiations with state government

    Subsequent (3) — N.E. United States selected

Case 8 — Eur. MNE

Background: Latin America considered of strategic importance to company, plus need to reenter fast growing market

Investment Capacity: Additional

Steps in Investment Decision:

    Initial — World market sutdy led to conclusion of need to focus on Latin American market

    Subsequent (1) — Detailed market studies in Latin American countries led to selection of Peru and Brazil, but rejection of Mexico

    Subsequent (2) — Negotiations with another foreign company for joint venture broke down. Negotiations with government; permission to invest denied until intervention of state government

    Subsequent (3) — Location in state selected

Case 9 — Eur. MNE

Background: Decree for the Promotion of the Automotive Industry. Restructuring of existing operation following company's merger with another major auto producer

Investment Capacity: Additional

Steps in Investment Decision:

    Initial — Study of Latin American country, Canada, and EC home country

    Subsequent (1) — Latin American country first choice because of need to comply with regulations, but strong lobby inside company urging investment in home country[a]

    Subsequent (2) — Negotiations with government of Latin country[b]

    Subsequent (3) — Latin country selected

Case 10 — U.S. MNE

Background: Decree for the Promotion of the Automotive Industry

Investment Capacity: Replacement — engine plant in Canada shut down (potentially this could be fired up again)

Continued

Table 3-3, continued

Steps in Investment Decision:

   Initial — Number of studies undertaken on products that might be put into Latin country to earn export credits. Considered and rejected station wagon because of impact on U.S. jobs.

   Subsequent (1) — Negotiations with government

   Subsequent (2) — Investment made

Case 11 — Japan MNE

Background: Increase in local content requirements; oil crisis and effects on packaging and freight costs

Investment Capacity: Additional

Steps in Investment Decision:

   Initial — Study of products that might be introduced to fulfill local content requirements

   Subsequent (1) — Negotiations with government and start of engine manufacture. Body production added because economics of former choice changed

   Subsequent (2) — Asian country selected for two projects

Case 12 — Japan MNE

Background: 1977 regulations, giving time schedule by which a specific list of truck items were to be produced locally

Investment Capacity: Additional

Steps in Investment Decision:

   Initial — Five items listed for local production by 1979, so company had no option but to introduce these to stay in the market

   Subsequent (1) — Negotiations with government

   Subsequent (2) — Asian country selected

---

[a] Arguments related to Mexico's chaotic currency policy and strength of U.S. dollar (and linking of peso to the dollar).

[b] In return for investing in engines, company wanted commitment on reciprocal investment by associate company in assembly and removal of price controls on types of vehicles.

Source: Compiled by the authors.

frequently this then goes back to the prime minister. It is true, nevertheless, that in all recent investments, as news of the auto firms' investment intentions has spread, the company itself has invariably been the subject of approaches *from* governments. The Austrian government has been most active lately in this regard: according to reports, Porsche, Volkswagen, Chrysler, Fiat-Lancia, Mitsubishi, and Ford had been approached, in most cases personally by Chancellor Kreisky, before General Motors eventually signed a deal with the country.[15] The investments in Latin America, Southeast Asia, and Oceania are in a quite different category, because, for the companies concerned, refusal to commit investment funds would have required divestment of their operations in the country. The two European auto makers did look at a number of different countries within Latin America, but there was no evidence of countries approaching the auto makers seeking investment.

Before leaving this brief discussion on investment decision making, it is worthwhile making some comments on the way in which investment incentives and performance requirements are incorporated into investment calculations. One company commented that they were treated as variables in calculating return on investment like any other, and an assessment of their impact emerges automatically from the calculations. While this is true, as an earlier comment indicated, companies have generally reached the stage of screening out all but a very small number of countries before detailed negotiations with governments take place. And in host countries in Europe and North America, the exact nature of the incentives/requirements package is not known before these negotiations. The approach outlined by one U.S. company in relation to its recent investments is instructive in this regard: in each of the three investments, considerable importance was attached to cost calculations referring to expansion on existing sites in Europe. Whether the company would actually have committed resources to facilities' expansion, given space shortages, man management, and other problems is beside the point. The fact remains that the company then set about "looking for something better" on greenfield sites, going into the negotiations with clear views about what incentives were necessary or what requirements could be tolerated to give an improved return as compared with expanding existing sites. This same company was interviewed both in Europe and in the United States, and similar types of issues emerged in discussions at parent headquarters, although some differences of opinion were admitted between various groups within the corporation. Thus the environmental analysis and, probably, finance groups stressed the role of incentives in reducing the capital required for new investment projects. Capital conservation reasons underlay, in addition, the moves offshore for selected components, such as the decision to buy certain components from Japan, even though the landed price in the United States was little different from the price of the same component produced in the United States. The planners by contrast argued that the cost of capital was less important than the long-run cost of doing business — where the corporation made an investment it had to be assumed that it would be present in the country for 50 years or more.

In case 6, the availability of a shell auto plant was important in reducing capital requirements, with the main effect of incentives being in cutting launching costs. The company comment on incentives was that they were "of no importance in determining strategy, but of some immediate importance tactically." In this instance, of course, the decision to enter the United States had already been made; the only decision remaining was then one of site selection within the country rather than, as in cases 1-3 above, selecting one country instead of another.

With regard to the Latin American investments, there appeared to be little room for negotiation over performance requirements or incentives, and the up-front incentives were negligible. In theory, on the one hand, this would make it easier to ascertain project viability at the prenegotiation stage. On the other hand, the potential for changes in regulations was an additional factor of importance. As one company commented, "What one thought was a good deal could turn out badly, as in Mexico, because of changes in Decrees." Particularly when companies were effectively investing for the future, changes in regulations could mean a long-term drain on corporate resources. Therefore, a factor in the equation that becomes relevant is the stability of the agreement with the country.

For the Japanese investments, finally, it was argued by one of the firms that in no instance had they ever received an incentive package, beyond that generally available in the host country, whereas in case 7 the incentives available were widely known and fairly nonnegotiable. The implication would be that incentives would at least be incorporated into investment appraisals.

Country and Site Selection

Countries Considered in Site Selection

The factors considered in site selection within the sample of investments are summarized in Tables 3-4 through 3-6. As was noted previously, in the investments located in Europe, typically the prospective auto investors arrived at a short list of countries, discussions were held with governments, delegations were received from other governments, and other steps were taken until a final choice was made. Table 3-4 identifies the countries on the short list for the various projects and the reasons for rejection. France emerges fairly commonly, principally because of its large market and the limited penetration of that market by the U.S. producers (in turn associated by the firms with the lack of a major manufacturing presence in the country); rejection seems to have derived mainly from the French government's requirement that any project be located in the northern steel regions and, allegedly, from pressures exerted on the French government by the indigenous auto makers. Somewhat similar reasons underlie both the potential attractiveness of Italy and its final rejection. The U.K. position is interesting in cases 4 and 5: as Table 3-3 revealed, in the European country analysis commissioned by the U.S. auto maker, the U.K. was top ranked on both recurring and nonrecurring factor costs, yet the company argued that their "unsatisfactory experience with the labor structure and labor stoppages overwhelms everything."

In the investments in the United States (cases 6 and 7), the decision question was, of course, different. Here, the choice was between continuing to export to the United States (albeit faced with restrictions in volume in one case) and manufacturing in the country: for the European multinational, changing international exchange rate and cost relationships were working against the home country as an export base. It is relevant, nevertheless, that the strength of the dollar has changed the economics of the latter enterprise since that time. At the current exchange rate the U.S.-produced automobile concerned is a good deal less competitive relative to imported rivals than it was at the time manufacture commenced.

For case 9, the auto producer's home country was the only seriously considered manufacturing location aided by the depreciation of the home country currency. Quality and greater control were

TABLE 3-4
Countries Considered in Site Selection

Case	Countries Considered in Site Selection and Reasons for Consideration/Subsequent Rejection
Case 1 U.S. MNE	Existing EC location – Shortage of space (necessary to strip out many profitable components to make room for new engine line); already large enough from man management viewpoint
	Berlin – Logistics
	Luxembourg – High wage rates, incentive offer inadequate
	Belgium – High wage rates
	Spain – Insisting on Valencia location where no incentives available
	France – Directing company to Communist-dominated steel area; incentive offer poor
	Rep. of Ireland – Highest incentive package; but other factors in favor of existing EC country
Case 2 U.S. MNE	Italy – Emerged from investment appraisals largely because a major market in which company had no manufacturing presence; rejected because of labor problems, corruption, political violence
	France – Emerged from investment appraisals as major market lacking important manufacturing presence; previous commitment by former president of company; rejected when French government withdrew incentive offer after intervention of Renault and Peugeot; incentive package moderate and French government insisting on undesirable N.E. France (Metz) site
	Non-EC European Country[a] – Substantial investment incentives offered, but still not financially attractive compared with alternative of expanding existing plants; high labor rates; doubts on labor availability; no way to offset tax losses in early years; offer of markets outside Western Europe could not be fulfilled
	Expansion of existing facilities – Seemed most likely when company approached by another non-EC country
Case 3 U.S. MNE	United Kingdom – Britain had substantial ($300-400 per unit) operating cost advantage over Germany; disruption in Britain a major deterrent; potential additional sales of 70-80,000 units in non-EC country tipped the balance in favor of latter. Without these, country less financially attractive than Britain

116

Case 4 United Kingdom
Case 5 Rejected because of company's unhappy experience with United Kingdom subsidiary and problems with labor
U.S. MNE structure and stoppages
France – Some in company favored France because stable country, large market, and corporation's low penetration of the market. Rejected because French government offered unsuitable sites in northern steel areas, where incentives large but labor discipline bad; view that French manufacturers put pressure on government to keep company out; French engineering technology different, creating problems for standardization
Italy – Rejected because market could be served reasonably well from Germany; big incentive areas were in south where there were labor and corruption problems[b]
Germany – Major existing European production base and unsuitable for further expansion from management viewpoint; labor supply situation tight

Case 6 Macro- and microeconomic trends in United States, W. Germany, and Japan studied before decision to locate in
Euro. MNE United States. Cost trends favoring manufacture in United States and need for manufacturing presence to rebuild market share in United States crucial

Case 7 Only Japan and United States
Japan MNE

Case 8 Mexico – Not thought of as an alternative to Brazil but question of which country to try to enter first. Rejected
Eur. MNE because truck concept different and structure of competition different (all major producers from the United States); Mexico more important to U.S. producers because of neighboring markets; situation changed since acquisition of U.S. firm that has Mexican licensee

Case 9 Home EC country – With depreciation of currency, country attractive as an export base and pressure from gov-
Eur. MNE ernment to invest domestically. Rejected because of need for continuing presence in Mexico, implying compliance with regulations

Continued

Table 3-4, continued

Case	Countries Considered in Site Selection and Reasons for Consideration/Subsequent Rejection
Case 10 U.S. MNE	None – Choice related to product to be manufactured in Mexico
Case 11 Japan MNE	None – Choice related to product to be manufactured in Australia
Case 12 Japan MNE	None – Question of which parts could be produced with the minimum cost penalty

[a]Published reports at this time give a different view of this. A company official is quoted as saying that the project was too costly and the finance was required in America to bring U.S. models to required fuel efficiency, pollution, and size standards.
[b]It was argued that in any event Fiat would have pressured the Italian government to keep company out.

Source: Compiled by the authors.

118

significant factors, together with the requirement from the government for domestic investment. But the need to comply with performance requirements in the Latin American country, however,
proved crucial, as they did in cases 10-12. In case 8, finally, Mexico
was considered and rejected, although the company's long-term plans
still see Mexico as an important area of operation. Essentially, the
different nature of the truck concept in Mexico, given the U.S.
influence and the different competitive structure, led the company to seek entry into another Latin American country.

Reasons for Choice of Country

The reasons for actually selecting the countries in which the
projects were finally located are given in Table 3-5. Market access
emerges as the crucial factor in most of the non-EC European investments. In case 5, however, the factor was expressed in terms of European market access, which is a reason for investing in Europe and not
any one country specifically. Incentives were mentioned frequently,
and some attempt at ranking their importance within the overall
range of variables indicated by companies is made later in this study.
What is interesting to note is the mix of qualitative and quantitative
factors apparently influencing particular decisions. In the former
category are factors such as the European subsidiary's influence on
one U.S. company's expansion program in Europe, intangibles in
non-EC Europe, and sensitivity to potential job losses.

Whereas there is room for debate on the influence of incentives/
requirements on European investments, cases 9 and 10 in Latin
America seem to have been overwhelmingly affected by performance
requirements, and the same is true of the Japanese investments in
Asia (cases 11 and 12).

Reasons for Choice of Site within Country

Taking the sample of investments as a whole, host government
influence becomes even more important at the final level of decision
making, namely that of site selection within the country (Table 3-6).
In the EC, incentives are (notionally) only available in depressed,
peripheral areas. Therefore, a desire on the part of the company to
obtain incentives must be matched by a willingness to locate outside
central areas — that the trade-off may prove unacceptable is shown

TABLE 3-5
Reasons for Choice of Country Selected

Case	Country Selected and Reasons for Selection
Case 1 U.S. MNE	EC — Preference to remain in existing EC country because of fears relating to 2-3,000 potential job losses at another site in country; productivity reasonably comparable with other European locations; then question of "What will it take?"
Case 2 U.S. MNE	Non-EC Europe — Incentive package. With incentives, country more attractive as location than any other alternative; without incentives, marginally less attractive than expanding existing plants; low wage rates; possibility of using as supply point for other non-EC European operations
Case 3 U.S. MNE	Non-EC Europe — Need for market presence — access to rapidly expanding auto market; labor costs; incentives small, but performance requirements question of "What will it take?"
Case 4 U.S. MNE	Non-EC Europe — Underdeveloped automotive industry in country with large market (company had tried unsuccessfully to enter market several years earlier for same reason); access to the EC; labor cost advantage (although believed this would be eliminated over 10 years); incentive package
Case 5 U.S. MNE	Non-EC Europe[a,b] — Access to European market — potential arising from fact that country was Europe's largest auto market without a major production facility; high ranking of intangibles (political and economic stability, good labor record, low inflation rate); incentive package; previous engine manufacture in country so experience of the technology
Case 6 Eur. MNE	North America — Medium-term objective of gaining 5 percent share of U.S. market; reduction in transport costs compared with importing; taking advantage of changing international cost relationships
Case 7 Japan MNE	North America — Circumvent import restraints; satisfy U.S. demand for company products; improve market position vis-a-vis Japanese competitors; political factors; rising labor costs in Japan; reduction in transport costs compared with importing
Case 8 Eur. MNE	Latin America — Fast-growing and large market for type of trucks in which company specializes; nature of competition understood;[c] concern about other companies building market shares and sales volumes

Case 9 Eur. MNE	Latin America – To comply with Mexican regulations on foreign currency balances. But need to distinguish between this particular decision and company involvement in Mexico as a whole; some of the following reasons may have played a part in the engine plant decision: Mexico a country target for company because of strongly expanding sales and large market potential, adjacency to United States, existence of associate company in country, and pressure from Mexican-minded managers. N.B. Wage cost differentials *not* a factor
Case 10 U.S. MNE	Latin America – To comply with Mexican regulations – underlying this was desire to remain in Mexican market where company is market leader in cars and highly profitable until 1982 – sourcing decision based on Mexico as part of U.S. auto market
Case 11 Japan MNE	Asia – To comply with Australian regulations; to remain in market where other major auto manufacturers have established position
Case 12 Japan MNE	Asia – To comply with Indonesian regulations; to remain in market

[a] Close links with company operations in an EC country also important in terms of communications, understanding of labor situation, and culture.

[b] High labor costs admitted but considered secondary in mechanized, high-technology industries; company confident of obtaining labor supplies and skills.

[c] Foreign companies represented in the market were those with which the firm was in competition in Europe and other parts of the world.

Source: Compiled by the authors.

TABLE 3-6
Reasons for Choice of Site within Country

Case	Sites Investigated/Offered	Factors Influencing Choice
Case 1 U.S. MNE	Three assisted area sites offered by government	Incentive package offered identical; wage rates identical; infrastructure similar; one site rejected, too close to existing poorly performing plant; labor performance similar in other two sites; company already had two satisfactorily performing operations in favored location, so decided to consolidate in this one area (subject to agreement on incentive package)
Case 2 U.S. MNE	No details obtained because company still negotiating	
Case 3 U.S. MNE	Three sites offered	One site in undesirable tough shipbuilding area; second site was company's preferred location as offered 25 percent investment grants by local government but pressure on company from central government; third site only feasible alternative
Case 4 U.S. MNE	Various	Other MNEs' experience in the country; avoid one area offered because of political problems, although incentives high; two other sites undesirable, tough shipbuilding areas (but see below); selected site close to border and to an international airport; but company had to agree to set up small operation in one undesirable location to obtain permission for large scale investment in preferred site
Case 5 U.S. MNE	Capital city site offered	Easy access to company's largest plant in neighboring country
Case 6 Eur. MNE	Many of the 200 sites and facilities offered were quickly eliminated because of three constraints — one	Site chosen because of existence of unused plant and investment in infrastructure. Other factors in favor of chosen location: logistics for distribution and the import of components from Europe; company market share

automotive model, an existing plant, and most components to be supplied domestically. Thereafter, focus on social, technical, and economic infrastructures

Case	Number of sites investigated	
Case 7 Japan MNE		higher in area; demographics of area favorable (cultural, origin, ability to retrain); plant area designated a foreign trade zone; redundant factory; available incentives
Case 8 Eur. MNE	Most major cities and their surrounding areas investigated	Option on land expiring in 1982; advantages in being adjacent to another company-owned facility; logistics of operating
Case 9 Eur. MNE	Various sites mainly in border area investigated	Choice of site mainly influenced by support that regional government would give for investment application
Case 10 U.S. MNE	Various	Government would not allow company to invest in border area, allegedly because U.S. MNE already there; site chosen because "labor is calm"
Case 11 Japan MNE	Not apparently an issue; determined by location of existing assembly facility	Selected site adjacent to foundry supplying castings for engine plant; adjacency to highways for exporting; adequate power and water supplies
Case 12 Japan MNE	Not apparently an issue	

Source: Compiled by the authors.

clearly in the inability of the French government to persuade companies to set up in northern regions of the country. In case 3 in non-EC Europe, the position was complicated by both central and local government involvement. The U.S. MNE noted that its preferred site was in a location where the local government offered 25 percent investment grants. But it was effectively forbidden from locating there by the central government and given the choice between two sites; one was in a tough shipbuilding area (which according to the company was "no choice"). The U.S. auto maker commented that the central government was trying to break the strength of the local council in the area offering 25 percent grants, financial strength that dated back to the 1930s and allegiances during the Civil War. The other U.S. MNE followed a different strategy (case 4), agreeing to establish a small operation in an undesirable location in return for the opportunity to go to their preferred site.

In case 8, site selection within the country was intimately connected to overall negotiations on permission to invest at all. Thus, the central government was reluctant to increase the number of truck producers in the country and, in any event, would give no thought to investment in the area or close to other major cities. Permission was granted only after the European MNE managed to enlist the support of the state government for its investment application.

As regards cases 9 and 10, plants were located in order to have access to the main industrial area, access to the border, reliable transportation and utilities, and government incentives.[16] The incentive program is designed to promote industrial decentralization, and, as part of this, industrial zones have been established and companies that locate in the zones become eligible for various types of subsidies. In case 10 specifically, however, access to parts suppliers and access to markets were major factors. Like another U.S. MNE, with facilities only two miles away, the company receives its major castings from a local company and is soon to receive heads locally. Transport costs on the export of finished engines, moreover, are minimized through excellent road links with the United States.[17] In case 9, the European company was subject to government influence on site selection because its favored sites were all close to the border. According to the firm, these locations were prohibited because a U.S. producer already had investments in the vicinity.

Only in the cases of the two auto assembly projects in North America were there definitely no governmental pressures on site location, although pressure also did not figure importantly in cases 11 and 12 either.

The Incidence of Incentives/Performance Requirements

The incentives/performance requirements packages applicable to each of the investment decisions are summarized in Tables 3-7 and 3-8. As had been expected, this was a very sensitive area for some companies, and a number would not disclose the precise terms for their investments: this problem applied particularly to cases 4, 5, 7, 11, and 12. From information obtained from companies and data gleaned from other sources, however, it appears that within the developed countries the incentives reached a maximum of about 67 percent of the investment cost in case 1. For cases 5 and 6, the incentives were worth 35-40 percent of the capital costs, and in the other two cases in non-EC Europe (3 and 4), their value was about 15 percent. The major component of these subsidies was the cash grant element and/or subsidized loans, with free or subsidized land and infrastructure investment in road and rail links and utilities being general for all projects (in both developed and developing countries). In addition, assistance with recruitment or training was sometimes part of the package, particularly in areas without a tradition of auto industry activity.

Some of the most revealing insights would emerge from comparisons between incentive packages in competing areas. Regrettably, in only a small number of instances were these directly available, the most interesting being case 1 — the attempt by one EC country to entice a U.S. engine plant investment away from another EC member. Within one week of, as they put it, "sniffing around," the U.S. MNE was inundated with requests from a range of European countries. One of the smaller EC countries was quickest off the mark and came up with the most attractive offer. The company was offered attractive terms based on the country's existing system of financial incentives, but the auto producer's response was that it would prefer a straight cash grant. Its view was that to benefit from the package offered, the company needed a balance of high-tax and low-tax locations in the world, which it did not have. The development authority in the host country, therefore, converted this into a cash grant equivalent and came up with a package worth about

TABLE 3-7
Incentives Package

Case	Incentive Package in Selected Location	Best Alternative Incentive Package (Where Available)
Case 1 U.S. MNE	Assisted area grants worth $88m.,[a] $122m. cash; connections to plant (electricity, water, other utilities); subsidized land; government assistance to build rail spur; total value $210m. (of which government received just over half back from EC Regional Development Fund); *plus* $38m. subsidized loans from ECSC	EC country — Cash grant equivalent of discounted value of original incentive offer; training grants; subsidized loans; special lease deals; free land; total value $213m.
Case 2 U.S. MNE	No details obtained because still negotiating. Stated to be much superior to next best offer of one-third cash grants plus free land and infrastructure (see across)	Non-EC European country — Cash grant amounting to one-third of investment cost; free land; infrastructure investment in road and rail connections; assistance with recruitment and training; prime site in capital city; total value $320m. (same offer in percent terms as to another company)
Case 3 U.S. MNE	Subsidized loans, net present value $25m.; $2m. in training grants; 95 percent exemption on import duties on capital goods (NPV $32m.); total value $59m. *plus* export subsidies at level of 11 percent of export value for five years	EC country — $25m. of investment grants; company stated it was unaware of the possibility of additional investment finance available in country and did not get to stage of negotiating with government
Case 4 U.S. MNE	Major location: cash subsidy of 10 percent and another 10 percent in official credits Other location: cash subsidy of 20 percent and 20 percent credit package *plus* infrastructure investment	Not applicable

126

Case 5 U.S. MNE	Cash grant of $210m.; free land on 99-year lease; infrastructure investment in road and rail connections; assistance with recruitment and training; prime site in capital city	Not available
Case 6 Eur. MNE	$40m. loan to be repaid over 30 years at 1¾ percent for first 20 years and 2 percent thereafter; $6m. loan at 8½ percent; substantial relief from property taxes for first five years; road and rail connections ($30m. raised by state through bond issues to fund these); $3.8m. to assist company with recruitment and training; total public investment $86m. *plus* import duty relief for locating in the free trade zone	Not applicable
Case 7 Japan MNE	Infrastructure support in railway spur and road access to new plant; subsidized loans (but value not disclosed)	Similar offers from elsewhere, but details not obtained
Case 8 Eur. MNE	Subsidized loans ("few million"), 10-year grace period and low interest rate; subsidized price for land ($1 per square meter); export incentives of 26 percent on total cif price when company operates at 80 percent local content; subsidized export financing (five years financing with repayments due semiannually at interest rate of 7½ percent); roads and services free up to site	Not applicable
Case 9 Eur. MNE	100 percent exemption from duties on imports not produced in Mexico; rebate of 10 percent of costs of exporting; export subsidy (15 percent f.o.b.), CEDI program; subsidized export financing (Fomez); free land; services free up to site; special exchange rate ($1/70 pesos for exports; $1/50 pesos for imports)	Not applicable

Continued

Table 3-7, continued

Case	Incentive Package in Selected Location	Best Alternative Incentive Package (Where Available)
Case 10 U.S. MNE	Duty exemptions; export subsidy (15 percent f.o.b.); subsidized export financing; free land; services free up to site; tax credits for initial construction	Not applicable
Case 11 Japan MNE	Not disclosed but stated to be identical to that obtainable for local projects	Not applicable
Case 12 Japan MNE	Exemption of import duty on materials and machinery for three years; exemption from profits tax for five years (stated to be "irrelevant"); above derived from joint-venture relationship	Not applicable

[a] Assisted area grants available to all investors at standard rate.

Source: Compiled by the authors.

$213m. This was rejected in favor of a slightly lower package from the EC country eventually selected (the company was insistent that neither side was aware of the other's offer), the cost of which was largely recouped from the EC Regional Development Fund; also involved were loans from the European Coal and Steel Community because the site selected was a designated steel closure area. Mention has already been made of the package in case 5, negotiated by one U.S. manufacturer but then picked up by another. That the latter was able to conclude its deal so quickly indicates a general level of awareness of how much would be required and how much would be available in such circumstances.

Before discussing the incentives applicable in the remaining projects, it is worthwhile commenting on the nature of performance requirements in cases 1, 5, 6, and 7. In at least three of these (there were apparently no requirements in case 7), the requirements must be regarded as informal in the sense that they fit within no underlying legal framework. This is not quite true in case 1, where legislation dating from 1972 and later does apply. And in the U.S. investment project in that country, there were, in theory, penalties for nonattainment of the objectives of the program. Yet in a dynamic market situation, it would be difficult to insist on compliance without endangering the viability of the project. The company objected to these (informal) performance requirements, but the host government insisted that it could not make the financial commitments without inserting the clause that the minister had, at his discretion, the right to recoup part of the cash grant if the objectives of the program were not met. In case 5, a series of informal undertakings were reached between the U.S. firm and the government, although the company was insistent that, for example, local suppliers would only be used if costs and quality were competitive. In the European company project in North America (case 6), because the community was risking its finance, it wanted guarantees on the level of activity at the plant over time. This was based on calculations of the input/output effect of the plant in the local area. The multinational auto producer refused to countenance such guarantees, but accepted some employment targets.

The non-EC country involved in cases 3 and 4 is different in that the incentive package available in percentage terms was much smaller than in the other developed countries and in the formal legal framework within which the incentives/performance requirements package

TABLE 3-8
Performance Requirements Package

Case	Performance Requirements Package	Performance Requirements Package in Alternative Location
Case 1 U.S. MNE	Objectives of program: create 2,500 jobs by date of maximum production; ensure engine was the sole engine for the car concerned; ensure volume forecasts attained (calendarized through 1988); ensure investment intentions kept (including basing carburetor manufacture for new car in another region of same country)	None
Case 2 U.S. MNE	None at all	Company not to employ more than 10 percent non-nationals in hourly workforce
Case 3 U.S. MNE	60 percent local content; market share not to exceed 10 percent of previous year's industry level; export/import ratio of 2:1 by value; two-thirds of output from plant to be exported	Not negotiated
Case 4 U.S. MNE	60 percent local content; 75 percent of 270,000 cars to be produced in first year of production to be exported	Not applicable
Case 5 U.S. MNE	Undertakings for direct employment of 2,800 workers and undertakings relating to production volumes; buy in country all inputs that are fully competitive in terms of price, delivery, quality, and vendor's capacity to supply; acquire in country equipment and building materials for plant construction equal in value to government cash subsidy (described by company as "informal undertakings")	Not applicable
Case 6 Eur. MNE	Nothing formal, but three related questions featured in negotiations: because community risking finance it wanted guarantees on level of activity at plant (company refused); employment targets established; emission overload in area (damping effect on some developments planned at site)	Not applicable

130

Case 7 Japan MNE	None	Not applicable
Case 8[a] Eur. MNE	Exports to be three times the value of imports albeit with buffer of $34m. during period of incentive agreement (but can make duty free importation of components and parts needed for exportation without this being part of 3:1 ratio); 80 percent local content to obtain export incentives; 94 percent local content to obtain floor financing facility with subsidized interest rates (company does not qualify)	Not applicable
Case 9[a] Eur. MNE	Imports of materials to be balanced by exports and preparation of annual foreign exchange budget: the budget is based on a company's sales program and export requirement defined by means of complex formula; minimum local content, based on material cost formula, of 60 percent; price controls	Not applicable
Case 10[a] U.S. MNE	Imports of materials (both original equipment and replacement) to be balanced by exports; minimum local content of 50 percent (rising); price controls	Not applicable
Case 11 Japan MNE	85 percent local content on a company-wide basis; unspecified level of exports[b] (but able to negotiate replacement of some locally made parts with cheaper imports in return); import duties of 57.5 percent on completely built-up units plus import quotas of 100,000 units per annum[c]	Not applicable
Case 12 Japan MNE	Very vague on performance requirements; main requirement was specific time schedule for items to be produced locally *plus* insistence on specific scale of projects; limitations on local borrowing v. MNE capital (was 2.5:1 ratio, now negotiated to 3.5:1). N.B. No export requirements	Not applicable

[a]Main elements of extensive regulatory framework only.

[b]Emerged when another auto producer obtained agreement that export proportion should count as equivalent to local content. So Japanese manufacturer forced (unofficially) to export something.

[c]In fact, these import restrictions are less onerous than those applying at time investment decision was made. But company had committed itself verbally so had to proceed.

Source: Compiled by the authors.

131

was implemented. As in Latin America, therefore, the subsidies need to be considered together with the package of performance requirements. So export subsidies ranging from between 11 to 26 percent on the f.o.b. or cif values existed in these three countries as the necessary other side of local content requirements, commitments to export, and other requirements. The European country, nevertheless, differs from the South American nations in at least one respect. The regulations that applied to the case 3 investment of the mid-1970s emerged directly from the U.S. corporation's own negotiations with the host government. Before entry, five manufacturers in the country shared the market between them. Performance requirements specified that no foreign company was allowed to own more than 50 percent of the capital of any enterprise in the country; 95 percent local content was required; and 30 percent customs duties applied to imported parts. By offering a large, export-oriented stamping and car assembly facility that would increase total output by half, the regulations were eventually changed on each of these items. Aside from the items mentioned in Table 3-8, wholly owned foreign subsidiaries were permitted, and customs duties on imported components were reduced to 5 percent. By the time of the case 4 investment in the same country, it was believed that the agreement outlined above had apparently expired; more recently still a further relaxation of regulations has taken place. The regulations now specify:

Maximum 12 percent market share from locally produced vehicles
The possibility of negotiating import licenses up to another 4 or 5 percent of the market
Local content requirements of 50 percent

This form of negotiation between company and country has existed in the formulation of the regulations in Mexico and Brazil, and extensive discussions were held with one auto maker on corporate lobbying before the enactment of the 1977 Decree in Mexico. This company (and perhaps others) was requested to make submissions to the government on changes in automobile policies that might be implemented to ameliorate the country's serious foreign exchange difficulties. Four alternative proposals were put to the government: prohibition of imports; raising local content to 100 percent; requiring imports to be compensated by exports; or some mixture of these. The company recommended the first of the alternatives but suggested that any decrees be relatively nonspecific, leaving flexibility for ministerial discretion; time for adjustment to any new regulations was, finally, recommended. The principal problem when the 1977 Decree appeared was that it allowed a much shorter time for attainment of foreign currency balance than the company considered feasible. The interaction in this instance was quite different from that involved in the buildup to the case 3 investment in Europe, because no direct negotiation was involved.

The evolution of regulations in Mexico has been principally designed to improve the economic contribution of the foreign-owned auto sector, and the problems in this regard have been extensively documented. Without going into detail at this stage, the 1962 Decree changed Mexico from an assembly to a manufacturing nation with the specification of 60 percent local content requirements and the establishment of production quotas. The 1972 Decree introduced a series of amendments to stimulate exports through tax rebates (CEDI); quota restrictions were lifted, but price controls were maintained, and product competition was limited by preventing manufacturers from entering any market segments other than those that they were currently supplying. Finally, as the trade deficit in autos and parts continued to deteriorate, the 1977 Decree was introduced. The main elements of this were the requirements for foreign currency balance and local content specifications that were set at a base level for the year 1978 and then progressively increased through 1981. On the other side were a number of fiscal incentives, which were available to companies that achieved this equilibrium between exports and imports in their foreign exchange allocations and abided by the minimum local content requirements. Basically, the regulations applied to all manufacturers, but the existing level of local integration and the degree of Mexican ownership were taken into consideration. The planning of the European company involved in an investment has had the latter issue very firmly in mind, and its corporate restructuring aims to continue majority local ownership. It is worth noting, nevertheless, that the firm has been insistent on control of its new facility and a wholly owned subsidiary has been formed to handle this project.

The position of the European firm is, in fact, rather different from that of most other manufacturers: the intention is to form a new umbrella organization in Mexico, which will be majority Mexican owned. This is seen as a high status venture for the Mexican government, as it will allow the government to claim control of a significant part of the automobile industry. By the same token, it has allowed the European firm to extract certain concessions outside the terms of the 1977 Decree — certain guarantees against competition and price increases for certain models, and government investment in car assembly.

As for case 8, the European company was subject to the terms of the various regulatory agencies in the country regarding export commitments and incentives, local content, and so forth. The trade-offs between these various elements mean that the firm does not, for example, qualify for local financing. Over 90 percent local content is necessary to benefit from this as compared with the present company position of about 85 percent. As will be noted later, the multinational auto companies are more concerned with high local content requirements than with the foreign currency balance regulations. Much of the concern derives from supplier problems, and under regulations the European company studied here is not permitted to integrate backward. This is not hard and fast, however, because various examples were quoted in interviews with U.S. producers, in which permission had been given to integrate vertically, although the government had to be shown that excessive prices were being charged by local vendors.

Major interest attaches to the projects in which Japanese auto companies have been involved, principally cases 11 and 12. In both instances, there is a distinct parallel with South America, with recent investment projects being largely necessitated by a progressive tightening of host country regulations. In case 11, the company had been involved since 1968 on a KD import and sales basis through a joint venture. In the early 1970s, the Japanese firm started to make a serious study of adding further value in the country. The government had two related performance requirements based on volume and local content: at an output of under 7,500 units per model, 60 percent local content was required; at 25,000 units the local content requirement rose to 85 percent. The Japanese company was assembling three models at the time, all on the lower volume/local content plan, but the government was proposing to change all assembly to the 85 percent basis. To achieve this required either engine or stamping production, and the former was chosen because the cost penalty was smaller at the time. But body production became necessary soon afterward, when oil price rises adversely affected packaging and freight costs on exports from Japan. The company claimed that the 85 percent rule was a consequence of political pressure from the U.S. multinationals and that it has faced considerable problems with changing policies since this decision to add further value locally. Thus, before it had actually commenced production, policy had changed to lower import restrictions.

The same types of issues emerge in case 12. Here the government has had no local content requirements for passenger cars, and the policy has been rather to encourage an increase in the supply of commercial vehicles. By 1977 this was expressed in terms of a time schedule by which a specific list of items was to be produced locally, and the company's investment in the manufacture of truck bodies and components was related entirely to this decree. It was stated that the Japanese firm did enjoy some "advantages" as a joint-venture operation, but some of these, such as five years' profits tax exemption, have proved to be irrelevant.

Experience with Incentives and Performance Requirements

Table 3-9 summarizes the companies' experiences with incentives and performance requirements. In two of the 12 projects studied, companies did not receive the full incentive package promised them. In both cases problems related to the provision of utilities and road connections. In case 3 difficulties in obtaining duty exemptions were also noted. In this latter instance, the government insisted on a search for local vendors before giving import duty exemptions. The search was claimed to take inordinate time. Equally interesting, conversely, is that in cases 1 and 6, incentives were obtained despite a failure to comply with the informal performance requirements.

In Mexico, none of the companies interviewed had achieved foreign currency balance as required by the 1977 Decree.[18] The companies negotiated separately with the government to set a new date for breaking even on foreign exchange balances, but in each case 1985 appeared to be the final date established. The 1977 Decree allowed the government to impose fines for noncompliance, and one firm admitted to having paid such a negotiated fine in 1979. According to the company, a small trade surplus in 1978 turned into a deficit of over $100m. in 1979 and increased further to more than $150m. in 1980. The reason for problems in the interviewed

TABLE 3-9
Experience with Incentives and Performance Requirements

Case	Extent to Which Incentives Offered Were Obtained	Extent of Company Compliance with Performance Requirements	Penalties for Noncompliance with Performance Requirements
Case 1 U.S. MNE	Fully, despite noncompliance with performance requirements (see across)	All objectives missed: missed employment target by 700; put alternative engine into car; failed to achieve volume targets because of loss of Far East business; carburetor manufacture located elsewhere in EC for fear of overdependence	Government had at its discretion right to withdraw 50 percent of $122m. cash grant if objectives not met. But did not enforce
Case 2 U.S. MNE	No experience as yet	Not applicable	Not applicable
Case 3 U.S. MNE	Not fully. Local authority agreed to provide electricity, storm drainage, and service road, but last two commitments not fulfilled because of lack of funds. Government took over obligation but still not fulfilled. Also problems with obtaining duty exemptions	Fully	Not applicable
Case 4 U.S. MNE	No experience as yet	Not applicable	Not applicable
Case 5 U.S. MNE	No experience as yet	Not applicable	Not applicable

136

Case 6 Eur. MNE	Fully	Failed to meet employment targets	None
Case 7 Japan MNE	Fully	Not applicable	Not applicable
Case 8 Eur. MNE	Fully	Fully, albeit with difficulties: finding export markets (chose Saudi Arabia, which would have been supplied from home country); problems with suppliers' costs; end result that Brazil not internationally competitive even with investment incentives	As outlined
Case 9 Eur. MNE	Not fully. Agreed to have free water, electricity, and other utility connections to plant, but municipality ran out of money	Along with other companies failed to meet foreign currency balance	Negotiated 1985 as break-even year for foreign currency balance
Case 10 U.S. MNE	Fully	Failed to meet foreign currency balance	Have paid fine in past; now negotiated 1985 as break-even year for foreign currency balance (on cumulative basis including interest on past deficits)
Case 11 Japan MNE	Fully	Fully, albeit with difficulty: wide range of items to be produced to get to 85 percent level; problems because of complete model change in Japan between 1976 and 1980. Australian models now have heavier	Not applicable

Continued

Table 3-9, continued

Case	Extent to Which Incentives Offered Were Obtained	Extent of Company Compliance with Performance Requirements	Penalties for Noncompliance with Performance Requirements
		bodies and less powerful, less fuel efficient engines	
Case 12 Japan MNE	Fully	Vague. Feeling that once in market with an investment of some scale, pressure decreases. But now insistence on engine and transmission production; company introducing this in 1984. Problem that government has given company no privileges on market access and other manufacturers entering market	Not applicable

Source: Compiled by the authors.

138

companies derived partly from the U.S. recession and higher than anticipated domestic demand in Mexico at the end of the 1970s. Even without these factors, the underlying import/export position for the companies could not sustain foreign currency balance on a regular basis. And the surge of engine investments into Mexico (see Figure 3-1) was an attempt by the auto makers to remedy this situation.

The required reaction of one U.S. company to the 1977 Decree went even further than this. Aside from the engine plant decision, the company response has been to set up a support group within the company in the United States to look into the purchase of Mexican components (which also count as export credits for the terminal manufacturers); to organize seminars for U.S. suppliers in Mexico itself with the aim of encouraging joint ventures; to investigate the possibility of selling engine components from its Mexican subsidiary to other engine manufacturers in the United States; and, finally, to set about exporting a strengthened version of a successful U.S. model for sale as a taxi and police vehicle. While not referring to the engine plant decision, it is worth noting that this same company has also experienced problems in complying with the Mexican local content requirements. The latter refer to all products individually, and in 1981 the company found itself short of local content for conventional rear-wheel drive vehicles. These vehicles were estimated to have a life span of only two years and did not have any engineering development support from the United States. So the decision was made to convert the subsidiary to produce front-wheel drive vehicles, and the changeover took place in the six months to February 1982. Local content requirements, therefore, promoted a much faster changeover than would have otherwise occurred.

Other companies are having problems fulfilling the requirements. A U.S. producer (not included in the 12 cases) argued, for instance, that the recent round of engine investments in Mexico will not be sufficient to achieve foreign exchange balance, so there will be a need for further investments or higher local content. Because the latter would be difficult to achieve, it was stated that additional export-oriented investments would be required. Problems with indigenous suppliers were noted by all companies with investments in Mexico and Brazil: in one case, difficulties were mentioned with the supply of four-speed transmissions in Mexico, which were to have been obtained from a local enterprise. Because of developmental

FIGURE 3-1

Major Mexican Investments in Engine Plants and Exports to the United States

Major Investments in Engine Plants (announced or under construction)

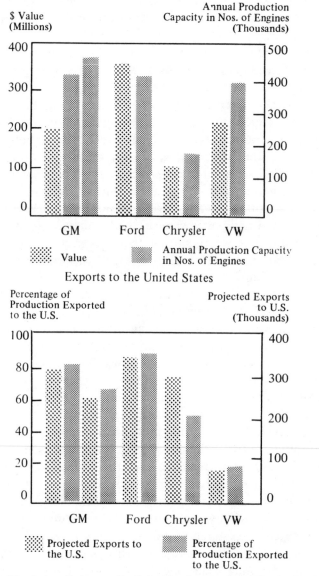

Source: The Labor Industry Coalition for International Trade, *Performance Requirements: A Study of the Incidence and Impact of Trade Related Performance Requirements and an Analysis of International Law*, LCIT, March 1981.

problems, the U.S. MNE eventually had to go to a U.S. supplier, but the domestic producer managed to persuade the government to grant dispensation against the payment of import duties. Various comments were made to the effect that indigenous investment in the supplier industry was less attractive in Mexico than in Brazil, principally because of price controls in the former country. Yet the inefficiencies in the supplier industry in Brazil were highlighted very forcefully in information received relating to a suppliers' meeting organized by one European manufacturer and in comments made by all interviewed companies with investments in that country.

In general, companies with experience of conditions in both Mexico and Brazil preferred the former. The reasons were, first, that the Mexican regulations allowed companies to make a choice between increased exports and increased local content. In Brazil, 85 percent local content means a requirement for stampings as well as engines and the usual "hang-on" parts. To make efficient use of stamping facilities, companies have to keep the product in existence longer to get adequate volume. Second, there was a view that Mexico had not done as much as Brazil to restrict profitability. One company remarked that Brazil granted export incentives but then offset them with domestic price controls. Third, it was felt that the decrees were more flexibly administered in Mexico or, at least, the government was not completely inflexible.

The first point noted in the previous paragraph emerges very strongly in case 11. The Japanese company concerned committed itself to both engine and stamping production for the local market, just at a time when a vast reequipment and model change program was taking place in Japan. Thus, the Australian market has older, less powerful, and less fuel efficient engines, and the Japanese MNE cannot export those based on new technology. Similarly, the models based on lighter bodies cannot be exported to the country. A further problem experienced in this country surrounds the emergence of new items in the performance assessment. It started when a U.S. MNE indicated that it would establish an export-oriented engine plant, and it wanted the export proportion to count as the equivalent of local content. The government apparently accepted this, and, as a result, the Japanese auto maker was forced (unofficially) to export something. They now export aluminum cylinder heads to Japan; even though not economically sound in itself, it satisfies the government and has a trade-off in that the company has been able to replace some locally made parts with cheaper imports from Japan.

The Impact of Incentives and Performance Requirements

*Incentives and Performance Requirements
and the Investment Decision*

In trying to summarize the impact of incentives and performance requirements, the starting point is clearly to ascertain the overall effect on the investment decision. A ranking of factors according to their relative importance is, thus, attempted in Table 3-10. In most cases these rankings were inferred rather than obtained from respondents directly. Performance requirements were undoubtedly the major determinants of the engine investments in cases 9 and 10. Another U.S. MNE, not included in the sample of decisions, also noted that its engine investment was simply to keep the company in the market. Only the final member of the Big Three U.S. auto MNEs, unconvincingly, gave a contrary response: here it was argued that the considerable economic potential and a change of administration improved the company's sights toward Mexico at a time when the company needed an engine.

In the other sample investment in Latin America (case 8), the performance requirements and incentives were relevant only in that they did not cause a serious disadvantage for the company. Market access was crucial. The difference in this case derives, primarily, from the company's seeking market entry. The investments in cases 9 and 10 were designed to protect what was already in existence; a U.S. MNE not included in the sample decisions regarded its recent investments in Brazil, a country in which it had been operating for many years, in this same defensive category.

The investments in Southeast Asia/Oceania were chiefly a consequence of performance requirements. This becomes very apparent when consideration is given to the responses on the questions concerning the hypothetical effects of the absence/removal of these requirements (Table 3-12).

Among the Northern Hemisphere developed country investments, incentives are probably the major factor in the yet to be announced

TABLE 3-10
Ranking of Factors in Investment Decision — on a Country Basis[a]

Case	Ranking	Comments on Influence of Incentives and Performance Requirements

Case 1
U.S. MNE
	1. Costs of set-up and manufacture
	2. Existing facility and expertise in country. Incentives enter at second level of decision, in choosing green-field site rather than expanding existing facilities and ranking as follows:
	  1. Incentives
	  2. Labor attitudes
	  3. Communication advantages from consolidating in one area
		General experience that when undertake studies, expansion at existing sites turns out most financially attractive because of reduced capital cost requirements. Aim in looking at new greenfield sites is to "get someting better," meaning that significant weight is placed upon investment incentives. Case 3 is rather different where access to large internal market was very important

Case 2 U.S. MNE	1. Incentives[b] 2. Labor costs 3. Market access	
Case 3 U.S. MNE	1. Access to market[c] 2. Source point for EC market Incentives minor and of little influence. Performance requirements more important (see note c below)	
Case 4 U.S. MNE	1. Market size and growth (country and continent) 2. Labor costs 3. Other recurring factor costs 4. Government and political factors 5. Incentives	Incentives not a major factor in the location decision. Admitted company had made mistake in past of rank-ing incentives more highly and going into "tough areas" where incentives were higher. In this case, government wanted company to go to such an area <div align="right">Continued</div>

143

Table 3-10, continued

Case	Ranking	Comments on Influence of Incentives and Performance Requirements
Case 5 U.S. MNE	1. Market size and growth (country and continent) 2. Intangibles (labor stability, work ethic, political and government stability) 3. Incentives	In spite of ranking, clear that incentives were important in the choice of this country as against other European locations. [d] It is interesting that another MNE rejected the country because, in total, return expected (even with incentives) well below alternative of expanding existing plants. This suggests that incentives more important than shown
Case 6 Eur. MNE	1. Rebuild market share 2. Production and distribution costs Incentives enter at second level of decision making, within the United States where ranking as follows: 1. Transportation costs and logistics for U.S. distribution and import 2. Nature of sites 3. Incentives	Main impact of incentives at set-up and launch phases where cost reductions helpful. So incentives "of no importance in determining strategy but of some immediate importance tactically"
Case 7 Japan MNE	1. Circumvent restrictions on car imports 2. Satisfy demand 3. Improve market position vis-a-vis Japanese competitors. Incentives not even important in choice of site	Incentives viewed as of little relevance. But import restrictions and "threats" crucial

144

Case 8	1. Market access	Investment seen in strategic terms. Need for "patient money" argued. Net effect of incentives and require-
Eur. MNE	2. Latin America of strategic importance to company	ments negative in that exports not as profitable as alternative supply sources. Belief that negative effect of requirements largely offset by positive impact of incentives, so neutral as investment factors
Case 9	1. Performance requirements	Desire to achieve foreign currency balance of over-
Eur. MNE	2. Secure market access for cars and trucks	whelming importance
	3. Adjacency to a major market	
Case 10	1. Performance requirements	Desire to achieve foreign currency balance of over-
U.S. MNE	2. Use of country as a source point for N. American market	whelming importance in decision to build engine plant
	3. Consolidate market position in country	
Case 11	1. Performance requirements	Performance requirements of overwhelming impor-
Japan MNE	2. Secure market position	tance in decisions
Case 12	1. Performance requirements	Performance requirements of overwhelming impor-
Japan MNE	2. Secure market position	tance

[a] As inferred largely from interviews, although in some cases respondents were prepared to commit themselves to rankings.

[b] Major factor tipping the balance in favor of country, given that without incentives selected country less attractive than some alternative investments.

[c] With the performance requirements that existed on market access before company entry, the project would not have been viable. With the renegotiation of these requirements, arguably performance requirements might be rated quite highly in the ranking.

[d] Adapted only slightly from ranking given by company.

Source: Compiled by the authors.

145

non-EC European project (case 2). The investments in cases 3 and 4 and 6 and 7 were largely market access oriented, but there is a clear difference between the European and Japanese investments in North America. Case 7 was undoubtedly influenced by actual and threatened import restrictions and has to be seen alongside the comment made by the interviewed executive in the company concerned.

Incentives and Performance Requirements and Aspects of Decision

Incentives and performance requirements could conceivably have other effects on factors such as plant characteristics. In all the sample investments, however, neither the scale of the facilities nor the degree of mechanization/labor content was deemed to have been affected by incentives or requirements (Table 3-11). The general view was that in such matters companies were captives of technology and economies of scale, and sometimes, of what was already in existence. Within auto assembly plants, possibilities for demechanization exist in the in-plant movement of materials, and various respondents noted instances in which these had occurred, but in response to lower labor costs, not incentives or requirements. In regard to the engine plants, different pressures could prevail, and one European company has planned a highly automated facility in Mexico in order to avoid problems with skilled labor.[19] On the question of scale, the response was almost always that world scale plants were planned. The possible exceptions concern the Japanese investments (cases 11 and 12). While agreeing that performance requirements were not a factor affecting the scale of the project in case 11, it was argued that the company did design the investments around the market and "what it could stand." The implication was that lower scale/higher cost output was possible because the company has passed on the penalties in price increases to the consumer. In case 12, performance requirements did affect the scale of the operation, causing the company to introduce larger scale manufacture than would have been desired.

In case 12, the performance requirements clearly influenced the products to be manufactured because the regulations specified items to be produced locally. It is arguable that, indirectly, the regulatory package also influenced the engine investment decisions in cases 9 and 10. The advantages of an engine facility were seen as:

TABLE 3-11
Influence of Incentives and Performance Requirements on Aspects of Decision

Case	Influence
Case 1 U.S. MNE	No influence
Case 2 U.S. MNE	Site location
Case 3[a] U.S. MNE	Level of imported inputs
Case 4 U.S. MNE	Timing of entry; site locations; level of exports; level of imported inputs
Case 5 U.S. MNE	Level of imported inputs
Case 6 Eur. MNE	No influence[b]
Case 7 Japan MNE	No influence
Case 8[c] Eur. MNE	Timing of entry; level of exports; level of imported inputs
Case 9[d] Eur. MNE	Type of product; timing of entry; site location; level of exports; level of imported inputs
Case 10[d] U.S. MNE	Type of product; timing of entry; site location; level of exports; level of imported inputs
Case 11 Japan MNE	Type of products; timing of entry; level of exports and imports
Case 12 Japan MNE	Type of products; timing

[a]In addition, the government more or less directed the company to its site. Argued that level of exports not affected by performance requirements because company always saw country as an export base and did not expect to get more than 10 percent of market with only one product line.

[b]But local concern about EPA regulations led, for example, to changed technology in the paint shop.

[c]Timing of entry affected because firm wished to enter earlier. In addition, governmental influence on site selection.

[d]Arguably, the choice of engine manufacture was related to performance requirements.

Source: Compiled by the authors.

An engine facility is relatively more self-contained than an assembly plant

An engine facility is relatively more machine driven and, therefore, is less subject to skilled labor constraints

Engine design does not change frequently (compare an assembly operation where there is a need to retool every time there is a model change)

The product has a high value added relative to freight costs

For the U.S. companies, sheet metal can continue to be shipped to Mexico.

It was noted by one respondent that the alternative to an engine plant would be a stamping facility, but this facility could not be an optimum size.

The influence of performance requirements on the level of exports and imports in cases 3, 4, 8, 9, and 10 is very clear. For the European company in case 9, 90 percent of the output from its engine facility is to be exported to the United States, with the remaining 10 percent being used domestically; for the future, possibilities of exporting to its home country were to be investigated. In case 10, 80 percent of engine output is to be exported to the United States while a smaller, one-third of case 8 truck production is exported. Some revealing comments were made on the choice of export markets in the latter instance. Peru, where this company's sister Latin American plant is located, is the biggest export market for the facility, because of access to contracts through the Peruvian company. Because of the closed nature of many South American markets, exports within that continent were inadequate to satisfy the performance requirements, and the European manufacturer was forced to look for a large volume market elsewhere. Its requirements were, first, a steady market demand, thus ruling out a socialist country where large, but irregular, contracts were the rule, and, second, a market where there was an acceptance of the company's trucks whether manufactured in its home country or Latin America. Eventually, Saudi Arabia was selected, although it was stressed that in the absence of performance requirements, the market would certainly have been supplied out of the home country in Europe.

There were no export requirements in case 12, and the Japanese company made it clear that it could not sustain any, except perhaps within ASEAN countries. The small volume of exports to

Japan (case 11), under the influence of performance requirements has already been noted.

Incentives and Performance Requirements and Efficiency/Profitability

Closely related to the issues discussed above are questions concerning the efficiency and profitability of the sample of foreign direct investments. Essentially, two important questions need to be answered. The first relates to whether at the time the initial investment decision was taken, the expected payout was better than in alternative locations; and the second refers to whether the outturn since the investment was made has been as expected. In fact, these were not clearly distinguished in responses, and the discussions tended to revolve around company experiences in particular locations, which may or may not be related to incentives and requirements.

In respect to the Western European and U.S. investments, previous discussions have indicated that the chosen country location was virtually always that with the best projected financial return, although the pay-out before incentives may well have been poorer than that in alternative locations. Company experiences since then have not always matched expectations. For example, the economics of the European venture in the United States (case 6) have changed adversely. This was not related to incentives, and even though the outturn in case 1 has been rather different from that anticipated, once again this is a consequence of wider environmental factors. Only in cases 3 and 4 were any doubts expressed, and these concerned vendor performance.

The Latin American experience might appear to have been rather different, first, because a number of investments have been undertaken despite the fact that potentially higher rates of return were available elsewhere, and, second, because operating experience has turned out to be more difficult than envisaged. One view expressed was that the United States would be a lower cost source for engines at present, and similar sorts of factors seem to have lain behind the delays in case 9 in starting the engine plant. But exchange rate factors may be chiefly responsible for changing the economics of sourcing. Earlier projects undertaken by these companies appear to have been bedevilled by quality problems, and one U.S. MNE, in relation to its recent car project, commented on the high costs of vandalism and poor delivery performance. Supplier inefficiencies have already been noted in the European project in case 8. This is one factor underlying the company remark that trucks exported were not internationally competitive even after taking account of the incentives available. It has to be said, even so, that the recent economic difficulties of the country may be a large part of the explanation for this latter experience.

Particularly critical remarks were made concerning the efficiency/profitability of the two investments in the Asia Pacific region (cases 11 and 12). In case 11, despite passing on cost penalties in vehicle prices, the company stated that it was still not in overall profit and was operating at unacceptable levels of efficiency. In part this was because of the very wide range of items produced to achieve 85 percent local content and because the company has had a complete model change since 1977. In case 12, too, the project is very much poorer in profitability and efficiency than Japanese norms; and this view was confirmed by another Japanese company that extended this conclusion to its investment in Malaysia as well as Indonesia — at least for cars. There seems little doubt that major efficiency problems emerge in such small-scale, domestic market-oriented investments. Within these latter two countries, the company estimated that engines being produced were three times the Japanese cost, with production costs for car bodies being double those in Japan. The final cost price in both Malaysia and Indonesia is about twice that of Japan for an equivalent product, and the company argued that it could in effect export and pay the high import tariff (if the government were prepared to issue import licenses) and still undercut their subsidiaries located in these countries.

Hypothetical Effects of Absence or Removal of Incentives and Performance Requirements

Table 3-12 refers to having no incentive and performance requirements. In regard to the hypothetical effect of the absence of incentives or performance requirements, the responses confirm a number of earlier findings. Where market access was crucial, companies tended to indicate that the investments would still have taken place. Where the performance requirements were the main determinants

TABLE 3-12
Hypothetical Effects of Absence or Removal of Incentives and Performance Requirements

Case	Hypothetical Effects of Absence of Incentives and Performance Requirements on Decision	Hypothetical Reaction of Company to Removal of Incentives and Performance Requirements at Present
Case 1 U.S. MNE	Politically bad decision to go outside country and potential labor problems with redundancies at existing facility. "Probably have struggled" into existing facility	None; no incentives or performance requirements in existence; incentives related to capital cost
Case 2 U.S. MNE	Add capacity to each of existing assembly facilities. Interplant trade flows in Europe affected	Not applicable
Case 3 U.S. MNE	Possible deferral of decision; although strategic factors may have been important, namely that another MNE was seeking site in country at same time; import volumes probably greater	Incentives virtually nonexistent, so removal would have no effect. Performance requirements likely to be removed, so no effect; market will become much more competitive, but company always has edge as domestic producer
Case 4 U.S. MNE	None, market access crucial. Site location within country may have been affected. N.B. In absence of performance requirements, however, company would have entered market through acquisition several years earlier. Import volumes probably greater	Incentives virtually nonexistent, so removal would have no effect. Performance requirements likely to be removed
Case 5 U.S. MNE	Likely that investment would have gone to another country (but company not prepared to confirm or deny). Intra-European trade flows affected	None; incentives related to capital cost
Case 6 Eur. MNE	Market entry not affected. Plant location probably affected. No significant trade effects	None; incentives related to capital cost

Continued

151

Table 3-12, continued

Case	Hypothetical Effects of Absence of Incentives and Performance Requirements on Decision	Hypothetical Reaction of Company to Removal of Incentives and Performance Requirements at Present
Case 7 Japan MNE	Remain as an exporter from home country, because of cost/quality advantages in supplying from Japan (but subject to import restrictions)	None; investment committed
Case 8 Eur. MNE	None; market access crucial. Site location within country affected. N.B. In absence of regulations, company would have entered market in early 1960s. Exports from Brazil sharply reduced; imports increased	Not internationally competitive location. Need to be in market, world recession, and economic problems likely to lead to change in nature of operation in the country
Case 9 Eur. MNE	Unlikely that investment would take place. Decision uncertain even with performance requirements because of chaotic currency problems and quality problems. Exports from Mexico sharply reduced; imports increased	No investment in engines
Case 10 U.S. MNE	No investment in engines. Continue with assembly of completely knocked-down kits or built-up packs. Exports from country reduced	With loss-making situation in country and economic problems of country and of company, divestment likely. Argued that all U.S. manufacturers would lose out to Japanese in free market situation
Case 11 Japan MNE	Completely built-up units or completely knocked-down kits exported from home country ("This would have provided cheaper and better cars to the consumer and much better profit to the company"). Exports eliminated	Probably close and export completely built-up units. Still not in overall profit in Australia and operating at unacceptable levels of efficiency. But difficult to say now that company has a heavier investment in the market

Continued

152

| Case 12 Japan MNE | Remain as an exporter from home country | Withdraw ("We would probably throw the production unit into the Java Sea"). Operation much poorer in profitability and efficiency than Japanese norms |

Source: Compiled by the authors.

of the investments their absence would most likely have led companies to continue as exporters only. In Europe, investment at a greenfield site in another country, expansion at existing sites, or deferral of the expansion decision would have been indicated. Finally, in the U.S. investments a difference was noted in the European and Japanese company responses. The former indicated that market entry would not have been affected, whereas the Japanese MNE was quite adamant that manufacturing in the United States would not have been considered.

Aside from the hypothetical effects of the absence of incentives and performance requirements on the investment decision overall, an important issue concerns the possible influence on exports and imports, and some comments on this are also included in Table 3-12. Where any effect is hypothesized for the investments in Europe, only intrafirm and intercountry trade within the region would be affected. The major trade effects would occur in the Latin American and Asia Pacific investments, particularly the former where world scale, export-oriented projects are involved. Even in case 8, where the investment would still have gone ahead in the absence of incentives and requirements, trade patterns would likely be very different: here, exports would probably be eliminated except perhaps to the company's sister plant whereas the removal of the constraint on the use of local suppliers would likely generate substantially increased imports. The same pattern would tend to apply in cases 9 and 10. No exports are involved in case 12, and exports in case 11 are quite small; in these cases import volumes would change. When considered in trade terms, it becomes very obvious that the adverse balance of payments implications of these changes could not be tolerated by the host countries concerned. Because the auto industry is such a large contributor to the balance of payments of these nations, alternative action directed at this sector specifically would have to be anticipated.

As a further check, an attempt was made to assess what would happen if incentives and performance requirements were removed at the present time. In some cases no change would be indicated because incentives were payable on the capital cost at the time the investments were made, and no other incentives or requirements applied. In relation to the removal of performance requirements, the one common theme was the increased competitiveness that would occur in a more open market situation. Thus, despite the problems of operating with performance requirements, increased competition from the Japanese might be the greater of the two evils. In addition, all companies reported that the operating environment in Latin America had become much more hostile, so a cautious approach would be indicated. One U.S. company went so far as to indicate that divestment of its entire Mexican operation was possible, but interestingly, and reflecting earlier remarks on poor performance and other problems, the Japanese companies involved in cases 11 and 12 indicated closure as a strong possibility.

Other Issues

The questionnaire used in the interviews covered a number of other issues. Some issues were specific to the particular investment decisions, and some were more general. This concluding section notes the type of information available on these issues. The information obtained was far from comprehensive, and no attempt is, therefore, made at detailed analysis.

Renegotiation of Agreements and the Use of Counterproposals

The question of renegotiation relates to the discussion on Table 3-9, referring to companies' experiences with incentives and performance requirements. Clearly, attempts at renegotiation will be involved where companies fear they will be unable to comply with certain terms, as, for example, when the Mexican government allowed the auto firms an extended period to comply with the regulations on foreign currency balance. In these instances the companies warned the government of their impending problems as part of their regular system of reporting and presented plans to extend the term. A U.S. MNE (not included in the sample) reported that the extent of the term of their BEFIEX contract was renegotiated at the request of the Brazilian government.

In Europe as noted earlier, the U.S. company involved in case 1 failed to achieve the objectives of its program. Here, bimonthly meetings were held with governmental officials to inform them of progress; eventually the relevant minister's discretion was obtained in the company's favor in January 1981, when it was agreed that it had met all its commitments. In case 3, the same company renegotiated higher shares of the domestic market, lower local content requirements, and less strict export/import value ratios. This was part of a program by which an engine plant was added nine months after the assembly operation began (in this instance no comprehensive site selection review was involved).

The Japanese companies interviewed made reference to cases of renegotiation in the Asia Pacific region "on almost a daily basis." One of the firms mentioned its operation in Thailand, where the government was persuaded against operating a particular law on foreign direct investment whereby machinery would be imported duty free but not sold duty free after it had been used. Much more recently in its current negotiations to enter Taiwan, the company had persuaded the government to drop a 50 percent export requirement. Another Japanese MNE noted pressure to accelerate local content from 40 to 50 percent in the early years after establishment in Malaysia, but this was successfully resisted. With regard, finally, to the specific investment projects studied in detail, frequent renegotiation was the rule in Australia, and the company had benefitted, for example, by being granted temporary exemptions on local content requirements when new models were being introduced.

Investment with or without Incentives

Looking more generally at auto investments, all companies noted that in recent years, where foreign greenfield projects had gone ahead, some incentives were almost always involved. But this says nothing about whether such incentives had any influence on the project decisions. In any event, the position was different with expansions on existing sites. This is particularly relevant in Europe, where most of the auto companies' largest and oldest facilities were in areas that did not qualify for incentives (as part of regional assistance schemes). Substantial expansions still occur in such locations; witness the case of one U.S. manufacturer that spent $350m. on its assembly line for the launch of a new model in Europe during 1982.

Whereas regional variations in incentive levels are apparent everywhere, the European system of regional aids seemed to cause particular concern among the companies studied. The aids had been a factor in the dispersal of the motor industry in Europe since the 1960s, but in instances, the experience of past investments made as a consequence of government regional policies had been poor. Partly reflecting that experience, Tables 3-3- 3-5 showed that companies are now very wary of selecting sites within a country purely on the basis of the differential incentive levels available.

Incentives and Performance Requirements and Divestment

The U.S. companies admitted to various divestments, in Latin America mainly, as a consequence of changing performance requirements. For one MNE, withdrawals have taken place as follows:

Peru. The government insisted on a local partner

Argentina. Price controls were a factor also; the operation was structured incorrectly

Chile. The auto producer withdrew the first time because the company could not repatriate earnings except by the purchase of gold, and this was prohibited by the U.S. Treasury. The company returned after the offer of protection against import competition; this is being removed as the country attempts to implement free-trade policies, and it was reported that they were "likely to be out again soon"

Saudi Arabia. The U.S. manufacturer withdrew from a truck plant venture because an agreement to provide loans and protection from assembled imports was not fulfilled

Another U.S. MNE withdrew from two of these same countries, Chile and Peru, in the 1960s because of changes in performance requirements. In Peru, the company was given three years to get from 15 percent to 70 percent local content; it was argued that this was impossible, but the government did not respond, so the company divested. Such changes are very relevant to the Mexican case, where again the companies have changed decisions as the regulations have altered. The difference is that the much larger market in Mexico raises the stakes in divestment decisions and improves government bargaining power.

Some auto firms are very cautious about making divestment decisions because of fears that such a decision may exclude them permanently from the market. A Japanese manufacturer involved in a 100 percent locally owned assembly operation in one of the smaller European countries is in this category. The company, aware that the venture is very unprofitable, was attempting to negotiate with the government to close the plant and shift the 150 or so workers into another product (for example, exhausts, plastic components) in return for retaining access to the market.

APPENDIX

This brief section provides notes on a number of investment decisions that are not included in the main text. They are included to indicate something of the diversity of investment incentives that may be offered and performance requirements imposed by countries in the automobile industry.

European MNE Investment in Bus Manufacture in the United States

This company's strategy in buses, simply stated, is to survive as a worldwide manufacturer at a time when mergers and rationalization are the keynotes of the industry and to take whatever steps are necessary to penetrate international markets. It was argued that international investment decisions in the sector were always related to trade barriers, leading to a highly inefficient and fragmented industry. With regard to the United States, the company view was that a major restructuring of the bus business was likely with the emergence of larger, more competitive units, and the European firm wanted to have a foothold in the market before this occurred.

The company decided to manufacture buses in the eastern United States at a plant acquired some years ago with a view to setting up a car assembly operation. The major reason for setting up this operation was the Buy America Act. Under the terms of this act, public bus operators can get 80 percent of their capital investments paid by the federal government if the supplier meets specifications and the product is a U.S. product (which means that more than 50 percent of the value is U.S.). The outcome of this is that the European company developed, for the first time ever, a factory for the complete production of buses — both body building and chassis manufacture. Body building is regarded as a low-technology, labor-intensive activity requiring low investment, quite the opposite of chassis manufacture, and has not traditionally been an activity undertaken by this company. In this case, the company bought body designs from Switzerland and developed and adapted the product, taking the view that this is the price it has to pay to get into the U.S. market. Underlying the decision, in addition, is a fear that the terms of the Buy America Act may be toughened. U.S. product liability legislation is also relevant.

The European firm could, of course, sell to private companies where the local content requirements do not apply, but there are other reasons for concentrating on the public market. In particular, the public operators run local services only, so it is possible for them to operate with centralized depots for parts and special tools. With the private operators there would be a need for a service network covering the whole country.

In the absence of U.S. performance requirements, it was stated that this European producer would service the market from exports and cooperate with a local body builder in the United States.

European MNE in West Africa

This case is illustrative of the type of arrangement that auto companies have negotiated in countries in the early stages of industrialization, where the real incentive is commonly the agreement to give tariff protection against imports from overseas to any company setting up a local operation.

The decision by this European auto maker to consider entry was based on the higher incomes expected from natural resources, and the company was favorably impressed by the industrial strategy that was emerging in the country at the time; the investment was planned between 1970 and 1972 and signed in the latter year. Leading companies were invited to tender, and the company was selected for a project in which the host country government had a 50 percent stake, home country banks 10 percent, and the firm 40 percent.

The arrangements for the project were as follows:

1. Level of local taxes raised to normal levels over a period of years as the project developed

2. Tariff protection against overseas competitors for 10 years after start-up. (Note, the consequences in terms of higher local prices were accepted by the host country in negotiation as the premium to be paid for the development of the industry)
3. "Investment contract" between European and host country governments whereby latter took some responsibility to act if the project ran into trouble
4. Local content requirements and achievement of employment levels
5. Specified indigenization of management, beginning three years after commencement of operations
6. Production of a specified product range, complementary to that of the other major manufacturer in the country
7. Requirement for latest technology at time of entry

The European auto maker's priority was how to protect what it knew would be an "unproductive investment": this was tackled partly through the investment contract and partly through the retention of home country management for a ten-year period. No export demands were to be placed on the company for the first ten years, and it would not have considered accepting this because of the scale of the operation and the pricing structure.

This investment is an interesting case. The market offers substantial potential even if this is very long term. In the short term, however, companies in the market are anxious to be protected against import competition; the European MNE indicated that it would withdraw if further franchises were granted in the country. On this point, in discussions with a U.S. auto firm, mention was made of the strenuous efforts being made by the corporation to gain entry to the market. The company had gone as far as offering to build a company town in return for market access and the relinquishment of certain performance requirements. To date, such efforts have been unsuccessful.

European MNE Investment in Canada

This company decided in the mid-1970s to try to develop a "duty-free" entrance route to Canada but not to consider establishing an assembly operation there. The company declared a distrust of the future of the Automotive Pact between the United States and Canada, deciding that there must be another way of entering the protected market and offsetting the customs penalty of 15-16 percent. After many years of looking at alternative possibilities, an agreement was signed in the early 1980s but has not been implemented yet because of economic conditions.

The executive interviewed described this deal as the "most detailed and constrained performance requirement agreement ever signed by . . . [the company] anywhere." While no details would be divulged, the essence of the matter was clear. The company had agreed to invest in a $100m. components plant in Canada giving employment to 500. The product was to be relatively high technology, involving parts of the power train. There was considerable debate with the Canadians as to what product would meet their demands, taking into account factors such as value added, filling local automotive industry supply gaps, the generation of auxiliary activity, and so on. Dependent on the performance of this plant in terms of value added, output volume, and employment, a specific proportion of company imports into Canada would be allowed to enter duty free — whether from the United States or Europe. While the details of the formula were not disclosed, it would appear to be based on absolute volumes and relative volumes (Canadian or non-Canadian sourcing). It was estimated that perhaps 35 percent of duty remission would initially arise from the plant volume with the rest from the use of Canadian sourcing.

It is interesting to see how the company regarded this deal. It was compared to its Brazilian experience, which was described as "an industrial steering decision," whereas Canada was a project designed to "adjust the Canadian trade account." It was made quite clear that the agreement involved severe penalty clauses whereby the duty exemptions would be lost if volume, employment, and value added were not maintained. Having said that, the deal had worked out close to optimal from the company viewpoint.

SUMMARY AND CONCLUSIONS

Drawing together the results of this study, the conclusion confirmed is that foreign investment decision making in the auto industry is closely bound up with government intervention whether in the form of incentives or performance requirements, albeit with market access considerations on occasions of even greater significance. The European Community emerges from the discussion as an area where competition between nations exists in the granting of investment incentives and where incentives influence the location of foreign direct investment projects. The payment of incentives through regional aid schemes has been the subject of much controversy, and the EC Commission has attempted since 1971 to coordinate and harmonize such schemes. Initial steps were aimed at limiting competitive bidding for mobile industry in the most prosperous regions of the European Community and at preventing regional financial incentives from being used to distort competition. Later, aid ceilings were established for each of five categories of regions, distinguished in terms of the severity of their regional need: the percentage of investment costs that can be funded by member states ranges from a norm of 20 percent to a high of 75 percent in especially deprived areas. In addition, the system of European Community evaluation of aid given was extended to include a cost per job limit. Despite such efforts, differences between country policies have made progress difficult, especially with high job-creating automobile projects.

Some of the most controversial cases recently have involved the United Kingdom, witness the £162.5m. support package for the rationalization and reinvestment of Chrysler U.K. in 1975; the £80m. package for the De Lorean sports car project in Northern Ireland, after, allegedly, the project had been offered to but rejected by the Irish Republic; and most recently the intensive discussions with Nissan, which promised to bring the first wholly owned Japanese assembly plant and manufacturing complex to European soil — despite earlier concerns over issues such as local content, fears of labor problems, concern over market access to continental EC markets, and the world recession. The United Kingdom is interesting also in illustrating the long-run problems that may be derived from directing and inducing the motor industry to suboptimal locations. Under the influence of Industrial Development Certificate (IDC) policy and the offer of loans and grants, Ford, GM, and Rootes (later Chrysler) all located new assembly plants in peripheral, nontraditional producing areas in the early 1960s.[20] Looked at 20 years later, the picture is a sorry one: the former Chrysler plant at Linwood in Scotland was closed in 1982; Ford's Halewood facility poses continuing problems because of disruption and low productivity; and the GM operations in Britain have been run down very significantly.

Even though incentives have had an influence on the dispersal of the auto industry in the European Community, many EC auto investments are not influenced by regional incentives. For example, the main European production bases of Ford and GM are at Dagenham, England, and at the Adam Opel operations in Germany respectively. Substantial investment has continued in these facilities over time, despite the fact that neither is an area eligible for regional aids.

In the long term, the formal linking of performance requirements to the granting of incentives would seem to be more likely. To date, it has been shown that informal performance requirements do exist but have not been implemented. Now, however, there is growing concern over, for example, the net job-creating effects of auto assembly plants, as the Nissan case illustrated very clearly. Yet because of competition between countries for projects, EC action would seem to be necessary before any such policies are implemented, and, as the following paragraph reveals, the short-term likelihood is for even greater incentive bidding.

Outside the EC in Europe, the position is more complex and more difficult to discuss without breaching confidentiality commitments. Essentially, if a country is relatively small and poorly developed but still offering some degree of access to the large EC market, then substantial incentives will be necessary to attract any auto projects, and companies would be likely to rank incentives as a major factor in investment decision making (case 2). Larger domestic market size and higher levels of development would be likely to reduce the importance of incentives in corporate decision making, particularly where countries have no or underdeveloped motor industries at present. Indeed, protection in the market against imports might induce companies to accept various performance requirements as the price for entry (case 3). It is doubtful if there are any countries in the latter position left in Europe now, and both the likely enlargement of the EC to include Spain and Portugal and the growth of association agreements between other European countries and the EC mean that incentive bidding may become more intense. This is particularly the case when only a few countries remain that have a large domestic market, but no auto industry.

The two investments in the United States (cases 6 and 7) offer a contrast. In one instance, location-specific factors, namely changes in relative wage and exchange rates were of considerable importance in the investment decision. As an exporter, market share in the United States was being lost to lower cost competitors. In the other case, cost factors favored the continuation of exports from Japan, but investment was prompted by import restrictions. The appendix to the second section contained an example of a further investment in the United States, this time made in response to performance requirements; it seems that both market access variables and import restrictions will induce further investments in the future. Incentives are unnecessary as an investment-inducing variable and, in the investments studied at least, are relatively unimportant at the stage of site selection also because of the similarities of the packages on offer from the various states.

The remaining group of investments, namely those in Latin America and Asia Pacific can almost be taken together. The main variable determining company responses was the extent of existing involvement with the market. On the one hand, where companies had significant investments in the country, the major factor determining new investment was performance requirements. The investment projects were, thus, undertaken for largely defensive reasons. Where, on the other hand, a company has been excluded from a large market, market access becomes a critical determinant of investment. The role of incentives did not emerge clearly in the interviews, except in case 8, but incentives may be viewed as an important factor in export-oriented investments (cases 8-10). Thus, it is doubtful if companies would have invested in export-oriented projects, despite performance requirements, if most of the cost disadvantage had not been offset through the payment of incentives. The Asia Pacific investments (cases 11 and 12) differ from those in Latin America in this respect because both of the former were domestic market oriented. In many ways these investments are similar to those undertaken in Latin America during its import substituting development phase.

Taking the investment cases together, the major variables determining the importance of incentives and performance requirements in corporate decision making at the country level would seem to be the following:

Host country variables	Market size
	Degree of development (in general and of auto industry in particular)
	Common market membership
	Market accessibility (through exports from parent or other subsidiaries
Company variables	Extent of existing investment in market
Investment orientation	Domestic or export market oriented

For incentives or performance requirements to be ranked highly as factors in the foreign investment decision, some illustrative combinations of these variables can be shown. Incentives would tend to rank highly for greenfield investments in the EC common market, unless there were substantial cost differences between countries as production locations. The position is quite different in the Andean Pact countries where market access can be used as a lever. Incentives would also be important in certain non-EC countries in Europe in which market size is small and the degree of development low (so that the countries are not attractive as export bases, despite low wage costs). Performance requirements, conversely, are likely to be important in developing nations for domestic-oriented investments, and for projects in countries where the auto producer already has investments, particularly where the market size is significant. Both of the latter factors raise the stakes substantially when companies are contemplating withdrawal, whereas excessively stringent regulations in countries with small markets and a low degree of development can and have led to divestment. Export-oriented investments differ from the domestic market-oriented category in that incentives will almost certainly be required in the former, in addition to any performance requirements, to facilitate international competitiveness.

The data in the case analysis section also showed that incentives and performance requirements have had an influence on various other dimensions of the investment projects concerned, such as site selection within the country, entry timing, types of products assembled or manufactured, and levels of exports and imports. The latter are especially important in the context of this project, and it can be said that patterns of international trade are being affected particularly, for example, the trade patterns between Mexico and the United States. At the same time, however, the balance of payments position of a country such as Mexico has to be borne in mind, and the trade flows implied by cost competitiveness would place an unacceptable strain on the foreign exchange position of the country. One of the major reasons for Latin American countries embarking upon strategies of auto industry development was precisely that of reducing the foreign currency drain.

NOTES

1. See, for example, K. Bhaskar, *The Future of the World Motor Industry* (London: Kogan Page, 1980); G. Maxcy, *The Multinational Motor Industry* (London: Croom Helm, 1981); United Nations Centre on Transnational Corporations, *Transnational Corporations in the International Auto Industry* (New York, 1982); and D. H. Ginsberg and W. J. Abernathy, eds., *Government, Technology and the Future of the Automobile* (New York: McGraw Hill, 1980).

2. Commission of the European Communities, *The European Automobile Industry: Commission Statement*, Bulletin of the European Communities, Supplement 2/81 (Brussels, 1981).

3. *Transnational Corporations in the International Auto Industry*, Part II.

4. M. v. N. Whitman, *International Trade and Investment: Two Perspectives*, Essays in International Finance, No. 143, Department of Economics (Princeton, New Jersey: Princeton University, July 1981), p. 10.

5. L. T. Wells, Jr., "The International Product Life Cycle and United States Regulation of the Automobile Industry," in *Government, Technology and the Future of the Automobile*, ed. Ginsberg and Abernathy (New York: McGraw Hill, 1980), pp. 270-92.

6. Whitman, *International Trade and Investment*, p. 13.

7. M. Wilkins, "Multinational Automobile Enterprises and Regulation: An Historical Overview," in *Government, Technology and the Future of the Automobile*, ed. Ginsberg and Abernathy (New York: McGraw Hill, 1980), pp. 221-56.

8. Maxcy, *The Multinational Motor Industry*, p. 270.

9. D. T. Jones, *Maturity and Change in the European Car Industry: Structural Change and Public Policy*, Sussex European Papers No. 8 (Sussex European Research Centre, 1981).

10. R. B. Cohen, *The Prospects for Trade and Protectionism in the Auto Industry*, paper presented at a conference on Trade Policy in the Eighties, Institute for International Economics, Washington, D.C., June 23-25, 1982, p. 29.

11. BIAC Committee on International Investment and Multinational Enterprises, *Relationship of Incentives and Disincentives to International Investment Decisions* (New York: OECD, 1981), p. 7.

12. Whitman, *International Trade and Investment*, p. 20.

13. Interestingly, this applies only to trucks and buses. In cars, the company aims to continue as a specialist producer, but it is not a major objective to be significantly internationalized.

14. A U.S. producer noted that they had rarely looked outside Europe in site selection. The company's world headquarters had made suggestions in the past that the company should, say, consider Mexico or Brazil (and Mexico was considered as a source for engines), but invariably such investments were not financially attractive.

15. "GM Bringing Austria into Auto Industry," *New York Times*, July 9, 1979. There is no implication from this that Austria is one of the investment decisions studied in the project.

16. American Consulate in Mexico, *The Auto Industry in Northeast Mexico*, June 30, 1982.

17. As the company is a Mexican enterprise and not in a zone that receives large incentives, the only subsidies obtained were tax credits for initial construction. The company has found, however, that being a major employer in the town gives it significant leverage with the Coahuila and Saltillo governments; also mentioned as advantages were the reliability and productiveness of the workforce, most of whom came from rural/farm backgrounds.

18. It is not certain that this was the position for all auto multinationals in Mexico. At least two MNEs had healthy trade positions because of exports, principally to the United States.

19. A U.S. manufacturer, however, stated that the transfer line in its Mexican engine plant was not so automated as that in the United States.

20. The government could and did refuse IDCs for expansion at existing sites.

4

Computers

Robert R. Miller

ACKNOWLEDGEMENT

Studies of this type depend crucially upon the cooperation of knowledgeable executives in the industry. In this case, all companies approached by the International Finance Corporation agreed to participate fully in the research, in many cases because executives were keenly interested in the outcome. To all of the executives who devoted long hours to interviews, but who have chosen to remain anonymous, the author wishes to express his deep appreciation.

INTRODUCTION

The computer industry, as defined for this study, is comprised of a variety of manufacturing companies. The industry includes firms active in manufacturing virtually every size of computer assembled in the world – from large mainframe units, with assorted peripherals needed to complete a system, through minicomputer systems to small desktop units sold through retail distribution channels. Moreover, because producers of such equipment invariably specialize in their individual manufacturing units, some of the investments examined here involve in addition to central processing units a variety of closely related products. For example, a particular factory might manufacture disc storage units or smart terminals, items sometimes

168

called peripheral despite their essential role in a functioning computer system.

It is important, however, to specify some boundaries, even if this can be done only by noting firms not to be included within the scope of the study. As an example, firms specializing in semiconductor fabrication, so-called "merchant" producers, are not covered here, although it is true that many of the companies discussed here do engage in semiconductor manufacture. Nor have firms concentrating on such peripheral items as high-speed printers or tape drives been included. Once again, however, several of the companies classified here as computer firms do, in fact, also produce many of the same items in which excluded companies specialize. Finally, the increasingly important set of activities associated with applications and systems software development is not included in the broad industry definition used here, despite the fact that it is also becoming central to the companies' foreign investment strategies.

Executives from 11 companies were interviewed. Eight companies were based in the United States, with the remainder located in Japan. In terms of international investment in the computer industry, these companies account for a large proportion of corporate involvements. The relatively little remaining foreign investment is almost all made by a small number of U.S.-based firms. Few European investments have been accomplished and, where they have, they are not generally considered to be effective competitors by executives in the companies included here. The corporations covered in this study are, in other words, all international leaders in technology developments in the industry.

In sales volume, the companies range in size from less than $500 million to multibillion dollar firms. Some specialize only in computer system manufacturing and sales; for others, computers are a modest part of their total business. Some companies maintain extensive manufacturing operations abroad, whereas others are relative newcomers in establishing overseas plants. As a consequence of such differences, firms in the sample vary substantially in their approaches to the world market and in their investment strategies. This means, too, that investment incentives and performance requirements are not viewed identically by all firms. General tendencies can be identified in managerial attitudes and reactions to governmental policy measures intended to influence investment flows, but such measures can affect individual firms quite differently. Finally, companies in the sample ranged widely in the level of sophistication with which they approached the investment decision. Some were highly analytical; some were almost intuitive.

Managerial perceptions of the effects of governmental policies may not in every case be consistent with what would seem to be underlying forces shaping the pattern of overseas investment. Executives tend by the nature of their tasks to focus on quite specific factors that affect particular investment decisions. They may be unaware that these same factors are the consequence of explicit policies of governments, policies that are intended to and can alter the pattern of international trade and investment. Most executives, for example, would not view tariffs as a form of investment incentive.

International investment strategies in the computer industry differ not only between various types of firms but also between the nationality of the companies. Japanese managers necessarily view international competition differently than U.S. managers. Partly, such differences can be explained by the lateness of entry as effective competitors of the Japanese. But, dissimilarities in the Japanese approach to investment decisions go beyond just these market positioning considerations. They involve as well quite fundamental differences in the way large Japanese companies have conducted their businesses, as compared with U.S. firms. For example, whereas U.S. companies have tended to be aggressive international investors, Japanese firms generally have been more reluctant, moving only when external events have forced a change in strategic posture.

The remainder of this part of the study begins with a brief description of the global computer industry. It will become apparent in this review why the study has concentrated only on U.S. and Japanese companies and has virtually ignored competitors elsewhere in the world. We then discuss the apparent investment strategies of both U.S. and Japanese companies and the general ways they have reacted to investment incentives and performance requirements. In the fourth section, each company's experiences are described individually. Every attempt has been made in these case descriptions to conceal corporate identifications, and they have been reviewed by responsible executives to ensure their satisfaction with the confidentiality level resulting. It should be noted also that executives were asked to review the summary section of the report for general accuracy. Even though most expressed approval, it should not be inferred that the opinions expressed here represent those of any individual manager or group of managers. Corporate confidentiality was guaranteed to each executive participating in the study as a condition of the interview.

The cases are followed by a compilation of more than 30 investments, detailing the level and type of incentives offered. In this compilation, neither company names nor countries are revealed. Conclusions and policy implications are the subject of the concluding section.

THE INTERNATIONAL COMPUTER INDUSTRY

The computer industry, more than virtually any other, can be characterized by a single word: dynamic. Fifteen years ago, the global industry was overwhelmingly dominated by a single company, International Business Machines (IBM). Although this firm is still enormously important, especially in large, general purpose equipment, today the industry also includes a substantial number of aggressive and rapidly growing companies. Data General, for example, did not exist 15 years ago; in 1981, the firm's revenues were three-quarters of a billion dollars. Another U.S. company, Digital Equipment Corporation, five years ago was about the size Data General is today; it has grown more than fourfold since then. Such growth is not confined to U.S. corporations alone. In Japan, Fujitsu, Limited, has become that nation's largest computer manufacturer, now surpassing IBM in sales there. Other Japanese producers, such as Hitachi, Nippon Electric, Mitsubishi, and Toshiba also are expanding rapidly. Recent worldwide market growth has been the by-product of continuous and still ongoing technological change, mostly coming from the microelectronics sector. The ability to incorporate more and more electronic functions into single integrated circuits has resulted in chips that are smaller, much faster in operation, and considerably cheaper in terms of cost per function. Such chips, moreover, use little power, reducing heat output, and are extremely reliable in operation. All of these characteristics have combined to make possible increasingly dependable, yet inexpensive, computing power for a wide variety of uses. The explosion in worldwide use of computers is a direct reflection of the miraculous technical changes occurring in the computer's primary components, semiconductors and integrated circuits. The continuing process of successful microminiaturization in these vital components has made possible further evolution in the computer industry as well.

It should not be inferred, however, that technical developments in integrated circuits are the only driving force in dynamic changes occurring in computers. Increasing capability in system design and software is also an important factor. In fact, several quite successful competitors in the industry depend almost entirely on their skills in these areas, and for all manufacturers, system design is becoming more vital than is hardware manufacturing itself. Larger producers, therefore, focus on developing internal capacity for producing semiconductors, the key manufactured element, and in maintaining competence in system design and applications software development. Smaller firms, because of the immense costs involved today in establishing integrated circuit production, purchase such components from merchant vendors. Even here, however, some semiconductors may be tailored to the firm's specific design requirements.

The reason for this attention to both software and critical hardware items is that increasingly the two are substitutable, as it becomes possible to incorporate more logical elements into the chip design itself. Many computer manufacturers believe that in the long run, competence within the firm in the design and production of integrated circuits will be essential to continued competitive viability. That is, it will not be possible to rely on others for technical components while concentrating on system software development, because from an overall design perspective, component and software production will become inseparable.

In any case, it is fair to say that the explosive growth that continues to characterize the computer industry has been technology driven. Increased computing capability has become available well before new applications made possible by this capability have become well defined. But the existence of low-cost computational power has spurred the discovery of new applications not previously considered in a serious way. Such a cycle, typifying the industry's development, continues to unfold today.

This evolution has generated a wide assortment of types and categories of computer equipment. On the basis of size, for example, computers range from very small units for home use costing, say, $100, to giant computers intended for scientific use and priced well over $10 million. Between these extremes is a plethora of intermediate-sized units: small business computers, dedicated minicomputers for such uses as process control or inventory management, and general purpose mainframes for a variety of business uses. In addition, of course, enormous numbers of microprocessors find their way to such highly specialized purposes as automobile engine monitoring or cameras.

For purposes here, this latter category is ignored and, to the extent possible, data will refer to three broad categories of equipment.[1]

1. Microcomputers, in which the central processing unit (CPU) consists of a single chip and where the typical "word" length is 8 bits. Priced between $1,000 and $10,000.
2. Minicomputers, where the CPUs may or may not be on a single chip, but where the word length would usually be 16 bits. The distinction between micro- and minicomputers is today becoming increasingly blurred. Priced between $10,000 and $100,000.
3. Mainframes, in which the CPU typically contains scores of logic chips and for which trained operators are normally needed. Word lengths are commonly 32 to 64 bits, yielding much faster operating speeds for more demanding applications. Priced between $100,000 and $5-10 million. Again, the difference between larger minis and mainframes is fuzzy, at best, especially in a temporal sense. Today's minis are larger and faster than many mainframes of five years ago.

Computers require a variety of so-called peripheral devices to function. Most use external memory capacity, which might be either magnetic discs or tapes, both requiring drive units for data input or output. In addition, computers require other output devices that may or may not be built into the computer itself. Video monitors or printers are examples. Peripheral equipment incorporated in computer systems normally would be included in value figures related to manufacturer shipments.

Companies that design and manufacture computer equipment are domiciled in only a few countries of the world. Most importantly, these countries are the United States, Japan, West Germany, France, Italy, and the United Kingdom. In each of these countries, however, an important part of total manufacturing activity in the industry is carried out by U.S.-based companies. In fact, in terms of market share, U.S. companies predominate in every country except

Japan, and even there U.S. companies (or joint ventures including such firms) account for nearly half of the market. Table 4-1 gives data for a recent year. The preeminence of a single company, IBM, is clearly evident from the figures, but it is also clear that U.S. firms generally figure prominently in the markets of all countries. The converse, however, is demonstrably not true; that is, companies from other countries hold only a trivial part of the U.S. market. Although some may be quite important in their domestic markets, none are a significant factor elsewhere in the world. Thus far, therefore, it can be concluded that only U.S.-based firms have become truly international competitors in general purpose computers.

Another way of viewing the U.S. predominance in global manufacturing and marketing of computer equipment is to consider total corporate sales. According to an analysis conducted by the U.S. Department of Commerce's Bureau of Industrial Economics, worldwide revenues of the top eight U.S. computer firms were $43.7 billion. The comparable figure for non-U.S. companies was about

TABLE 4-1
General Purpose Computer Market Shares by Country, 1981
(In Percent of Sales)

Company	U.S.A.	Germany	France	U.K.	Italy	Japan
IBM	67.7	62.9	56.3	43.0	65.7	27.6
Honeywell	6.8	6.5	25.0*	7.5	15.4	—
Univac	6.7	5.4	3.4	5.0	8.0	10.4*
Burroughs	6.2	—	4.1	4.3	—	4.1
CDC	3.0	2.0	2.4	1.5	—	—
NCR	2.1	—	—	—	—	2.0
Siemens	—	17.4	2.3	—	3.2	—
ICL	—	1.2	3.1	32.0	—	—
Fujitsu	—	—	—	—	—	21.1
Hitachi	—	—	—	—	—	16.6
NEC	—	—	—	—	—	14.1
Others	7.5	4.6	3.4	6.7	7.7	4.1

*In France, Honeywell Information Systems is part of a joint venture forming CII-Honeywell Bull. In Japan, Univac is part of a joint venture with Oki.

Source: Fujitsu Ltd., *Fujitsu and the Computer Industry in Japan* (Tokyo: Fujitsu Ltd, 1982), p. 16. Data based on sales value.

$10.0 billion. Thus, U.S.-based companies accounted for over 80 percent of total global sales of these larger companies. In larger-sized equipment, the figure is even higher, with some estimates putting the figure at well over 85 percent (Eastern European production excepted) for U.S. firms. The remainder is divided between Japanese companies, which probably account for about 8 percent of total sales, and European firms with about 5 or 6 percent, divided mostly between British and West German companies.

Part of the rising importance of Japanese companies in the computer industry can be traced to that country's growth in the use of such equipment. Japan today is undoubtedly the most important single market for computer equipment outside the United States, and, within that market, Japanese companies have moved to positions of leadership. On the one hand, while still relatively small by U.S. standards, the Japanese market now is nearly half the size of that of all Western European countries combined. On the other hand, although Japanese firms have entered into joint marketing arrangements in both the United States and Europe for the sale of Japanese-made equipment, they are as yet insignificant competitors in markets outside Japan.

Given past experience with Japanese competition in other sectors, some closely allied with computers, virtually no one in the industry expects this situation to continue into the indefinite future. The Japanese themselves see the development of international competitiveness in computers to be a goal of critical importance to the continuing movement toward technically based industries and are expending considerable effort to improve their position in markets outside Japan. Already, Japanese firms predominate in the production of some peripheral items of consequence in computer systems. Such products as dot matrix printers and terminals have become particular areas of Japanese strength. From a total of about $337 million in computer-related exports in 1979, Japanese shipments of peripherals accounted for $247 million. In comparison, central processor exports amounted to only about $84 million.[2] Thus, while achieving success in related items, Japanese companies have not become a major factor in international shipments of computers.

Some additional insight into the state of international involvement in the computer industry can be gained by reference to trade ratios for the various countries. These ratios relate exports and imports to total new supply and are given in Table 4-2 below for a recent year.

TABLE 4-2
Trade Ratios for Computer Equipment, 1980

Country	Exports/New Supply	Imports/New Supply
United States	.293	.045
France	.225	.267
W. Germany	.364	.423
Japan	.121	.156
United Kingdom	.426	.492
Italy	.348	.519

Source: *1982 U.S. Industrial Outlook*, Department of Commerce, Bureau of Industrial Economics, Washington, D.C.

Of the nations reported, Japan is lowest in the relative importance of exports to new supply, defined as local production less exports plus imports. By comparison, the U.S. ratio is more than double that of Japan, despite the fact that U.S. producers of computer equipment rely importantly on output from wholly owned subsidiaries abroad to supply foreign markets, a practice not duplicated by Japanese firms. Japan, however, is far less dependent upon outside suppliers in its own market although, as mentioned above, several U.S. firms maintain manufacturing facilities in that country.

In summary, the picture that emerges in the international computer industry is one of continued and pervasive U.S. dominance, a picture that has not changed significantly for many years. Even in newer product lines, little evidence suggests that companies elsewhere in the world are achieving substantial inroads into the overwhelming U.S. position. For example, it is estimated that three-quarters of total sales of personal computers are made by U.S.-based corporations. In the product category that still accounts for the predominant share of total value, general purpose mainframes, U.S. companies furnish 70 percent or more of the markets of every country in the world except Japan and the United Kingdom. While the proportions are somewhat smaller in these nations, especially Japan, they are still very large (in value, about two-thirds in Britain and nearly half in Japan).

Most industry executives would agree that if increased international competition is to develop in the near future, it would almost necessarily come only from Japanese companies. Certainly such expansion onto the international scene is the expressed objective of both the Japanese government and companies there, and there is common agreement among industry representatives that the Japanese possess the technological wherewithall to become more significant competitors. Most agree as well, however, that there is much more involved in international competition than technical competence and in other areas, Japanese competitors have thus far lagged significantly behind their U.S. counterparts. For example, major firms long in the business have developed systems and applications software with which customers have become intimately familiar and, in some senses, dependent. As a consequence, customer loyalty to existing systems and their successors is enduring and difficult for newcomers in the market to overcome. This problem is one reason that firms, including several in Japan, have developed "plug compatible" equipment, designed to run on IBM software.

INVESTMENT STRATEGIES AND GOVERNMENTAL POLICIES

U.S.-Based Companies

As was evident in the previous section, U.S. computer firms are far and away the international market leaders. Moreover, unlike other electronic sectors, the dominant U.S. position has not as yet been substantially eroded by either European or Japanese competitors, even though governments in both areas have made substantial commitments to development of an indigenously viable computer industry. In Japan, such local firms as Fujitsu, Hitachi, and Nippon Electric have displaced U.S. companies as the major suppliers, but U.S. subsidiaries still enjoy substantial shares of the local market. Elsewhere in the world, Japanese companies have made only marginal headway. European firms, however, have lost market position to U.S. companies both at home and abroad. Several of the larger European producers today rely on the Japanese to supply technically acceptable systems at competitive prices.

This historic and continuing dominance by U.S. companies in the computer industry, both in market share and in technology development, has had significant influence on the distribution of investment, especially in Europe. Most obvious, perhaps, is that market competition virtually everywhere in the world has been conducted largely between U.S. companies. This observation is true not only in large mainframe computers but also in minicomputer systems and desktop units, market segments where U.S. firms also predominate. In such a setting, early moves to set up manufacturing activities abroad by one company inevitably draw the attention of other U.S. firms. The original motivation to invest, therefore, can be a response to a competitive advantage perceived to exist for another company through its foreign investment.

In addition to this type of duplicative investment activity, however, U.S. dominance has had other effects. For example, country governments desiring to establish local competence in rapidly evolving computer technologies have in recent years been forced to contend with companies already having the skills. These have been mostly U.S.-based corporations. Thus, when governments provide investment incentives for the purpose of stimulating technical transfers, the incentives are necessarily directed mostly toward U.S. companies. Similarly, performance requirements, sometimes only implied or suggested by governments, affect largely U.S. companies. As one example, when Mexico's government invited proposals to manufacture minicomputers under the new regulations in that country, 30 of 31 early responses came from U.S. firms. The mirror image of this effect has been that where U.S. companies have been repelled by performance requirements, the countries have been able to attract only investors not technologically qualified to compete elsewhere in the world.

U.S. computer industry executives state that foreign investments have been made essentially for two reasons: (1) to better serve an already existing market and (2) to reduce manufacturing costs in labor-intensive phases of production. Although the majority of interviewed companies have made investments of both types, a few have made only one type or the other, not both, sometimes as a matter of policy. Market-directed investment of the first type obviously is located where markets either exist or where their development seems imminent. Europe and Japan would be major locations in the first category, whereas Mexico and Brazil could be described as developmental in computers. Sites chosen to reduce labor costs are largely in the Far East (Singapore, Hong Kong, Malaysia, Philippines, Taiwan), but other locales are also mentioned (Puerto Rico).

Of course, a few areas combine characteristics of the two general classes. One thinks, for example, of Spain as a low-cost labor area prospectively within the European Common Market.

Labor costs are also a significant consideration in the choice of location within a developed market area. Still, such costs are not likely to be a paramount consideration in choosing a site in these circumstances. More typical are the criteria mentioned by several managers with regard to Europe:

1. To be within the Common Market.
2. To be near a major university. High-technology companies frequently desire to establish research links with scientific and engineering departments within universities. In fact, in several cases, firms were instrumental in having university programs established to service their needs.
3. To be near a major airport. Many companies, although by no means all, set up training and educational facilities adjacent to manufacturing locations. Typically, training is done for a quite sizeable region, and efficient transportation is vital. Some companies also need nearby airports for shipments of components and parts.
4. To have access to first-rate communications facilities, both mail and electronic.
5. To be in an area where professionals, both expatriates and locals, prefer to live. This type of criterion becomes more important where engineering design or software departments are part of the firm's usual manufacturing activity.
6. To be able to attract a competent workforce, where competence usually is defined not only in skill terms but also in work habits. Clearly, cost of labor would also be a relevant consideration here.

The point to be made is that labor costs and, indeed, costs of capital are only two of several factors considered in establishing manufacturing subsidiaries in developed country markets.

The typical operations carried on in an area such as Europe are associated with assembly and test of final equipment. These operations tend not to be labor intensive. A "normal" plant might be 250,000 square feet, employing perhaps 300 to 400 people, with the output supplying two or three national markets. Part of the task in such a plant is tailoring products for particular countries or specific customer needs, and the proportion of skilled technicians is both high and rising. One interviewee stated that in a typical situation, well over half the workforce would be salaried. Another executive stated, "Hardware costs are becoming trivial, and systems capability, together with software, is now the vital element in sales, a trend that is likely to continue and perhaps to accelerate."

Because of this production characteristic, some firms have backed away from earlier commitments to manufacture almost everything sold. Today, several companies farm out manufacturing to outside vendors, except for those technical components (for example, integrated circuits) where managements believe either that their companies have unique capabilities or that internal technical skills should be maintained for competitive reasons. In fact, some rapidly growing and highly successful firms manufacture, in the usual sense, virtually nothing, preferring instead to purchase "off-the-shelf" components or parts made by outside vendors to company design specifications. These companies rely completely on their demonstrated systems and software competence to serve their customers' needs. In any case, market-oriented investors in such areas as Europe maintain as an additional and highly important decision criterion the nearby availability of proven vendors to supply the firms' component requirements.

None of this is meant to imply that investment incentives or performance requirements are unimportant in such a setting. According to most interviewees, on the one hand, incentives are not likely to result in an investment's being shifted from a less developed area to an industrialized locale, simply because most of the broad decision criteria are unaffected by the incentives. On the other hand, *within* the relevant market (again, say, Europe), investment incentives could be quite important in determining the specific location for a plant. As one executive put it, "We look to the 'fundamentals' first; only after they are satisfied do we consider investment incentives at all." This type of statement, of course, may or may not have much meaning. It leaves for definition "fundamentals." Is a threat to remove a market unless an investment is made — certainly a form of incentive — a fundamental? Is the promise of new business from the government a fundamental?

Formal performance requirements seem not to exist in any substantial degree in market-oriented investments, even in cases where incentives have been part of the picture. Usually, executives state that the only expectation of the government, sometimes but not always spelled out, is to provide a specified number of jobs or level of investment. Implied actions, however, are another matter. According to several managers, governments in Europe and elsewhere often threaten to direct government procurements, and even government-influenced procurements, away from otherwise qualified computer vendors unless local production is initiated. The teeth in such threats vary with the company's dependence on governmental business, but it has been a major factor influencing a number of investment decisions. In the usual case, however, such implied threats were more likely to affect the timing of an investment rather than the location.

Not all executives were unanimous in agreeing with this conclusion, and investment strategies again come into play. For those who disagreed, the emphasis was on the necessity of building an integrated worldwide manufacturing structure for their companies. Computer firms, where possible, like to have multiple sources for products and components vital to the sale of important systems. If government procurement restrictions force the firm to locate manufacturing facilities in a particular location, it is said, and if the facilities are used as a global sourcing point, it can severely constrain the company's flexibility in making investment decisions elsewhere. As a hypothetical example, if Canada forces a firm to construct a plant that, to gain productive efficiencies, must supply an outside market, the company will view subsequent investment possibilities, say in Mexico, differently. In this view, few investment decisions in an integrated firm can be made in isolation, and where the market power of an industrialized country is brought to bear on a company through procurement policies, poorer nations without equivalent power are likely to be the losers.

The other form of foreign investment decision, that made to reduce manufacturing costs, presents a somewhat different picture in some respects. First of all, while all interviewees operated plants in industrialized countries, not every U.S. manufacturer sources parts and components from owned factories in low-wage areas. Some producers, in other words, confine their international investment activities solely to countries or areas where the companies already have well-developed markets. Some well-established computer manufacturers fit this category. However, even where such an investment posture has been taken, low-wage areas are not necessarily unimportant in the final composition of the firm's products because component vendors frequently are located in such areas. Whether or not a company operates plants in less developed areas depends in part on the degree of integration in the firm's manufacturing activities. As a general rule, although not one without exceptions, firms that eschew manufacturing of labor-intensive products avoid production in low-cost areas.

Even where manufacturing is conducted in areas outside the industrialized countries, it is almost never found in the poorest nations. Computer components and peripherals production demands a disciplined and reasonably skilled workforce, and such a labor supply seems to be restricted mostly to nations where some form of previous electronics production, for example, semiconductors and consumer electronics, has been undertaken. Most prominently, these conditions exist in Singapore, Hong Kong, Malaysia, Taiwan, South Korea, and the Philippines, all nations in the Far East. To a lesser extent, Puerto Rico has been the source of some production, but most executives interviewed state that today the island is advantageous more for tax reasons than for low labor costs. In any case, plant location to achieve lower labor costs by and large involves newly industrializing, not less developed, countries.

Many managers believe some types of production would be located in the Far East even in the absence of labor cost differentials. This view reflects the seemingly widespread experience that higher quality standards are easier to achieve there. Still, the driving force behind most existing Far Eastern investments by U.S.-based computer manufacturers has been the availability of lower-cost labor, not superior quality standards.

This basic motivation carries some implications for the effects of investment incentives on locational decisions. First and foremost, the majority of manufacturing executives would agree that incentives are not likely to lead firms to shift investments from newly industrializing countries to developed nations, and vice versa. The locations, in other words, are not usually substitutable. In addition, investment incentives, even very attractive ones, would not be sufficient to persuade company managements to shift the types of operations now found in the Far East to lesser developed countries. Computer companies require certain infrastructural arrangements that simply do not exist in poor nations. Even if this were not the case, most executives believe that lower hourly labor costs could not be converted effectively to low production costs in such a setting, because comparable labor productivity could not be obtained.

The upshot of these considerations is that investment incentives seem to matter only in deciding between a number of similarly placed countries, all newly industrializing. For example, U.S. firms probably would compare incentive offerings of Singapore and Malaysia quite carefully, but not Singapore/Malaysia and, say, Papua New Guinea. In fact, for reasons discussed subsequently, it is unlikely that investment alternatives in different regions of the world would be compared, even where both countries might be classified as newly industrializing in some broader sense. Singapore and Spain, for example, would never be viewed as substitutes on fundamental grounds.

It should be emphasized, however, that none of the foregoing should be interpreted as meaning that firms never shift *production* between regions. They do, with some frequency. Circuit board "stuffing" might be moved from Scotland to Singapore, with the released space possibly being used for new test and assembly facilities. Or, conversely, new manufacturing technologies might obviate the need for low-cost labor sites, and production in such cases might be shifted to a developed country location. Even so, at the time new investment decisions are made, when technologies are a given, substitutability of investment alternatives between regions does not seem to be a normal circumstance.

It should be stated, too, that past practices of the type briefly outlined above may be in the process of changing. Far Eastern production locales, which earlier had been a source for components and peripherals shipped to other parts of the world, are increasingly becoming assembly centers for finished systems sold regionally. Thus, assembly and test facilities in addition to software development centers, both more typical of fully industrialized countries, are beginning to make an appearance in the Far East. In part, these changes reflect rapid regional growth, but they mirror as well the increasing concern felt by all industry executives about expected major competition from Japanese producers. Japanese expansionary efforts might be anticipated to be initiated in adjacent areas to the home market.

Thus, investment incentives in newly industrializing nations are clearly important in company locational decisions between sites within a region, but they are not generally significant between regions. Occasionally, incentives can be instrumental in persuading a management to relocate existing production to a new site, usually involving a move from an industrialized area. More typically, however, the incentive affects the timing of a move that was already being considered and that probably would have been made eventually with or without the incentives. The decision to relocate production depends on more basic and longer-term considerations such as low-cost and skillful labor, good communication and transportation facilities, and the ease with which needed components, especially integrated circuits, can be obtained locally. Such elements severely constrain sites to be evaluated, and incentives come into play only after firms are satisfied with such more fundamental aspects.

The fact that in both developed and newly industrializing regions investment incentives have influenced decisions mostly within an area has had an important side effect. Country governments desiring to attract investment have been forced by circumstance to at least match incentives offered by similarly placed neighbors. The consequence of this tendency to match competitors has been the development of a broad sameness in incentives packages between countries within a particular region. It is no accident that managers perceive incentives to be much alike as between, say, Singapore and Malaysia or Ireland and Scotland. Company managements, faced with essentially equivalent sets of incentives, have frequently been able to make their comparisons on approximately the same economic grounds that would have existed in the absence of any financial assistance.

Again, it should not be inferred that this phenomenon necessarily implies that incentives have had no influence over investment flows. The existence of financial incentives in a region has, as mentioned above, been sufficient to alter the timing of some investments. And, if incentives are defined to include tariffs and other barriers to trade, it is probably true that incentives, in themselves, have attracted *some* investment that would not otherwise have occurred, especially in industrial areas. Still, while incentives have sometimes been decisive in bringing investment to a region, the evolution of similar incentive packages has often neutralized intraregional competition between countries.

The matter of performance requirements in the newly industrializing nations discussed above can be disposed of quickly: they are virtually nonexistent. Executives, in fact, mention the complete freedom from performance requirements in the Far East as one of the attractive elements of doing business there. Incentives usually relate to a predetermined product output deemed desirable by the local government, and, as long as the company provides the specified level of investment or employment to produce that product, it is free to conduct its business. Performance requirements are simply not a factor to be considered (Taiwan may be an exception).

Thus far, the interesting cases of Mexico and Brazil have been ignored in the foregoing discussion. These two countries, more than most, have combined incentives and performance requirements in unique ways in an effort to develop an indigenous computer design and production capability. Yet, neither country really fits within the two classes of investment decisions discussed above. Of the two nations, only Brazil has the beginnings of an industry. It is mostly a U.S.-based mainframe industry existing for many years behind protective tariffs. Its minicomputer industry, tightly constrained by governmental policy, has not attracted U.S. companies, and there appears little likelihood that it will under the present circumstances. Mexico, possibly having learned some lessons from the earlier Brazilian experience, has been able to attract several U.S. minicomputer manufacturers with regulations that, while stringent, are apparently negotiable on an individual basis. Neither nation, however, has developed as a significant source for manufactured components or peripherals. There are a few exceptions to this rule, mostly along the U.S.-Mexican border, but it is fair to say that they are minor compared with Far Eastern sources. Both Brazil and Mexico are discussed in several company cases covered in the fourth section of this study.

Japanese Companies

The problem confronting Japanese manufacturers of computers is easily stated: outside Japan itself, the companies are an insignificant market factor, commanding only about 7 percent of the global market in value terms, compared with well over 80 percent for U.S.-based companies. In important world markets, namely Europe and the United States, the Japanese have neither the distribution apparatus nor technical infrastructure necessary to compete effectively against their much better situated U.S. companies. There is no indication, moreover, that Japanese inferiority is lessening, even in portions of the market where such improvements might have been anticipated from other, earlier market successes. In particular, the Japanese position in desktop computers is little, if at all, better than that in other, more established product areas.

Japanese manufacturers, along with a cooperative government, are aware of their difficulties in the computer business and have developed long-term strategies to improve their situation. As in earlier export product successes, an important part of these strategies revolves around technology development. The Japanese government has announced its objective to assist materially in the development of a "fifth-generation" computer. Japanese managers using this assistance intend to bring their companies to world technological leadership within the next 10 to 15 years. Based upon this technology, together with an already acknowledged technical parity in communications equipment, Japanese companies plan to market systems that will literally make existing equipment and its related software obsolete.

Such long-term plans may or may not succeed against aggressive competitors also dedicated to preserving technological leadership. In the meantime, given their relatively weak position internationally, Japanese firms have few viable marketing options. Some companies have concentrated, for example, on supplying such peripheral equipment as terminals and printers and, in some cases, have achieved quite notable success. In addition, to circumvent the problem of lacking very costly distribution and sales facilities, Japanese firms have used their existing technical skills in forming joint relationships with a number of foreign companies. These ties are implicit recognition of the Japanese near parity with U.S. technology and of their commensurate emerging superiority to manufacturers elsewhere. Fujitsu today supplies both ICL in the United Kingdom and West Germany's Siemens with large-scale systems. Similarly, Hitachi ships computers to BASF (Germany), Olivetti (Italy), and National Advanced Systems (United States). It should be remembered, however, that none of these companies are truly significant competitors in today's market, often depending on sympathetic governmental procurement policies to maintain viability.

The Japanese recognize that this strategy of supplying existing, but weak, foreign companies cannot succeed in the longer term in realistically establishing Japanese companies as globally competitive equals to U.S. firms. To achieve this ultimate goal, Japanese firms will need to develop much closer relationships with major users of computers, a move that will necessarily involve the creation of an integrated worldwide manufacturing and distribution system. Because of the enormous potential costs of such a system and because of their own lack of experience multinationally, Japanese executives are proceeding cautiously in establishing an international presence. First steps in manufacturing abroad, for example, have not been in computer assembly but rather in semiconductor fabrication. (Unlike in the United States, major merchant producers of semiconductors are also Japan's largest computer companies.) In some semiconductor products, Japanese manufacturers already have attained market leadership, and local production can be used not only to supply existing customers but also to gain managerial experience. Plants of the study's interviewees have been built or are planned in the United States, Ireland, Scotland, West Germany, Singapore, Hong Kong, and Malaysia.

Another important consideration leading Japanese electronics firms to undertake offshore production relates to what company managements perceive to be incipient pressures against expanding Japanese exports of high technology components. In this regard, Japanese firms are today experiencing similar kinds of governmental pressures alluded to by several U.S. companies in earlier moves abroad. Japanese executives hope that local production will blunt country demands for Japan to reduce its exports or, short of that, will provide managements with extra degrees of freedom in coping with potential market losses. Without much question, some of this activity has been orchestrated by the Ministry of International Trade and Industry, but it is also a strategy that probably would have been adopted anyway, although possibly with different timing.

In any case, the newness of Japanese high-technology electronics companies operating abroad, combined with their relatively weak position, has made their attitude toward investment incentives and performance requirements somewhat different from that of their U.S. counterparts. Incentives have been more influential in locational decisions, and performance requirements have met with less resistance from the Japanese. With regard to the first, however, Japanese companies react similarly to U.S. corporations in that incentives are neither a necessary nor sufficient motivation for a regional investment to be made. Within a region, the Japanese thus far have been more sensitive to the availability of incentives than have typical U.S. companies. Stated differently, in their investments, the Japanese list of fundamentals to be satisfied before incentives are seriously considered has been somewhat shorter than comparable U.S. lists. In part, this tendency reflects the relative lack of experience of Japanese investors. There already is evidence that their level of sophistication has increased as a result of their early experience.

Performance requirements, however, may be a different matter. Although the available data are extremely limited, it appears that Japanese firms are considerably more flexible than U.S. companies concerning such governmental stipulations as local content requirements, shared ownership, technology transfers, and balance of payments restrictions. The obvious explanation for this more cooperative attitude is their need to establish some vehicle for market entry. The typical U.S. corporation, on the one hand, adamantly refuses to enter joint ventures abroad where technical sharing is part of the arrangement. Japanese firms, on the other hand, have entered shared relationships involving technology transfers in situations where the payout is, at best, in the indefinite future. No U.S. company has considered such an arrangement, even where the potential market is commercially attractive.

Still, investment areas where formal performance requirements are at all a factor are decidedly the exception rather than the rule for computer firms, U.S. or Japanese. Brazil and Mexico are the primary cases today. In the former, wholly owned U.S. subsidiaries participate in some parts of the market, subject to stringent performance requirements, but they have chosen not to supply technological and other information in other areas reserved to Brazilian-owned companies. At least one Japanese firm, however, has successfully negotiated limited entry, again under stringent conditions, but it has yet to establish any manufacturing and is reported to have had second thoughts about having entered into an agreement. In Mexico, a variety of U.S. firms are discussing possibilities with the government for minicomputer output, under regulations that apparently can be modified through negotiation. At this writing, only three have signed agreements, and, even for these, the current somewhat chaotic economic environment is causing added uncertainty. The degree of Japanese potential participation in Mexico is unknown, but it is clearly very modest compared with demonstrated U.S. interest. Elsewhere, formal performance requirements have not influenced the direction of trade or investment for either Japanese or U.S. firms in the countries considered here.

One final point needs to be noted in considering Japanese companies in the computer industry. Thus far, it is apparent that the influence of such firms on the international competitive structure of the industry has been quite modest. As a consequence, differences in their approach to the market could be safely ignored by competing U.S. firms. It is entirely possible, however, that if the greater Japanese willingness to yield to governmental policy measures affecting investment results in a significant gain in their worldwide market share, it could force a change in the strategic posture of U.S.-based firms. Several executives stated, for example, that they might be forced to meet Japanese competition in, say, establishing joint ventures being fostered by some governments. Under such fluid conditions, one might speculate that performance requirements will become more influential in determining the direction and form of international investment.

COMPANY INVESTMENT EXPERIENCES

The 11 company cases discussed in this section are each given a letter designation only to assure that confidentiality agreed upon as a condition of individual interviews is maintained to the extent possible. Each case has been reviewed by a responsible executive in the firm for two reasons: (1) as a check on the accuracy of the report, from the viewpoint of the interviewees, and (2) as further assurance that nothing of a proprietary nature is revealed. The company cases outlined below are arranged more or less randomly, and no categorization on the basis of size or type of business has been attempted. In each case, the focus has been on elements that are important in the foreign investment decision and on the manner in which investment incentives and performance requirements have influenced such decisions.

Company A

General

Company A, by computer industry standards, is an intermediate-sized firm manufacturing microcomputer systems, including many components and some peripheral equipment. Like many other companies in the industry, the firm is expanding very rapidly both at home and abroad. As a consequence, new plant capacity must be brought continuously on-line. Company A's management, particularly in manufacturing, is hard pressed to meet the demands being placed upon it, as it struggles under this pressure to develop an integrated international manufacturing system. Decisions must be made quickly, often with much less than complete information. In such a setting, rules of thumb become important in making investment decisions.

Growth difficulties are especially acute for Company A because the firm's management maintains a strong belief that most system components should be sourced internally. From a manufacturing viewpoint, this policy necessitates careful planning to take into account the inevitable interdependencies that will exist between producing units. Only relatively low-volume finished items are left to vendors to supply. Some of the rules of thumb flowing from such considerations are:

1. If a product is vital to the continued revenue stream of the firm, it will be produced in more than one factory. Thus, in situations where the absence of any important item would prevent delivery of a computer system, the item will be double sourced. Such a "manufacturing hedging" strategy is, of course, not uncommon in the industry.

2. The company will not invest anywhere unless the fundamentals are sound. In the perspective of this study, this means that investment incentives as usually perceived by company executives, would never become the basis for an investment that was unsound on other grounds. Such statements, too, are commonly mentioned by industry executives.

   A number of policies would be considered as incentives in the context of this study, but for executives in Company A they are fundamentals. For example, tariff protection or, more frequently, avoiding a tariff is an important fundamental for Company A. The firm has also been threatened with removal of important markets or, conversely, has been promised better access to a market as a stimulus for investment. For the management, such considerations are clearly fundamental. Policies that would be thought of as incentives would be such explicit government offers as grants or tax exemptions, and these are never considered in the investment analysis.

3. Company A invests only in areas believed to be stable politically and where it believes that government policies, not only in business regulation, will be consistently applied over time. Management worries about contracts being honored in terms of intent expressed at the time of writing and is wary of the possibility of contracts being constantly reinterpreted as governmental administrations change in some parts of the world.

4. Unlike some other electronics firms, Company A wants to be the major economic entity in areas where it chooses to locate.

5. The company is strongly concerned about maintaining employee loyalty and will avoid areas where labor problems would appear to be likely.

These were the stated rules of thumb that broadly guide the corporation in its investment activities. As will become apparent, however, there are some unstated policies that do make a difference in the distribution of the company's global manufacturing network.

Ireland

This investment, one of the firm's first overseas, is located in a semirural setting, consistent with the policy position outlined above. The company's management is very satisfied with its negotiations with the Irish Development Agency (IDA) and with the operation of the plant itself, so much so that expansion is contemplated. Except for its agreement to provide a specified number of jobs, the company is not subject to any performance requirements. In fact, one of the very attractive features of the plant site is the firm's complete operational freedom. The government frequently monitors the employment level, which has yet to reach the agreement level, but, thus far, the firm's management is quite satisfied with the government's patience.

The underlying motivation for locating a plant in Europe was to better serve a rapidly growing market from within the EC. As it turns out, however, the company uses the plant to supply other regions of the world, including in a minor way, the Far East. The specific location within the Common Market, Ireland, was selected partly because of the thorough professionalism of the Irish Development Agency, partly because of earlier Irish experience of some members of the firm's executive cadre, and, finally, partly because the nation is English-speaking. Other locational possibilities within the United Kingdom were considered, and information on incentives available in each area was compared internally. No effort was made, however, to use one country's incentives offer to improve that of the other.

In the end, even though the company took advantage of the incentive package set forth by the IDA, it was really not a major consideration in making the investment decision. The incentives, which included an attractive up-front grant, low-interest loans, tax exemptions, and training funds, were matched to a close approximation in the United Kingdom, and, in terms of making the investment at all, the company had earlier concluded that a European factory was required, given the company's expanding sales in Europe. Thus, it seems clear that the incentive package was neither a major element in the decision to transfer production from the United States nor important in choosing between competing sites within the Common Market.

On the other hand, it is also evident that had the Irish government not been forthcoming with its incentive package, the locational decision might well have been made in favor of the competitive (Scottish) site. Unfortunately, even in Company A's executives' minds, such possibilities remain speculative, simply because the decision never presented itself in that way. One gets the feeling, however, that the Irish location was strongly enough preferred on other grounds that the difference in incentive offers would have had to be quite striking to result in a different decision behavior. In any case, the Irish incentives were probably unnecessary to attract the plant.

Scotland

Two fundamental considerations were responsible for Company A's Scottish investment. First, like several other electronics firms,

Company A had received a number of hints that U.K. government business might be more easily obtained if the firm established a local manufacturing facility. Because this business was not unimportant to the company, earlier plans to expand in Great Britain at a later time were accelerated. Second, the particular reason for selecting a Scottish site within the country was the government's willingness to supply general assistance to the company. These incentives, while sufficient to convince executives to place the U.K. plant in Scotland, were probably not exceptional in comparison with other competing countries.

The financial incentives included a substantial investment grant, partially covering land acquisition, plant construction, and equipment purchases. For the remainder of the original investment, the company received a loan carrying an interest rate well below prevailing market rates. In addition, as in Ireland, generous training grants were provided for preparing the 900 workers ultimately to be employed in the facility. The plant is a greenfield investment, located away from other electronics factories but fairly near a university. The latter stipulation was quite typical for the company, which normally likes to establish cooperative research and development activities with university faculties in proximity to its various facilities at home and abroad.

Manufacturing operations carried out both here and in Ireland are similar to those found in the United States. Both are intended predominantly to serve the firm's European markets; therefore, output replaces exports earlier made from the United States. It should not be inferred, however, that incentives were responsible, in and of themselves, for transferring the production to Europe. The decisions were made mostly for more fundamental reasons relating to customer servicing and logistics, and the incentives simply made the decision a happier one. Neither plant is subject to performance requirements, except for the employment levels agreed upon.

Other Locations

Among Company A's other international locations, two are of some interest. In Canada, the company has established a small plant clearly because of government pressure made manifest through threats to stop sales to its various agencies. Sales in Canada, including those to the government, cannot generate the economies of scale necessary for an efficient plant; therefore, part of the output is being used to supply the firm's U.S. operation. Without the pressure from government procurement managers, the company would not have decided upon a Canadian location. Still, with shipments to the United States, the plant is an efficient unit; any losses occur as a consequence of added logistical problems.

Like many of its competitors, Company A is also considering production in Mexico, but the application made to the Mexican government is more an effort to keep the entry door ajar than it is a serious thrust to begin operation there. Company executives state that with very rapid growth rates elsewhere (higher than in Mexico), it is not at all clear that the perceived problems to be faced in Mexican manufacturing are worth expending a substantial amount of scarce managerial time over a period that the firm's management thinks could be prolonged. Among other problems, Company A executives doubt that they can achieve the local content requirements being asked of them. In addition, company executives know that the firm will be asked to share ownership in some phases of its operation in Mexico, and, while not adamant about wishing to avoid ownership sharing, they believe it could cause control difficulties in the Mexican setting.

Company A management is aware that failing to agree with the Mexican government now is tantamount to giving up both the existing modest market and the probable, much larger business of the future. Executives know that Mexican sales will simply disappear without an agreement, because of import licensing restrictions. Even present users of the firm's equipment would experience more and more trouble in finding adequate service and parts. But if the alternative is progressively tighter operational restrictions, as the management believes probably will be the case, the best arrangement might well be to forgo the market entirely and cease further efforts there.

Finally, Company A has not altered plant size or chosen different technologies for production as a consequence of investment incentives or performance requirements. The firm limits maximum plant sizes to avoid looming too large in any given location, but its policy of looking to fundamental business aspects of any investment decision militates against changing a plant significantly only because of the influence of governmental policies. Performance requirements have not been as yet a matter of concern to the company, but they could have some effect should they occur in the future. For example, agreement with the Mexican government would almost certainly entail adaptations of the company's normal manufacturing activities.

Company B

General

This firm is a diversified manufacturer of electronic equipment and is included in this survey because of its active participation in the minicomputer market. The company has been multinational for many years, producing and marketing its outputs in many countries. It is both profitable and growing very rapidly. Possibly because of its management's experience internationally, the company's philosophical position with respect to overseas investment can be characterized as somewhat more mature than is the case for many industry members. This maturity is especially evident in the way decisions are rendered, a topic to be covered in more detail below.

Like many of its competitors, the company is quite sensitive to difficulties that sometimes accompany unionization and cautiously evaluates situations where the prospect of difficulties might threaten. At the same time, maintaining employment, even during cyclical downturns, is an important goal. In addition, Company B in its foreign investments imposes upon itself certain performance standards. For example, the company routinely monitors its own trade performance for each international subsidiary. To some extent, the reason for such internally imposed restrictions is the supposition that in the future, governments would come up with standards anyway, and the firm would be better off by anticipating them. In addition, the company's management tries to foster local sourcing for as many components and materials as possible. Therefore, it does not in general desire that its investments be, say, pure assembly and test operations.

Company executives put these actions in the context of what they call "good corporate citizenship," particularly with regard to investment in developing countries. Managers believe that if the firm is to operate in some of these countries, it has a responsibility to assist in attaining the government's developmental objectives, to the extent that such assistance is consistent with the company's profit constraints. Such an attitude on the part of Company B's management cadre makes the firm more flexible than some other electronics industry members when it comes to governments attempting to impose restrictions. It should be noted, however, that there are limits beyond which the company will not go in its efforts to be cooperative. In particular, Brazil has imposed unacceptable requirements on the possibility of expansion there, and the firm has decided to continue in trying to persuade the government to alter its ways but to delay further investment there.

Singapore

The investment here was not influenced in any way by investment incentives, which were neither offered nor sought. The firm chose Singapore because of low labor costs, the knowledgeability of local officials and their willingness to cooperate on the planning of the project. In addition, there were no performance requirements attached to the project.

However, before any further investments in Singapore, the company would compare that country's incentive package with that of other possible locales in the Far East.

United Kingdom

Company B's decision to locate a plant here originally pitted Ireland against various U.K. sites, most particularly Wales and Scotland. Because both Ireland and the British government dangled financial enticements with respect to these locations, it is in some ways surprising that the company selected a plant site near London, England. No investment incentives, therefore, were proffered, except for a minor R & D-related grant available to all U.K. firms. It can be stated quite unequivocally that the company refused incentives in order to gain objectives considered to be more important. Because these objectives are not atypical of the industry, a few are listed below:

1. To be within a significant local market. This condition, in itself, militated against an Irish location, although it was not the only reason that country was eliminated from consideration. Like several other firms, Company B believes in establishing a local

presence within markets considered to be important to the firm's future. Management believes that "bricks and mortar" provide tangible evidence of the company's long-run commitment to the market and will be so recognized by residents of the area.

2. A major university must be located nearby. Company B, again like some others, likes to establish joint research projects with university personnel, particularly to reinforce the notion of a longer-term commitment but partially also to take advantage of university level research skills in science and engineering. Wales was eliminated as an alternative based upon this objective and others.

3. Transportation facilities must be efficient and available in close proximity. In this specific case, the company planned to bring individuals from throughout Europe for training and education at the plant site. The availability of Heathrow Airport was considered to be an important dimension of the decision. Scotland might have been marginally acceptable with careful selection of a specific location, but the English site was felt to be much superior.

4. The area must be attractive to professionals. Company B is not a believer in forcing people to live where it wants to put a factory for other reasons. This factor really was a basic and negative consideration for both Scotland and Wales, to say nothing of Ireland, where professionals are very difficult to attract, according to interviewees. This matter, perhaps more than others, pushed this firm toward the south of England.

5. The area must have efficient communications facilities. Company B managers were aware that other companies with subsidiaries in Ireland routed all messages through affiliates in the United Kingdom because of poor service, especially mail, in the Republic.

6. A competent workforce with good work habits must be available. Some computer firms would have eliminated England from consideration on this basis, but Company B had earlier experience in the United Kingdom that had been positive. Executives believed England to be at least as good as Scotland or Wales on this dimension and far superior to Ireland, where it was thought the labor market already was saturated from earlier electronics investments. Many companies, it was stated, went to Ireland to gain incentives and were finding the country a difficult place from which to operate.

In any case, the English location ultimately was selected for all of these reasons, despite efforts by the government to have the firm build elsewhere in the United Kingdom. There were no incentives and no performance requirements imposed. The company management, however, was strongly impressed by the proficiency of local officials in England, who were excellent in their willingness to provide support by assisting in the search for appropriate real estate and, subsequently, in the development of necessary infrastructural elements. Aside from such considerations, the investment was made entirely on business grounds.

Mexico

One of several firms now permitted to manufacture minicomputers in Mexico, Company B is engaged in planning its investment there. The agreement with the Mexican government was, perhaps, easier to negotiate for this firm than for others in the industry because of its somewhat unique operational strategy abroad. In fact, in opening the negotiation, the company's executives had only two "walkaway" conditions from which they would not retreat.

Ownership. The firm insisted upon 100 percent control and ownership. In common with other industry firms, Company B's theory was that it was bringing something (the ability to manufacture and market high-technology equipment) with it and, therefore, was unwilling to share ownership with a party who brought only money to the relationship. In fact, the firm did not even need investment capital from outside, being capable of internal funding.

Continued ownership of the firm's existing sales and service operations in Mexico. This matter was more of a sticking point for the government than was plant ownership, because it was felt that service was one thing that local businesses reasonably could be expected to supply. However, the company succeeded in convincing the government that computers were unique and that, in fact, sales, service, and manufacturing were inseparable for this product. Had the government not agreed to company ownership, the firm was willing to withdraw from the negotiation.

Aside from ownership considerations, the agreement struck was broadly within the published development program of the Mexican government, a program that stipulates export percentages and local content requirements. Partly because of the firm's attitude toward investment anywhere, such restrictions did not go beyond what the firm would have willingly accomplished anyway, even in the absence of the program regulations. It is likely that the precise timing of some activities, especially those relating to local content generation, might have been changed by the regulations, but executives insisted that expectations are well within the company's usual practices. There was, in addition, some discussion with government officials pertaining to detailed control, item by item, of the schedule for local content, but company officials sought and received more freedom within the overall integration guidelines.

Although the Mexican regulations restricted import competition through both tariffs and quotas, company officials insist that the investment was by no means contingent on this protection. The firm intends that the facility will become fully competitive by international standards. Stated somewhat differently, Company B executives believe that they can compete against other companies who come in later.

The plant receives no financial incentives from the Mexican government or from local or regional authorities. In fact, the firm cannot even receive grants that go to local companies because of its insistence on total ownership. The firm's management, after careful study of earlier agreements and contracts, is not concerned about future slippage in its dealings with Mexico and does not anticipate constant renegotiation.

In summary, the Mexican case for Company B hinges on the attractiveness of the market and the firm's general policy posture. First, the company has a well-articulated conception of corporate responsibility. This normally means that the company attempts to have each subsidiary live up to certain requirements, including internally imposed import/export limits, local content use, and use of local managers. Second, the company's management believes that when the firm operates in a developing country environment, it has a responsibility to assist in the government's efforts to promote industrial growth, to the extent feasible within normal business constraints. The management believes that almost inevitably poorer countries will try to guide industrial growth through such policy steps as incentives and performance requirements. It behooves company managements, in this view, to understand and accept such guidelines and, further, to assist governments in their goals. Together, these two corporate policies mean that Company B is far less sensitive to governmental restrictions than are some other companies.

Company C

General

Company C is one of several full-line companies in the computer industry, manufacturing equipment that, for the purpose of this study, ranges from minicomputer systems to large-scale networks. In addition, like some other firms in the industry, this company produces a variety of other products, mostly intended for sale to businesses. In its international activities, Company C has been well established for many years and maintains manufacturing plants in several countries, for the most part in industrialized countries where the firm has significant operations. In fact, it is company practice that the firm locate manufacturing facilities where markets have been established to support the activity.

Other corporate policies relevant to investment decisions are a cross section of policies found elsewhere within the industry. For example, the company tries to double source all important final products and components to ensure consistent availability. Recall Company A's similar objective. Another general policy duplicated in some parts of the industry relates to external sourcing. The company does not attempt to manufacture all parts of its products, instead concentrating its efforts on segments having strong technological content. Outside vendors, therefore, supply a variety of parts, assemblies, and "boxes." This focus means that this firm, like Company B, often goes to extraordinary lengths to encourage and, in fact, to actively assist in the establishment of proficient local vendors wherever the company does business. Without much doubt, this policy is at least in part a desire by corporate management to have the firm appear to both the government and citizens as a contributing member of the economy beyond the individual plant. In any case, the policy makes the firm more adaptable in some dimensions to possible performance requirements than some other companies in the industry.

As a general rule, investment incentives are usually not a determining factor in the firm's feasibility analysis of new international investment projects. The management's attitude is that incentives are always short-lived and, therefore, projects should be accepted or rejected on the basis of continuing and more basic business factors. This position does not mean that the company refuses to negotiate for incentives. It does push for whatever concessions might be forthcoming from host country governments. Still, availability of these incentives, and they can be substantial, never determines the choice of manufacturing site, according to company executives.

Brazil

Like all companies doing business in the computer industry, Company C has been foreclosed from operating in some parts of the market, most particularly smaller minicomputers. In addition, imports have been restricted, forcing the firm to manufacture equipment that otherwise would be imported. To gain economies of scale, Company C exports some of this equipment, even though Brazil would not normally be considered by others to be internationally competitive in such items. Such exports, of course, can be used as justification for import licenses.

The major producer being allowed to make minicomputers is COBRA, a Brazilian company that most U.S. firms, including Company C, believe is well behind the state of the art technology. Even so, its equipment is being forced on reluctant businesses, especially banks, that would opt to use better, bigger equipment, if permitted. Because regulations are based primarily upon defense and national security considerations, not commercial reasons, no one expects the stringent rules to be relaxed in the near future.

Still, in terms of the businesses in which Company C is allowed to participate, profitable operations have been maintained. The firm has received, and continues to receive, attractive financial incentives, but it has also been subjected to performance requirements. Most important, the company has agreed to local content stipulations, a requirement that, in this case, the firm does not find especially onerous. Of more concern are increasing difficulties in obtaining import licenses and exchange control affecting remittances. Executives foresee the time, if Brazil continues in its present policy direction, when business operations now allowed will become more and more constrained. In the meantime, the company's management tries to keep the subsidiary's activities flexible in an effort to be accepted within the increasingly difficult policy environment, with the hope that the future might show a more attractive business climate for foreign investors.

Mexico

As in other cases, the Mexican government's program for mini-computers is forcing Company C to consider local manufacture. Without the regulation, there seems to be no question that the firm would choose to continue serving the market by exporting from the United States. For example, the government is holding 83 percent of the market either for government firms or for approved local manufacturers. The remaining 17 percent presumably would be allocated among residual producers, hardly sufficient to maintain a viable business among the many competitors. In addition, of course, is the likelihood of a 30 percent tariff on imported systems. Given such restrictions, along with the inevitability of major competitor moves to produce minicomputers in Mexico, Company C executives felt that no alternatives to local production were available.

In return for agreeing to investment, the firm received a number of financial incentives: duty reductions on equipment and parts imports, tax credits, low-cost local currency financing, and permission to import other types of equipment. When sources of local supply can be developed, content requirements also are to be increased.

Others

There are one or two other examples that might be cited, but discussion would inevitably violate the confidentiality agreement made with cooperating executives. Details of the financial packages involved in these cases, however, will be included in the tabular summarization.

In summary, Company C's investment strategies appear, on the one hand, to have little room for financial incentives to alter materially the global distribution of the firm's resources. On the other hand, tariffs, another form of incentive, clearly have had an influence on the firm's decisions, as have incentives in regional context within host countries. Performance requirements, too, can be sufficiently stringent to discourage investment, although the firm's attitude toward local content requirements and the like make it less rigid in this regard than some of its competitors. Finally, even though the firm normally follows a practice of wholly owned facilities, because of plant interdependencies, sharing of ownership would be considered in other circumstances. Computer service centers might be an example of such a situation.

Company D

General

Like Company C, this firm is a manufacturer of computer systems of various sizes, as well as a producer of other types of equipment. The company has been multinational for many years, predominantly in Europe, but it also maintains production in Latin America.

In its international investment strategies, Company D has thus far considered market potential first and foremost in the location of its operating subsidiaries. This focus is not necessarily the same as concentrating on the present distribution of sales. If a market looks promising, even if sales now are modest, it could be considered as a potential manufacturing locale. For example, the company currently is considering a joint venture in a European country because it forecasts the market to be among the larger of the region within the next decade and is dissatisfied with its market share there.

After identifying likely countries for investments, the company takes into consideration various operational constraints that could influence the form of the company's participation. At the moment, the most important element affecting the firm's activities is implied government procurement restrictions. In fact, even in some developed countries, governments have not only restricted purchases to governmental departments but have also issued directives to certain institutions in the private sector, company executives state. This and other forms of nontariff barriers are becoming the most difficult aspect of the firm's international operations. In any case, many countries, including industrialized ones, strongly favor local firms in at least governmental purchases, and the practice is leading Company D's management to consider seriously the possibility of joint-venture arrangements. The problem is that even long established, but wholly owned, subsidiaries frequently are not equated with being a local firm when it comes to governmental procurement. Such subsidiaries are often excluded from the bidding process.

According to the interviewees, governments have found a variety of subtle means to evade the Tokyo Round international agreement on procurement practices. Whole governmental departments, for example, are removed from the "approved for open bid" list on the basis of national security. But even schools, universities, and municipalities have been affected. One corroborating example, taken from the *Wall Street Journal* and not necessarily involving Company D, concerns a British purchase for the Oxford Regional Health Authority, which awarded a computer contract despite a lower bid and technological superiority of a U.S.-based competitor. The company claims that similar restrictions, often only implied or suggested, are coming to be commonly applied throughout the world, especially in the computer industry. In any case, the heightened popularity of restrictive procurement policies is driving the firm to think of ways in which the effects of such policies might be softened. Joint ventures are one possibility.

The last step in the analytical sequence leading to investment is the decision of specifically where to site the plant. Here, of course, both investment incentives and performance requirements can enter the picture, but Company D's management claims that incentives alone would never attract the firm where other, more fundamental, elements were lacking. For example, the firm has been romanced repeatedly by the Irish Development Agency, but it does not now nor does it plan to have a plant in Ireland. There are two apparent reasons: no substantial market exists to support a plant in Ireland, and other markets that might be serviced from Ireland are already well covered from other places.

Company officials observed that the market-oriented strategy of this firm as well as others is a product of concern about procurement restrictions. Companies are worried that without investment, business will flow to local firms. "Sweetheart" deals with domestic firms, according to interviewed executives, are now standard practice in several nations, and the practice is becoming more widespread. The trend obviously upsets not only trade flows normally taking place but also investment flows, as companies vie with one another to place themselves in a position to be able to bid on business that, in the absence of investment, would be closed to them. Company D managers, along with those of at least one other firm, believe that

most computer companies would have much more modest investments in Europe and elsewhere were it not for these procurement
practices.

Brazil

The situation here can be described in terms very similar to those
of Company C: tight control over production of small and medium-
sized computers, which effectively keeps the firm out of the business, more operational restrictions on production that is allowed,
and forced exports. Still, whereas operating in the country does not
encourage the company to expand or to market products incorporating the latest technologies, the market is large and the business
has been profitable. In part, of course, the firm's success is due to
the policy position of the government itself. Constraints on imports
have reduced competition and allowed the company to raise prices
over those prevalent in the international market. Thus, the firm is in
the paradoxical position of disliking restrictions that prevent it from
operating in a very attractive market area while, at the same time,
enjoying protection in areas where it is permitted to sell.

Like other companies in Brazil, Company D also is required to
export a proportion of its output. Because the firm cannot manufacture competitively, given the exchange rate, it must accept losses
on these sales, particularly relative to returns that would be available if shipments could be made from alternative sources. To adjust
for these losses, the company engages in detailed cost-benefit analyses, trading off losses here with gains to be made on leases and
sales within Brazil. However, while manipulations of this type are
necessary to maintain viable operations, they also make the firm's
management highly sensitive to the possible imposition of financial
restrictions that would impair its ability to repatriate earnings or,
phrased differently, to shift funds internationally from Brazil.

As with Company C, the firm is confronting a number of operational restrictions in Brazil. For example, importation is possible,
but it is becoming increasingly difficult. All equipment imports must
be approved to obtain a license, and the procedure, which initiates
only from the customer, not Company D, can take 18 months for
final approval. The firm maintains a fairly sizeable staff in Brazil
whose sole task is to assist customers in demonstrating that the
imports are required to mate with existing equipment already in

service, to fill out the financial data requirements, and to complete other procedures. In addition, the firm has local content requirements to contend with but does not in general find them to be onerous, being well within the limits that the company itself would try to attain.

Each new product to be manufactured must be approved, even where the equipment is intended to replace discontinued product lines. The suspicion of governmental officials is that the company might try to slip into production of restricted items with its new equipment requests. The government's problem, of course, is to ensure that small and medium systems remain the province of indigenously owned firms.

Not surprisingly, company executives are unanimous in their belief that the government's policy mix with respect to the industry is inevitably counterproductive for a number of reasons. First, no company in the United States, in the opinion of these managers, will agree to license anything resembling state of the art technology to a Brazilian-owned firm. Thus, technology that would be transferred would be costly to the country and be generations behind. In the meantime, Brazil's other sectors are forced to accept equipment technically well behind even neighboring countries, rendering these sectors less able to develop international competitiveness. Second, governmental policies have resulted in nine companies manufacturing terminals and six making small computers. Even if these firms were technologically competent, in the opinion of interviewees, there is no possibility of generating economies of scale sufficient to compete internationally. In the key technology of semiconductors, moreover, the Brazilians have no production capacity and no research and development capability. The policies, in short, have led not only to lack of growth in technology but also, in this view, to relative decline.

Mexico

As with other industry members, there is little question that a Mexican investment in minicomputer manufacturing would not be considered by Company D were it not for the development program of the government. The fact is, however, that the firm is planning just such an investment in the near future. The market promises to be an interesting one, growing at an estimated 40 percent last year, and the firm's management believes import restrictions will allow prices to be sufficiently high to justify local production.

The biggest problem in dealing with the Mexican government has not been ownership, which would have been critical had not 100 percent ownership permission been granted. Instead, as with several companies, the firm could have difficulty with local content requirements or, as the Mexicans state, with local integration. The government, according to interviewees, approaches the problem on the basis of a formula, called the National Integration Factor. This formula combines the dollar value of vendor integration with local research and development activity. One could be low and the other high to satisfy the numerical calculation. In particular, if a firm undertakes R & D, it "levers" the index up, even without much local integration. Unfortunately, from a computer manufacturer's point of view, software development has not been counted as R & D. In any case, the company does not ultimately anticipate undue difficulties in living with local integration requirements.

Perhaps the most critical element in the negotiation was the import quota. Management feels it needs quotas not only to permit current levels of business but also to allow for significant expansion. Without a quota agreement, the firm would probably not have decided to undertake minicomputer manufacturing in Mexico. Not to get fabricator status would have made it impossible to continue servicing even existing markets, because fabricators will be getting 93 percent of the quota and will pay only a 20 percent tariff (as opposed to 40 percent for nonfabricator importers).

While company managers see the Mexicans as having learned from the Brazilian experiences and profited from their mistakes, they do not believe the evolving policies will yield the goals the Mexicans have set for themselves: to be able to make and market computers competitively in the world. These executives do not fundamentally believe that any Latin American country (perhaps no European nation as well) is equipped to duplicate the Japanese success in high-technology industries. In short, they do not feel that countries like Mexico can successfully force-feed high-level technology development when even highly industrialized countries fail.

Other

Only two other investments are to be covered here. The first, in Scotland, is a plant being constructed to second source equipment that is made also in the United States but that is a substantial seller in the United Kingdom. Despite attractive incentive offers from the government of Ireland, the company received only the standard 22 percent investment grant in Scotland. The location was selected because several other electronics firms were situated nearby, and the company believed that the availability of managers and technical people would be superior in this location. In addition, the company management wanted to stay within the United Kingdom to satisfy the British on government procurement. Based on earlier experience, it might be, however, that an indigenous location will not be sufficient.

In addition, as has been true for other industry firms, the company has sited a plant in Canada specifically to obtain substantial governmental orders. Even though the facility was constructed to serve a wider market outside that country, it would not have been built without the procurement stipulations. The Canadians also have subjected the firm to a "value-added" rating based on local content and labor employment. This requirement, however, has not been particularly difficult for the company to accommodate.

A few other points are worth mentioning in conclusion. It was noted by one interviewee that another firm had built a Quebec plant partly in response to Canadian government incentives. Three years later, the company closed the plant, returning the production to the United States. Legally, there was no obligation to continue operations, but most observers today would believe that there were implied obligations that went beyond contractual commitments. The lesson to be learned, according to this source, was that managements should never overlook such implied obligations and, therefore, should *never* determine project feasibility on the basis of incentives alone.

In the opinion of interviewees, major European computer companies are "out of the ballgame" technologically. Most now depend upon Japanese firms to remain at all competitive, and none are competitive outside traditional markets.

Hardware costs are becoming trivial; systems capability and software now are vital to sales. Manufacturing of technical components is heavily automated, and the amount of labor employment is small and getting smaller. For other components, the situation might be different, but most companies today farm out this production to outside vendors.

Company E

General

One of the industry's more successful firms in terms of sales growth, U.S.-based Company E already has manufacturing plants in several foreign countries. Like a few of its competitors, this firm has developed a healthy OEM (Original Equipment Manufacturer) market in which sales of the company's products are incorporated as a part of another firm's final product.

Thus far, the firm has followed a policy of 100 percent ownership of its manufacturing facilities, but management states that it is not dogmatic about this position. For example, if joint ventures were required in a country as a condition of doing business and if the country were important either as a current or potential market, then ownership sharing might be acceptable. However, such a decision would strongly influence the nature of Company E's commitment, because the firm would be most reluctant to share current technologies with a subsidiary in which there was a significant external ownership interest. This general type of policy statement, of course, is not at all uncommon in the computer industry.

Although it was implied in a number of interviews, Company E executives were the only ones to state openly that in their overseas decisions they are strongly sensitive to the issue of government corruption, quite broadly defined. Management does not wish to get into situations where such matters as bribes or peculiar payments arrangements are required as a way of doing business. As a general rule, therefore, the company is reluctant to open negotiations for entry where such possibilities are strongly expected to exist.

The company usually has looked to the costs of serving a market as its primary decision criterion in establishing new plants abroad. Thus, whereas tariffs might have been a stimulus, financial incentives have never entered formally into the decision process, except to improve upon an already attractive prospect. It should be noted, however, that this viewpoint is changing. Recent decisions to locate in one country as opposed to another *in the same region* have been based almost solely on the availability of some incentive. The company's recently developed investment guidelines, moreover, explicitly take into account cost advantages derived from the availability of investment incentives. The firm also would now attempt to quantify the effects of any performance requirements that might be a part of the investment package.

Like many of its larger competitors, Company E believes in creating plants as second sources for facilities elsewhere. This policy of global manufacturing integration reduces the firm's dependence on output from a single factory. In addition, the company is a strong advocate of maintaining employment and attempts to avoid reductions in workforce during downturns. Such a policy has been possible to follow in a business where growth has effectively disguised business recession, but its practical implication is that the company does not take the decision to expand into new facilities lightly. As a corollary to this policy, the firm seeks locations where employee loyalty is relatively easy to develop. Phrased differently, such a policy means that the company avoids locales where unions are likely to be a problem.

Finally, Company E generally dislikes industrial parks that it would share with a number of other firms. The company wants to develop a "high profile" in communities where manufacturing facilities are located. This policy means that the company is a believer in greenfield plant sites.

Singapore

This investment decision, involving a large components plant, originally was one of primarily adding more manufacturing capacity in the Far East to gain production efficiencies through lower labor costs. The search was confined to three or four countries on economic grounds, and the ultimate decision between the last two countries to survive early scrutiny, Singapore and another Far Eastern country, was based entirely on the difference in incentive packages. The company was neutral on economic grounds between the two nations. The incentive package was predominantly a tax holiday, but local currency bank loans were available for equipment purchases (including that purchased from the parent). In addition, the firm was offered a lease-back agreement on the manufacturing site and building (or, alternatively, subsidies for the construction of a company-owned facility).

The plant, a large one by industry standards, is intended to serve both as a component producer for export to other operating units of the company and as a potential site for assembly and testing of completed systems destined for sale within the region. There are no performance requirements, except for the firm agreeing informally to provide a specified number of jobs, a number well within the intended size of the plant under any likely circumstances. Even this figure, however, is not part of any legal contract.

In the negotiations, there was no attempt to play one country against another, as has happened in some other industry cases, to achieve a better incentive package. Executives did concede, however, that it was likely that governments were aware at least of the firm's discussions with other countries through sources of their own. Still, company negotiators did not reveal the nature of offers to opposing governments; instead they simply gathered data and then chose between the alternatives as presented.

Mexico

As in most other cases, Company E would not have considered manufacturing in Mexico at the present time. The firm's investments generally are either market oriented or manufacturing-cost oriented, and managers believe neither of these objectives is relevant in Mexico. The present market for this firm is far too small to justify an efficiently scaled plant, and manufacturing for export can be better achieved elsewhere in the world. Thus, even though there is presently no convincing economic argument for being in Mexico, company managers see the market's potential growth and the firm's part in that growth to be attractive under the appropriate conditions. It is nonetheless clear that without the government's investment regulations, the company would not have chosen now to make its first investment there.

When a plant is constructed, it will be a minimal commitment in common with most other U.S.-based computer firms. In addition, the company will be carefully restrictive about the types of technical transfers allowed between the parent and the subsidiary. The biggest concern is that local content requirements may not be achieved, given the kinds and qualities of local vendors, and the firm is most reluctant to be commiting itself to performance requirements that it would not be able to meet.

In summary, were it not for import restrictions that are making it most difficult for Company E to supply parts even to existing users of the company's equipment, there seems little doubt that no serious consideration would be given to establishing manufacturing facilities in Mexico at the present. Given the relatively small existing market, the availability of attractive alternative opportunities, and the pattern of the company's past investments, the necessary motivation to devote resources to Mexico simply would not be present now.

Scotland

The strong stimulus to invest in the United Kingdom was not the possibility of receiving incentives but the firm's desire to have production facilities in an important market. Once again, as in other cases, the U.K. government made it clear that it would find it easier to deal with a company as a supplier if it had a local manufacturing plant. The Scottish Development Agency provided interim facilities until the firm could build its plant, along with a standard 22 percent grant, some training assistance, and help with certain infrastructural elements related to the greenfield plant site. In addition, in lieu of low interest loans, the government provided interest relief grants of an equivalent amount.

Ireland was not used as a competitive wedge to obtain a better arrangement in Scotland, but company executives clearly felt that the Irish were somewhat easier to deal with in negotiating from other experience. IDA is more streamlined in locating plant sites, in making clear exactly what it is willing to do, and in going out of its way to understand the unique problems of expatriate firms. Such assistance goes beyond any financial incentives that might subsequently be offered. The competent "one-stop shopping" approach of the Irish had impressed Company E executives, as it had numerous other managers in the industry.

Other Points

Several other aspects of some general interest emerged from this interview. First, to the extent that a computer firm is engaged in an OEM business in a country, governmental expectations regarding the company can be modified. A firm's products are less visible, being incorporated into the final output of a local company, and the supplier is often perceived as a component vendor, not a computer company, a stance that appears less threatening. Thus, both explicit and implicit performance requirements may be less stringent.

Also in many situations, investment incentives are tied to providing employment, not to manufacturing *per se*. Thus, incentives can be and are received for sales and servicing facilities, in addition to manufacturing. The implication is that the study's focus on manufacturing might be too narrow, especially in the computer industry where it is quite difficult to divorce production from marketing activities.

Finally, the attractiveness of various types of financial incentives is, in part, a function of the recipient company's financial structure. For example, some firms maintain little or no debt and, because of this policy, are less interested in soft loans than other companies might be. Similarly, some managements are much more sensitive to exposure problems stemming from foreign currency financing, even soft financing, than are others. Again, loans may be less attractive.

Company F

General

Having grown at an astronomical rate, this company now bills a sufficient amount of sales to be called intermediate-sized in terms of the rest of the industry. Like some other industry firms, Company F manufactures relatively few of its system components. Instead, the firm views itself as a systems specialist, concentrating on such production as system interfaces, circuit boards, CPU assembly, and software and coding. Only in those items where the company can make a significant contribution from a technical point of view is internal production maintained. For ancillary areas, the company depends upon outside vendors who can specialize there. One of the firm's primary measurement standards, therefore, is value added per employee, a figure that is unusually high because of the high ratio of professional employees.

In some ways, Company F epitomizes the entrepreneurial firm in the electronics industry, especially in computers. Its brief history is one of taking advantage of technical gaps by providing systems assembled from more or less standard components, systems that take advantage of the company's software and design capabilities. That is, the strategy thus far has been admittedly opportunistic and relatively fluid. Thus far, the strategy clearly has met with outstanding success.

Entrepreneurial growth has had other results as well. The major one for purposes of this study is that the firm concentrates much more on purely financial criteria in its investment decisions than many other companies do. Others look at much longer term matters, such as nearness of universities, market stability, market size, and the like. Company F, by its nature, has been much more short-range in its assessments. As a consequence, investment incentives, especially those coming early in the project's life, are extremely important to this company, much more so than to other industry companies. In fact, one executive stated that the company looks almost exclusively at incentives when considering overseas locations. Certainly in the investments discussed below, incentives were paramount in the company's decision to go abroad.

Ireland

Analysis here involved a detailed cash flow analysis. The calculations took explicitly into account not only the incentives offered but also logistical elements and local sourcing possibilities. The incentives were exceptionally attractive, with plant start-up being virtually costless, but were no more so than has been the case with a number of other companies in this and other countries. Still, executives were explicit in stating that without the incentive package, the plant would not have been constructed. This experience is, in fact, contrary to that described by most other industry interviewees.

The plant was intended to serve mostly the company's existing European markets. In fact, tentative plans call for the plant to be doubled, with the negotiated incentives applying as well to the extension. The incentives involve a purchase-lease back provision for the equipment (much of it manufactured by Company F), a construction grant for the building, full training grants, and an extended tax holiday. The tax breaks were especially critical to the firm's plans, which involve intrafirm transfers among a set of affiliates.

Other Points

The company is negotiating in a number of other countries where market entry will be limited if investment is not forthcoming. The strategy in all cases will be to minimize corporate outlays through leasing, if possible, and to constrain technology transfers. In common with many other companies, Company F does not wish to transfer technology to potential competitors abroad.

Company F executives, moreover, differ in their approach to country negotiations with governments. They attempt to make sure that each government is aware specifically of incentive packages being offered elsewhere, that is, setting one country against another. Viewed less pejoratively, the company believes in open negotiations in which country governments know the type and magnitude of opposing incentives from other parties. This approach differentiates Company F from many others in the industry; the usual negotiating stance is to be aware of the likelihood that government officials know something about competitive bids, but to have company executives never discuss such offers at the negotiating table.

Finally, executives in this company believe that where companies are forced to negotiate with governments for access to a market, they typically do not then manufacture state of the art equipment. This is particularly true in situations where technology licensing might be required as a condition of market entry. No company, least of all Company F, in the opinion of interviewees here, will risk losing control of primary technology to potential foreign partners or affiliated firms.

Company G

General

A relatively new company in comparison to some of the larger industry members, Company G, nonetheless, is today successfully established in the market segments it has chosen to serve. The firm is primarily a supplier of minicomputer systems and is also one of several companies that operates actively in the OEM markets both in the United States and elsewhere. More than many of its competitors, however, the firm manufactures a substantial part of its product offerings, including a major number of component parts and assemblies. In its terms of reference, the company is vertically integrated in its global manufacturing activities. The company designs and manufactures most of its systems.

Because manufacturing is so basic to the company's operating strategy, cost competitiveness and production efficiency are central objectives. As a general rule, the firm operates overseas only when the operation promises to reduce worldwide production costs. And, partially as a consequence of the firm's complexity as a manufacturer, it strongly prefers to maintain ownership of its facilities in order to ensure necessary control over scheduling and logistics. Only where joint operations seem to offer some advantage not otherwise available to the company does the management consider sharing ownership, but even here it will not accept minority positions. As in most other firms in the industry, moreover, Company G prefers ownership as a way to reserve control over proprietary technology.

In assessing their own global operations, company executives believe that few firms can manufacture competitively in Europe, even when compared with the United States. The major reasons, therefore, for being in Europe are, first, to avoid tariffs, which are no longer a substantial barrier, and, second, to be considered as a local company when government procurements are up for bid. As a consequence of these considerations, Company G executives state that few computer firms are truly manufacturing in Europe; instead they usually confine activities to assembly and test, or related functions. Manufacturing economies of scale, both in the United States and the Far East, prohibit the establishment of cost competitive plants in Europe, with or without incentives. Some other industry executives disagree with this assessment, but there are a substantial number of essentially assembly and test facilities in the Common Market.

None of this discussion should be interpreted as suggesting that Company G has itself avoided the same motivating factors that have drawn others to Europe. However, for purposes of this study, interviews centered on coast-motivated investments in the Far East.

Singapore

The stimulus in this investment, as implied above, is strictly economic: the prospect of being able to lower manufacturing costs by locating a plant where hourly labor expense is much lower than in industrialized countries. In addition, company managers were fully aware of Singapore's reputation as having an industrious and motivated workforce, as well as a stable government. In addition, of course, government officials had been active in attempting to attract the company and were professional in their negotiations.

The incentive package included 100 percent financing, partly from the government and partly from lending arrangements with local commercial banks. No grants are involved, but the company was not required to use any of its own funds in starting up the plant. In addition, the firm receives extended tax holidays and full training grants. With these conditions, management believes the plant should be profitable even without the incentives and a very attractive investment with the incentives included in the calculations.

The alternative considered, and very nearly accepted, was in Malaysia, which offered a very enticing incentive package, especially if the firm would agree to a regional location request by the government. In addition, both individual and corporate income taxes would have been extremely low. Possibly the most appealing aspect of a Malaysian location was the possibility of developing a greenfield site. In either the Malaysian or Singaporean locations, the original investment showed the investment to be attractive on economic grounds. The incentive packages, therefore, were compared only in an effort to decide upon a specific location for an investment decision that had already been made in a regional context.

Philippines

The company is considering a new investment in this country, again to achieve low costs of production through labor. Incentives here were not detailed in the interview but are thought to be on the order of the decision in Singapore. Another motivation is the availability of an English-language workforce. Finally, in making all Far Eastern investments, the company is aware of the generalized tariff preferences of ASEAN, which are important for shipments between various plants and for the growing market itself.

Other Aspects

Company executives noted that the firm also owns service and design centers in various parts of the world, and such activities represent a growing portion of the business. In their view, as with others, manufacturing in the usual sense is becoming less and less important in the industry and is being overtaken by after-sale activities, including training, spare parts, and service. For example, it was pointed out that in Company G today fully one-third of the company's total inventories are spare parts tied to the firm's servicing establishment, both at home and abroad. Moreover, even the manufacturing workforce is nearly half exempt (nonhourly), and this proportion is growing rapidly. Such dynamic change means that the company's management places a high premium on ensuring maximum flexibility in its operations and avoids situations where rigid unionization might be a problem.

Also as a consequence of these changes, executives believe that governmental interest in industrialized nations in attracting computer manufacturing is sadly misplaced. First of all, production activities do not usually transfer the types of technologies that are the target of governmental officials. For these to be transferred in any meaningful sense, governments should concentrate not on attracting low-level factory jobs but on developing higher order skills in systems and application programming. Such skills seem inevitably to be in short supply and are a constraint on true technical transfer. In addition, of course, going after factory jobs ultimately places workers in the industrialized countries in direct competition with labor in such developing regions as the Far East. Generally, labor in the Far East not only is much cheaper but also, for the type of work involved, is probably more proficient.

The firm has also had dealings in Brazil and Mexico. In the former, the negotiations collapsed not so much over the ownership of production facilities as over the issue of control and ownership of system software. Brazil's government insisted on full disclosure, but the company, consistent with its policy position on technology sharing, refused. Like other executives in the industry, Company G managers strongly believe that Brazilian policies have relegated that country to the use of second-rate technology. In Mexico, an application has been made, but acceptance is not expected to be forthcoming anytime soon.

In summary, in the investment covered here, the firm's major motivation was lowering production costs. Investment incentives were not taken into account until after management was satisfied that its primary cost goals could be achieved without them. Where incentives are considered, they can influence the location of a plant within a region, but comparisons are more likely to be used as a negotiating wedge to acquire concessions in the place the firm has chosen for other reasons.

Company H

General

Being a relatively small company, but one where growth has been explosive, this firm's international investment activities thus far have been quite limited. Rapid growth has dictated that the company watch its investment commitments very carefully. Management already is overextended and cannot effectively deal with investment projects of any degree of complexity or that might be considered peripheral to the company's central problem: handling growth. Decisions must be made quickly; there is no large staff to do detailed evaluative work.

Company H is, for the most part, an assembler of purchased components. It does no board stuffing, buys its semiconductors, and does not manufacture peripherals or any other piece of equipment. The firm's management believes that its size now gives it an exceptionally strong position with potential vendors, enabling the company to dictate much more effectively on costs or quality than it could if operations were conducted inside. Still, in the opinion of a number of other industry executives, it leaves the firm open to future competitive pressures that could be devastating. Some observers, for example, firmly believe that without inside capability in the production of integrated circuits, any computer company will be left behind because more and more software functions are being incorporated on chips. If this turns out to be true, of course, Company H will not suffer alone because several firms rely upon merchant semiconductor producers for their needs.

Singapore

The two overriding reasons for going to Singapore were, first, to take advantage of low labor costs and, second, to achieve better purchasing efficiencies on products bought in the Far East. The company sources a fair number of materials and components there, and it was felt that a local plant could achieve economies in purchasing and logistics.

Only two potential sites were considered seriously. These were the subject of a quick survey trip by a manufacturing executive during which a tentative decision was reached. Top company managers usually support decisions of immediately responsible executives, for to do otherwise would require alternative strategies for evaluations. Little opportunity or staff exists to conduct such an evaluation. Singapore was selected over Hong Kong, the alternative, for the following reasons:

1. Stable government
2. English-speaking
3. Motivated work force, gauged by conversations with those who had previously established operations there
4. Superiority of the country as a place to live and work
5. Vendor relations would be superior

Malaysian labor problems, particularly the requirement to maintain balance in the composition of the labor force, eliminated that country early from serious consideration. The Philippines also fell from favor, mostly because its tax advantages were not as attractive and because the company suspected that the labor force was less competent. In any case, even though investment incentives entered the evaluation, they clearly were not paramount. Hong Kong's offer on taxes, in fact, carried no investment requirements, as did Singapore's, but the decision had been made on other grounds in any case.

The incentives offered by Singapore eliminated corporate taxes for a substantial period, provided subsidized loans, and reduced withholding taxes on interest and royalty payments. In addition, the company was impressed by the government's willingness to assist in adjusting the incentive package to the firm's peculiar needs. Finally, the company received tariff preferences on shipments back to the United States, a feature that was ranked highly in importance by the firm's management.

Ireland

This plant serves as an assembly and test facility for the company, furnishing completed systems to Europe, the Far East, and

North America. The major motivating factors were:

1. To manufacture more efficiently for the expanding European market from within the Common Market
2. To reduce distribution costs
3. To be closer to the market, a market that demands different product characteristics for each country
4. To have a European location that gives the firm a "European image," which the company believes is beneficial from a marketing point of view

Incentives included grants, tax holiday, training grants, and soft loans. Company management believes that tax incentives in Ireland are the world's best, with the possible exception of Puerto Rico. On the one hand, although the incentives did not dictate the choice of going to Europe, it is probably fair to say that they might have influenced the decision within the region. On the other hand, had the firm's management exhibited sufficient patience, it is probable that such countries as the United Kingdom would have closely approximated the Irish incentive package. Even so, the nature of the incentives in each case would have been important to Company H executives. The main Irish tax incentive is a permanent elimination of tax, whereas the U.K. incentive is a tax deferral. From an accounting point of view, tax deferrals give no earnings benefit. Still, given the company's desire to avoid protracted negotiations, the decision was made early not to become involved with such U.K. organizations as the Scottish Development Agency. As a practical matter, therefore, once the Irish had made their incentives offer, the locational decision was finalized quickly with no real comparisons made.

Other Aspects

A few other international matters deserve some notice. The firm has confronted not inconsequential resistance in at least one European country to continued reliance on imports to serve the market. The problem does not appear to be a local content or manufacturing problem, *per se*, but rather is couched more specifically in balance of payments terms. The government wants some exports to at least partially offset the company's imports. Company managers now believe the problem can be solved through propitious sourcing of components in the country, but it is clear that these implied performance standards have altered the firm's preferred sourcing patterns. The threat is the potential foreclosure of government business, which is apparently not trivial, to the company.

As in so many other cases reviewed here, Company H has applied for permission to manufacture in Mexico but is concerned about local content requirements. With protection, the firm believes that the investment prospect could be attractive if local content expectations could be reduced.

The real problem with the move toward both incentives and performance requirements, in the opinion of interviewees in Company H, is that the flexibility of the firm to create an internationally integrated manufacturing operation can be severely reduced. For example, being forced to set up manufacturing facilities in one country can limit a company's ability to respond to demands from another national, because often the only way that necessary economies of scale can be generated is for the first plant to export to the firm's other markets. Thus, the company might be foreclosed from reacting to attractive possibilities by earlier decisions forced upon it elsewhere in the world.

Company I

General

This firm is a large, integrated company manufacturing a variety of primarily electronic equipment, including computers in virtually every size range. The firm has relatively few manufacturing subsidiaries abroad but does maintain a network of sales and service centers for computer equipment. In addition, Company I has established sales relationships with a number of other manufacturing enterprises where it serves as a source of supply for some of the customer's final product offerings.

The newness of Company I to international investment has had the natural corollary of making its management quite cautious in approaching prospective commitments. It has also meant that the company's executives tend not to have developed the type of longer term strategies and investment criteria of many other industry firms. Together, these considerations have worked to make the company's management somewhat more sensitive to governmental offers of incentives. That is, investment incentives have loomed more importantly in the firm's acceptance standards for investments than would normally be the case for other computer manufacturers.

Ireland

The major motivations for this investment to have been made are, first, to get behind the EC's tariff barrier and, second, and perhaps more important, to avoid even more serious trade impediments that the firm's management sees coming in high-technology industries. Executives do not believe that industrial countries will allow such industries to be essentially taken over by overseas vendors. In terms of the decision to manufacture in Europe, therefore, the possible availability of incentives played little part.

In the more specific decision to choose Ireland over alternative sites in Europe, incentives as such also seem to have been only moderately important, certainly not central to the firm's evaluation. In fact, the search for possible alternatives to Ireland was really quite superficial. The company had been contacted by representatives of the Irish Development Agency who were, in the opinion of company executives, thoroughly professional. This high level of respect continued throughout the negotiations and through the establishment of the subsidiary. When other sites were evaluated, the assessment by then involved a comparison with the Irish experience already begun. For example, company contacts in Scotland were made, but the relationship with the Scottish Development Agency apparently was less happy than the relationship with the Irish. Germany also was briefly considered, but it was not felt that its superior labor productivity would be sufficient to overcome the wage disadvantage.

Incentives ultimately involved a fairly standard package of up-front investment grants covering land, plant and equipment, and training grants. Eventually, the company decided upon a leasing arrangement that management believes resulted in lower overall costs of operation. According to executives, there are no tax incentives, a matter about which executives demonstrated little concern because they did not anticipate significant profits from the subsidiary for some time to come. There are no performance requirements, aside from providing the specified number of jobs.

Other Areas

Although confidentiality considerations prevent identification of other countries in which the firm operates, there are two cases that should be discussed more generally. In one, the company was considering locating a plant in a low-wage region on economic grounds. The choice of specific country, however, was based on the threat to withdraw a large set of governmental procurements. In the other case, the firm has agreed to exchange technology for the right to manufacture minicomputers in cooperation with a local company. In addition, executives hope that this commitment can be broadened to include the provision to the market of a variety of other electronic equipment. Given other competitors' similar expectations, only time will tell whether these hopes will come to fruition.

Company J

General

A major producer of computer equipment, this company also manufactures and markets a wide variety of other equipment worldwide. The firm is only a recent investor in computer-related fields, but it has a longer experience in other product lines. This additional maturity, when compared with, say, Company I, has led the firm to be more analytical in its approach to the evaluation of investment opportunities.

West Germany

This investment was made as a consequence of the company's desire to locate manufacturing in Europe. In part, this desire was fostered by the belief that incipient pressures in European countries for control of high-technology imports would make it more and more difficult for the company to serve its markets there, markets that were becoming large enough to achieve adequate economies of scale in manufacturing. Major sales for this firm tend to be on the continent rather than in the United Kingdom.

The decision to invest in Germany was made after considerable deliberation and after a comparison of possible alternatives. The major alternatives analyzed were the United Kingdom (mainly, Scotland) and Ireland. Executives stated that in terms of incentives, the three locations were about the same. All offered up-front grants of about the same size covering total investment. Although Ireland also had certain tax advantages, these were not considered to be of significant additional benefit to alter the decision. In addition, Ireland was rejected on the basis of its lack of industrial infrastructure and its dearth of well-educated electronic engineers. Clearly, because many other companies have built plants in Ireland, such factors are a matter of managerial perception. In the United Kingdom, the major problem worrying executives was labor relations. Belgium, which received brief thought, was a place where wage increases had gone well beyond the general inflation rate. Although wages were also higher in Germany, the firm's management felt confident that high productivity would offset it.

Thus, because incentives essentially canceled out between countries in the region, the decision was made on more usual business considerations. Whether the decision would have been different had the incentive packages been markedly different is a matter on which executives could not comment.

Malaysia

Here, the company responded to an invitation by the government to consider investment. Upon investigation, the company believed that high productivity could be combined with lower labor rates to achieve an efficient operation. Because the firm has since decided to expand the plant and to change its output to more sophisticated products, the original expectation seems to have been realistic.

Incentives were limited to tax exemptions, but they were not in any case particularly germane to the decision process. There were no grants. In addition, there is little evidence that alternative sites were seriously considered once the original Malaysian assessment had been undertaken. The investment option was viewed alone and was found to be attractive on economic grounds, even without incentives.

Other Areas

In other computer-related investments, no incentives have been offered, although in at least one case, potential trade impediments were a factor. Here, the company's management, as in Europe, saw the likelihood of import barriers being erected in the near future. Even though there is no expectation that internationally competitive production is possible, the company has made an investment anyway to protect its existing market position. In other cases, investments have been made, usually for testing and export of components, on straightforward business considerations.

Company K

General

This firm is a diversified manufacturer and marketer of electronics products throughout the world. However, as in the case of Company J, the firm's overseas ventures in manufacturing computer-related products are quite recent, all within the past five to ten years. In all of these investments, the firm's management would have preferred to leave its production in home-based plants in order to gain maximal economies of scale and to better control output quality until the company obtains substantial overseas markets. For reasons discussed below, however, the decision was made to diversify geographically.

Ireland

As in several other cases, this plant location decision was motivated by a variety of considerations. First, European business had expanded rapidly and had become sufficiently robust to support at least a reasonably sized manufacturing facility. In addition, the company, again as in other cases, detected rumblings of the possible instigation of quantitative controls over technical goods and wished to defuse that possibility with production inside the Common Market. Finally, the availability of incentives in this case was a definite attraction, without which the investment probably would not have been made.

Incentives offered by the Irish government included incentive grants on capital investment and training, a tax holiday for up to 15 years, and, if desired as an alternative, subsidized arrangements. The government also accepted responsibility for infrastructural construction on a greenfield plant situated in a semirural area.

The company considered as alternatives both Germany and Scotland, and the Irish incentives were clearly decisive. In addition, in the interview there was some discussion about expectations regarding labor relations, and company managers believed Ireland would be an easier place to deal with employees than either of the other two locations. With respect to Germany, language was considered to be a potential problem in operating the plant. There were no performance requirements in Ireland, but none would have existed in either of the alternatives.

In retrospect, the firm might have second thoughts about letting incentives play such a central role in the decision. It is not that labor relations have been poor, but that the remote location chosen has not worked out ideally. As in some other cases, the company has had some difficulty convincing its own technical employees to relocate to Ireland.

Scotland

A more recent decision, the Scottish plant in some ways is the consequence of the earlier experience in Ireland. The major reasons for choosing the site were the nearness of technical talent at universities, availability of managerial staff, access to the EC market, proximity to other electronics plants (including its own), the availability of perquisites offered by more metropolitan areas, and incentive grants covering capital investment and training.

Although the company management maintains that the additional investment in Europe would not have been made without the incentives, it is also apparent that in choosing between the European alternatives in this case, the incentives did not play a primary part. It is clear as well that the move of major competitors to the European market probably also influenced the company in its own decisions to locate manufacturing operations there.

In summary, the major motivation for this company to make these investments, as with other investments not discussed here, was the expansion of business without causing trade constraints. Incentives were important elements in the decisions, but the distinct impression is that, with or without specific incentives, the management would eventually have found it necessary to make the investments anyway for reasons of longer-term market strategy.

CONCLUSIONS AND IMPLICATIONS

Foregoing sections have indicated the extent to which investment incentives and performance requirements have influenced the computer industry's pattern of international investment. For purposes of summary, it is useful to attempt to answer several questions:

1. To what extent has the existence of incentives and performance requirements attracted (or repelled) international investment?
2. To what extent has the pattern of overseas investment that has occurred been altered by the existence of investment incentives or performance requirements, especially as between industrialized and developing countries?
3. In what ways are patterns of investment behavior changing as a consequence of competitive conditions or governmental policies? That is, how, if at all, will the future differ from the past in terms of international investment behavior of industry firms?

On the first question, it is probably too facile to state unequivocally that investment incentives have had no influence on attracting investment that otherwise would not have taken place. Executives in the interviews cited above detailed a few cases where incentives were critical in the decision. Still, in the large preponderance of cases, most of which did involve incentives, managers state that the investments would probably have been made even in the absence of governmental sweeteners. The claim, made over and over again in interviews, is that investment is accomplished for quite basic economic or strategic reasons: for example, to lower costs of production or distribution, to better serve existing markets, and to achieve better international diversification possibilities. Investment analyses in the typical computer company do not even consider incentives until what are thought to be more fundamental decision elements are completely satisfied. Then and only then, in the repetitive opinions of industry executives, will the effects of financial incentives be calculated. That is, investment incentives tend to make an already attractive possibility potentially more so. Table 4-3 shows incentive offers for various regions.

Not all governmental policies directed to foreign producers are ineffectual in drawing investment into some countries. Mentioned frequently as being important aspects of the investment decision

TABLE 4-3
Compilation of Incentive Offers

Incentive Offer	Location
30 percent up-front grant on total investment; Tax exemption on virtually all income; Training grants of about $15,000 per worker	Europe
Government-leased land availability	Far East
Complete market protection for one major product; Promise of future government business	Europe
15-20 percent up-front grant on total investment	Europe
Complete exemption on income taxes	Far East
None	Far East
Implied threat of trade restrictions	N. Amer.
40 percent up-front grant on plant and equipment; Subsidized lease arrangement on land; Site preparation; Tax exemption on virtually all income; Complete training grants	Europe
40 percent up-front grant on total investment; Complete training grants	Europe
Implied threat of trade restrictions	N. Amer.
50 percent up-front grant on total investment; Subsidized loans on remainder of investment; Delayed interest and principal payments; Tax exemptions on virtually all income; Complete training grants	Europe
40 percent up-front grant on total investment; Subsidized loans on remainder of investment; Complete training grants	Europe
Implied threat to take away government purchases	N. Amer.
None	Far East
Small research and development grant; Some site development assistance	Europe
Access to market threatened	N. Amer.
Income from exports exempt from tax; Duty-free equipment imports; Preferential import licensing on equipment; Subsidized export financing; Strongly subsidized local currency financing; Substantial market protection	S. Amer.
Reduction in duty on equipment and maintenance parts; Strongly subsidized local currency financing; Tax credit on exports; Tax credit on local components purchased; Reduction in duty on component imports; Reduction in duty on other equipment; Availability of import licenses ensured; Market protection	N. Amer.

Continued

TABLE 4-3, continued

Incentive Offer	Location
60 percent up-front grant on total investment; Employment grants and complete training grants; Strongly subsidized local currency loans; Reduced corporate tax rate	Europe
Government threat of import barriers	Europe
Substantial market protection; Preferential import licenses on equipment; Subsidized export financing	S. Amer.
Market protection; Availability of import licenses; Reduction of tariff on imports of parts and components; Government rebate to equipment purchasers	N. Amer.
22 percent up-front grant on total investment	Europe
Award of large government order contingent on investment	N. Amer.
50 percent up-front grant on total investment; Strongly subsidized alternative leasing; Full training grants; Tax exemptions on virtually all income	Europe
Substantial market protection	Far East
90 percent subsidized government financing; 10 percent subsidized bank loans; Tax exemptions for first ten years; Full training grants	Far East
None	Far East
13-year tax exemption on income; Subsidized local currency loans; Elimination of tax on interest and royalty payments	Far East
40 percent up-front grant on total investment; Full training grants, subsidized commercial local currency loans; Tax exemption on virtually all income	Europe
Threat of market restrictions	N. Amer.
Tax holiday for ten years; Full training grants; Subsidized local currency bank loans	Far East
Threat of market restrictions; 22 percent up-front grant on total investment	Europe

Source: Compiled by the author.

were protective tariffs, which tend to raise internal prices, and government procurement policies, which have implicitly reserved important markets for companies willing to produce domestically. These types of policies prevent firms from competing effectively and, especially where these companies have already achieved an earlier position in the market, are considered by managements to be fundamental to their operating strategies for an area. It is fair to say that such policies, which are also clearly investment incentives in a more basic sense (although not usually perceived to be by corporate managers), are far more important as a determinant of patterns of investment than are the more visible financial incentives being offered by governments. In case after case, threats to existing markets or the prospect of operating behind some form of trade barrier, or a combination of the two, were cited as the proximate cause for considering an investment possibility.

However, even the influence of these indirect governmental policies should not be overstated. Although the motivational effects of such policy stimuli were mentioned quite frequently in interviews, they were often quickly followed by the comment that the government's policy position only accelerated an investment decision that would have been made under any circumstances for business reasons. That is, protectionist policies frequently change only the timing of an investment project. This observation is especially true, of course, in areas where market growth is very rapid and where the firm is gaining in market share.

Performance requirements seem to be a different matter and, depending on their nature, can have a marked effect on investment behavior. Although few computer firms have been affected by such requirements in their operations, those having experienced them can alter their investment behavior substantially. For computer companies, especially U.S.-based ones, the critical areas where performance requirements make a real difference are ownership and technical sharing. Most, although not all, computer firms avoid situations where they are required, as a matter of policy, to share ownership in their subsidiaries. The clear majority would choose not to serve particular markets if ownership sharing were a requirement of market participation. Even more managements would be sensitive to entering into situations where they were expected to transfer proprietary technology. Unlike the semiconductor industry, which has a history of licensing technology worldwide, computer companies jealously guard what they perceive to be the ultimate source of their comparative advantage, proprietary technology. Almost all would refuse to enter any arrangement where significant sharing of state-of-the-art technology were a part of the deal.

On the second question above, that having to do with how policies affect the pattern of international investment, the evidence is mixed. On the one hand, industry executives maintain that almost never would investment incentives draw projects from a less industrial area to a more developed region, and vice versa. Investments in the two areas are made for totally different reasons: the one to reduce labor costs, the other to better serve a market. For firms that have plants in both types of regions, and several important ones do not, the investments made in each case are quite different. For example, labor-intensive phases of production would no more be placed in Europe than they would be placed in the United States; final assembly and testing of systems being sold in Europe, however, would rarely be done, say, in the Far East.

On the other hand, when investments of one type or the other are being considered, company managements increasingly are taking into consideration the types and numbers of competitive incentives being offered by various countries within the particular region chosen. Five or ten years ago this was less the case, but today most firms considering investments in Europe would carefully compare Ireland, Scotland, and other continental locations. The same would be true in the Far East, where Singapore, Malaysia, Hong Kong, and, increasingly, the Philippines would be evaluated together. Because such comparisons are becoming more the rule, the kinds of competitive incentive packages being offered by governments are coming to look more and more alike.

But, even this case can be overdrawn. There are numerous situations where firms have refused extremely attractive financial incentives from a country government in order to achieve goals considered to be more important. Once again, it is important to stress that incentives usually affect only purely financial variables in the comparative analysis. As noted in the cases, there exist a variety of other considerations to be taken into account. In sum, even though managers would agree that financial incentives have influenced decisions on the location of a plant within a region, such incentives are rarely the major consideration entering into the evaluation.

Finally, on the last question above, any statements about the future, especially beyond five or ten years, are highly speculative. Thus far, the international competitive game in the computer industry has been one played, for the most part, by U.S.-based participants, and the rules seem to be well developed and understood by all. A single company, International Business Machines, has been the dominant force in the industry, particularly in general purpose equipment but increasingly in other segments of the industry as well. Other companies have grown and prospered in market niches left unfilled by IBM, and some, again mostly U.S. firms, have become major multinational corporations. These firms, along with IBM, historically have been the international leaders in technology and market developments.

It is also true, however, that the industry is changing internationally, most especially because of the advent of Japanese manufacturers as new and technologically competent competitors. The current efforts of such firms, with the active assistance of a sympathetic government, to achieve technological superiority to U.S. companies was briefly reviewed in the third section, and there is little question that these efforts are a major concern to U.S. companies. In almost every interview, the Japanese were mentioned as the only viable potential competitors on the international scene today.

Still, it is too early to gauge the future effects of Japanese companies on the world competitive structure. Thus far, the impacts have been minimal, but there seems little question that this will change, as it has in a variety of other industries. From the viewpoint of this report, the interesting element is likely to be the differences in the way in which Japanese companies approach the international market, as compared with earlier efforts by the U.S. companies. If Japanese firms further improve their relative technical ability, vis-a-vis U.S. companies, and if they continue to be more flexible in their responses to investment incentives and performance requirements, old ways of doing business could change markedly. The most likely firms to be affected early would be, of course, the smaller, financially weaker U.S. companies that have existed for years in the shadow of IBM. Such companies themselves would be forced to become more adaptable in their approach to world markets in such circumstances and may, in fact, become willing partners in joint efforts by the Japanese to open new markets. Already, several

European firms and a few U.S. companies have followed this course of action. In addition, companies that thus far have avoided joint ventures with local firms, either governmentally or privately owned, might well find such relationships to be more palatable as Japanese competition increases.

In situations where such joint ventures have been attempted in the past, they have not been notably successful in altering the competitive complexion of the worldwide industry. Combining two or more technologically weak companies has not tended to produce a demonstrably stronger offspring. Still, this situation could change if one of the partners brought into the relationship superior computing technology combined with innovative process and manufacturing technologies, as the Japanese fully intend to do. That is, the dynamics of the industry might be expected to result in shifting competitive strategies as established firms vie with newcomers for market share.

Thus, even though it is reasonable to say that neither investment incentives nor performance requirements have had much influence on the decisions of industry members, especially those who have counted, this posture could change materially if Japanese producers successfully follow a different technical and marketing strategy, forcing alterations in long-established competitive reactions of other industry firms.

From a policy point of view, competitive incentive programs between countries within a region seem to have been the only policy instrument, aside from tariffs, procurement manipulation, and the like, that has had much real effect on industry investment patterns. In the vast majority of cases in this study, incentives did not materially influence the decision to locate a plant in a region. Within regions, the picture is somewhat different, as company managements have investigated incentive packages of similarly placed countries quite carefully. But even here, the competitive responses of country governments in attempting to attract investment has resulted in very similar incentives within regions, and frequently the investment decision has been made on the same grounds that might have existed in the absence of any governmental interference. Where this has been true, of course, the incentives become unnecessary transfers from taxpayers to corporate investors. Because Japanese companies, as they have gained experience in the international arena, have reacted to investment incentives much as their U.S. counterparts do, there seems little reason to project any substantial change in industry behavior toward incentives.

As we have seen, the major area where governmental policy initiatives could make more difference in the future than they have in the past is performance requirements. Here, the more pliant attitude of Japanese company managers in accepting governmental requests for technical or ownership sharing could lead to the increased use of such devices by virtually any country with a market sufficiently large to be attractive commercially. This would include not only the well-known present cases of Brazil and Mexico but also various other more industrialized countries that have not been able to foster a competitively viable industry, despite quite substantial past efforts to do so.

Aside from such speculations about possible future developments, performance requirements today seem to be viewed as an element to be considered in an investment analysis much like any other factor. If, for example, local content requirments will constrain the firm from achieving sales or revenue projections, managements try to negotiate content reductions or, conversely, try to obtain protection that would enhance revenues on whatever sales volume ensued. Similarly, if exports are mandated by the government, even though local production cannot be achieved at internationally competitive prices, then firms attempt to find other ways in the local market to gain revenue amounts equivalent to the losses.

It bears repeating that for most computer firms, there are only two circumstances where performance requirements are likely to raise questions of operational principle. One is ownership sharing, which most firms attempt to avoid for a variety of reasons, mostly related to managerial control of the global enterprise. The other, sharing of proprietary technology, is related to the first, because firms see joint ventures with foreign firms as potentially tantamount to sharing technology. On this issue, most U.S.-based companies would shun situations where such an outcome appeared to be a prospect. However, as noted above, it is precisely in this aspect that Japanese competition in the international market, should it emerge, could make a substantial difference.

NOTES.

1. These definitions were proposed in the Office of Technology Assessment (U.S. Congress) *International Competitiveness in Electronics* (Washington, D.C.: Office of Technology Assessment, 1983), p. 83.

2. See T. A. Pugel, Y. Kimura, and R. G. Hawkins, "Semiconductors and Computers: Emerging International Competitive Battlegrounds," presented to a conference on International Transfer of Resources: Strategic Company Responses in the Dynamic Asia Pacific Environment, Montreal, September 1981.

5

The Petrochemical Industry

H. Peter Gray and Ingo Walter

INTRODUCTION AND CONCLUSIONS

This study is an examination of investment-related distortions of international production and trade patterns (investment incentives and performance requirements) in the petrochemical industry. The data base consists of an in-depth examination of 16 specific projects, with generalizations built up from these microlevel observations as modified in some cases by overall strategic perceptions of such measures on the part of the firms contacted.

The individual projects are not identified to preserve confidentiality to the extent possible. In each case, the investigators undertook personal interviews with responsible project planners, financial executives, and others at corporate headquarters, both in the United States and abroad. Among U.S. firms only one of those contacted (Union Carbide) refused categorically to participate in the study. Many of the others provided outstandingly helpful and frank information within reasonable limits of confidentiality. An effort was made to incorporate non-U.S. firms in the study to ascertain possible differences in experiences or perceptions, with mixed success ranging from good cooperation in the United Kingdom to great skepticism and reluctance among German firms. Despite lengthy efforts through Japan's Ministry of International Trade and Industry and appropriate industry groups, it proved possible to obtain meaningful information from only one of the Japanese chemical majors. Further indications of the behavior of Japanese firms were developed from other sources as well.

The first section of the chapter presents a profile of the petrochemical industry: processes, products, suppliers, markets, investment, and trade flows. The second section discusses the data base, provides a summary of the case studies in tabular form, and presents the overall conclusions that could reasonably be derived from the microlevel data examined. The third section attempts to summarize the overall study.

The study divides the petrochemical industry into three segments: commodity (primary) petrochemicals, intermediates, and petrochemical products — the latter again subdivided according to whether the product is further processed or sold for direct use. Fifteen petrochemical projects worldwide are classified accordingly and examined in depth with respect to the influence of investment incentives and performance requirements.

The principal investment incentive affecting factor costs is found to be concessionary feedstock costs, which influence the location of primary petrochemical facilities, sometimes coupled to subsidized credit terms and crude oil entitlements. Such measures are not, however, found to be distortive of international trade in the sense that they generally reinforce countries' fundamental comparative advantage in primary petrochemicals based on indigenous natural resources.

The principal investment incentive affecting product prices is a high rate of effective protection — essentially blockading domestic markets for petrochemical intermediates and products against import competition from world-scale plants elsewhere. This clearly affects the global pattern of petrochemical production and trade.

A variety of other investment incentives and performance requirements are encountered, some statutory and others discretionary, ranging from low-cost financing and tax holidays to export requirements and domestic-content regulations. These can be profiled as "net incentive/disincentive packages," and frequently governments appear to use incentives to offset disincentives, and vice versa. However, because of industry characteristics that drive production locations either to the source of raw materials or to the source of market demand, these packages are not found to have a significant impact on patterns of production and trade.

Whereas the 15 case studies that form the data base for this study represent a small sample of petrochemical projects undertaken during the past decade or two, the common threads are sufficiently strong to contribute a substantial degree of confidence in the results.

PROFILE OF THE WORLD PETROCHEMICAL INDUSTRY

The importance of investment incentives and performance requirements in the petrochemical industry must be evaluated against the backdrop of global developments affecting the industry as a whole. These developments have been dramatic indeed. In this section, we describe the industry in terms of processes and products, identify the major players on the international scene, describe patterns of production and trade, and project probable future developments in the industry.

Petrochemical Processes and Products

The chemical industry can be divided into petrochemicals and nonpetrochemicals. The latter include inorganics such as alkalies and chlorines as well as wood- and gum-based chemicals, which fall under the heading of organics. Most organic chemicals may be classified as petrochemicals (see Table 5-1). The chemicals operations of the major oil companies fall almost exclusively into this category. However the large, integrated chemical firms have elaborate product lines that span the entire spectrum of petrochemicals and nonpetrochemicals.

The petrochemical industry involves a variety of processes that begin with the breakdown of basic raw materials and end in the production of a wide range of end-use products. These products are either petrochemical or petrochemical-dependent in nature, as indicated in Table 5-1.

Crude oil and natural gas are the industry's basic raw materials. In Western Europe, crude oil is the predominant raw material used, while natural gas is the raw material of choice in the United States because of its wide availability and low cost. Crude oil is converted by refining process to finished fuel products such as gasoline and fuel oil, accomplished with relatively little significant chemical change. However, some of the heavier fractions such as ethane, kerosene, and naphtha can be cracked to produce primary petrochemicals.

TABLE 5-1
Classification of Chemical and Allied Products

Industry Sector	Classification
Industrial inorganics	
Alkalies and chlorine	Nonpetrochemical
Industrial gases	Nonpetrochemical
Inorganic pigments	Nonpetrochemical
Industrial inorganics	Nonpetrochemical
Plastics materials, synthetics	
Plastic materials and resins	Petrochemical
Synthetic rubber	Petrochemical
Cellulosic man-made fibers	Petrochemical-dependent
Organic fibers	Petrochemical
Drugs	
Biological products	Petrochemical-dependent
Medicinals and botanicals	Petrochemical-dependent
Pharmaceutical preparations	Petrochemical-dependent
Soaps, cleaners, toilet goods	
Soap and other detergents	Petrochemical-dependent
Polishes	Petrochemical-dependent
Surface active agents	Petrochemical
Toilet preparations	Petrochemical-dependent
Paints and allied products	Petrochemical-dependent
Industrial organics	
Gum and wood	Nonpetrochemical
Cyclic crudes and intermediates	Petrochemical
Industrial organics	Petrochemical
Agricultural chemicals	
Nitrogenous fertilizers	Petrochemical
Phosphate fertilizers	Petrochemical-dependent
Fertilizers – mixing	Petrochemical-dependent
Pesticides	Petrochemical-dependent
Miscellaneous	
Adhesives and sealants	Petrochemical-dependent
Explosives	Petrochemical-dependent
Printing ink	Petrochemical-dependent
Carbon black	Petrochemical
Chemical preparations, not elsewhere classified	Nonpetrochemical

Source: Compiled by the authors.

Other "feedstocks" are natural gas, natural gas liquids, and petroleum liquids and gases. Table 5-2 and Figure 5-1 describe basic petrochemical processes and products, indicating that there are three subgroups of chemicals which are based on these feedstocks — primary petrochemicals, petrochemical intermediates, and petrochemical products. Essentially, a material is classified as a petrochemical if it is originally derived from a hydrocarbon raw material and a chemical reaction occurs in the conversion of a feedstock hydrocarbon to a primary petrochemical or of a primary petrochemical to an intermediate or of an intermediate to a petrochemical product.

Primary petrochemicals are derived from feedstocks by chemical conversion, and are mainly utilized for the production of intermediates and/or some petrochemical products. They are usually large-volume commodity petrochemicals such as ethylene, propylene, butadiene, and benzene which are shipped in bulk to other industrial chemical producers.

The intermediate group of petrochemicals actually consists of more than 100 organic compounds of major importance, which in turn are used for a wide variety of chemical and other products. They are usually produced by the chemical conversion of primary petrochemicals to more complicated derivative organic compounds. Most of the products listed in Table 5-1 are derived from these major intermediates. There are more than 5,000 other intermediates of lesser importance.

Petrochemical products are derived from either primary or intermediate petrochemicals, and can be transformed into finished goods. This is accomplished by physical change such as the molding of plastic products or the forming of tires from synthetic rubber compounds. However, the distinction is not always clear. A product may be an end product in one use and an intermediate in another (for example, ethylene glycol) (see Table 5-2).

Numerous mixtures and compounds, while not actual petrochemicals on the basis of these definitions, are dependent on petrochemical intermediates or products, for example, paints, detergents, explosives, and printing inks. Further processing here may not involve chemical change of the petrochemical input, but rather physical treatment such as the mixing (see Figure 5-1).

A wide variety of industries is dependent on chemical producers as major suppliers. These include the textile industry (synthetic fibers), agriculture and food industries (fertilizers and pesticides),

TABLE 5-2
Material Classification Feedstocks and Petrochemicals

Petrochemical Feedstocks	Petrochemical Materials		
Raw Materials	*Primary*	*Intermediates*	*Products*
Natural gas	Unsaturates	Acetic acid	Plastic materials
Methane	Ethylene	Ethylene oxide	Synthetic rubber
Natural gas liquids	Propylene	Ethylene glycol	Synthetic fibers
Ethane	Butylene	Ethylene dichloride	Surfactants
Propane	Butadiene	Vinyl chloride	Medicinals
Butanes	Acetylene	Acrylonitride	Nitrogenous fertilizers
LPG	Aromatics	Cyclohexane	Phosphate fertilizers
Petroleum liquids	Benzene	Ethylbenzene	Pesticides
Naphtha	Toluene	Phenol	
Reformate	Xylenes	Styrene monomer	
Raffinate	o-Xylene		
Gas oil	m-Xylene		
Carbon black oil	p-Xylene		
Crude oil	Naphthalene		
ING	Methanol		
	Ammonia		
	Carbon black		

Source: Compiled by the authors.

242

FIGURE 5-1
Petrochemical Processes

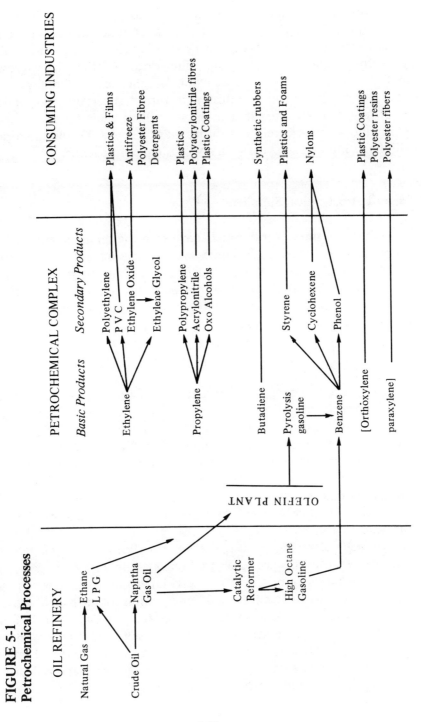

243

the construction industry (paints), automobile manufacturing (synthetic rubber, pigments, plastics) and the health care industry (pharmaceuticals). Chemical firms worldwide benefit from the strength of these "downstream" industries. As they have grown and developed, so has the demand for chemical technology and innovation. The chemical industry, in turn, has certainly responded creatively. It is reported that over two million chemical compounds exist, and it is projected that during the 1980s 1,000 new chemicals will be produced each year — many of them petrochemicals.[1]

Major Petrochemical Suppliers

The years since World War II have seen the dramatic rise of the petrochemical industry. Established producers expanded and prospered, and new firms entered the market. Although global competition has remained strong, a group of major international participants have emerged whose strategies and technologies affect the entire industry at the present time.

France

The French recognized the importance in growth in the chemicals sector immediately after World War I and erected tariff barriers to protect their industry. Until the 1960s it was characterized by small, inefficient, undercapitalized, family-owned firms. In order to raise capital and achieve economies of scale, they frequently participated in joint ventures, and prevailed through the early postwar years. Finally, advancements in petrochemicals provided the catalyst that led to mergers and consolidations of many small firms into major chemical combines.

Rhône-Poulenc S.A., was formed in 1961 and is the largest chemical and textile producer in France, sixth in size in Europe. The company is comprised of four divisions, one of which is responsible for base petrochemicals and combinations of their derivatives, many of which in turn are utilized in the company's own film (polypropylene) and textile (polyester) subsidiaries. Rhône-Poulenc has suffered from a lack of company-owned natural gas and crude oil resources, a disadvantage in a very competitive market. During the expansion period of the 1960s and early 1970s, company sales grew rapidly as the entire French chemical industry prospered. Foreign chemical investments in France were encouraged, and a massive ethylene capacity buildup occurred. Demand recession caused 1975 to be a disaster, with plants operating at 50 to 60 percent of rated capacity. Rhône-Poulenc recorded its first annual losses ever, a total of $312 million in 1975 and 1976.

Although French companies such as Rhône-Poulenc were strong in individual product lines such as fertilizers and fibers, they lacked both depth and diversity to cope with rapid shifts in demand. For example, Rhône-Poulenc had massive capacity in synthetic fibers. Not only did feedstock costs increase dramatically during the mid- and late 1970s, but demand decline hit the firm at the same time as cheaper fibers from the Far East and the United States. In the future, management plans to cut back on commodity petrochemicals, where imported oil dependence has made operations very vulnerable. Emphasis is on diversification, and the firm has become involved in overseas sales of a wide variety of French industrial products. It has also adopted a very aggressive foreign investment policy, particularly in the United States, never a notable characteristic of the French industry in the past. Rhône-Poulenc is attempting to become a more fully integrated chemical major. Such plans are now subject to the French new economic policy, which includes the nationalization of Rhône-Poulenc announced in 1981.

Great Britain

The chemical industry, one of Britain's oldest, has been one of the country's most continuously successful, consistently maintaining its competitive position in world markets. This is in sharp contrast to other British industries, such as textiles, steel, and automobiles that flourished for many years but have entered a long period of decline.

The British chemical industry has consistently maintained good profit margins that have, in turn, spurred investments in research and development. Two important factors have fueled this growth. Before World War II, a shift was made from coal to petroleum as a raw material, which led to an increased involvement of the oil companies — both as suppliers of feedstocks and as producers of petrochemicals.[2]

Imperial Chemical Industries, PLC (ICI) was formed in 1926.[3] This was, in part, a competitive response to the German formation of

IG Farben in 1925. ICI was formed by the amalgamation of five major British producers. The company currently operates worldwide with 250 affiliates. ICI produces numerous intermediates, and more than half are used internally — in plastics and fibers — as well as paints, pharmaceuticals, and dyestuffs. A worldwide business has also been established for bulk petrochemicals.

The company has pursued an active policy of exporting and foreign investment to take advantage of world chemical demand. International sales accounted for about half of total sales in 1981. Much of the company's petrochemical manufacturing is done at the Teesside, England, plant, one of the world's largest chemical complexes.

The discovery of oil and gas in the North Sea has important implications for the U.K. petrochemicals industry. For the first time, hydrocarbon feedstocks are assured and import dependence has declined. ICI has an 18 percent share in Ninian oil field, one of the three largest discovered, and the company's downstream activities are being protected by upstream investments.

The British government has viewed the availability of North Sea resources and EC membership as an attraction to foreign chemical investment and expansion of exports. However, since 1976 the British share of basic petrochemical production (ethylene, propylene, and benzene) has declined. Although chemical investment has increased as a percentage of the EC total, British petrochemical exports have declined, especially plastics. The government has blamed construction delays on a new ethylene cracker and a deterioration of export competitiveness because of adverse exchange-rate movements.

In 1981, ICI decided to combine its plastics and petrochemical operations in order to strengthen the company's position as a major European manufacturer, despite existing and prospective petrochemical oversupply. The main strength of the British chemical industry has been ICI for over 50 years; in 1981 the company accounted for 32 percent of U.K. chemical sales.

Germany

This country has been prominent in the chemical industry for decades, both as a major source of capital equipment for the industry and a leader in the export of chemical products, especially petrochemicals. Only machine tools outrank chemicals among Germany's exports. Germany's strength was achieved by a combination of scientific progress and industrial cooperation. The large firms have a long history of market sharing and cartellization. In 1925 eight German companies, including the three largest (Badische, Bayer, and Hoechst), joined to form IG Farbenindustrie A.G. IG Farben dominated both German and world chemical markets, becoming the leading exporter during the interwar period.

IG Farben's involvement in World War II led to its being dismantled in the early postwar years. Its assets were divided among four companies — BASF, Bayer, Hoechst, and Hüls. A strong technical base and aggressive management have caused BASF, Bayer, and Hoechst not only to dominate the German market, but also to rank at the top of world chemical producers. At present, BASF is the foremost German chemical company in terms of sales. In the past, the company has specialized in petrochemicals and fertilizers. In 1978 basic petrochemicals accounted for 21.2 percent of sales. The company utilizes a good deal of its basic petrochemical output as feedstock for its own downstream activities. Although it markets 6,000 products in 140 countries, BASF has the smallest international involvement among the German Big Three and is also the smallest in terms of export activity. Over 70 percent of capital expenditures in 1979 were slated for domestic programs. The United States constitutes the company's largest foreign investment base.

In 1979 Hoechst A.G., a leader in synthetic fibers and dyestuffs, ranked twelfth in sales among the European industrial companies, with about 67 percent of sales originating outside Germany and 6 percent from U.S. operations. Bayer A.G. has historically been a leader in specialty chemicals and synthetic rubber. Like Hoechst, it has a longer history of foreign investment than BASF. Foreign investment represented about 35 percent of total capital expenditures in 1979.

The German chemical industry traces its underlying success to a smooth transition from coal to petroleum-based production in the 1960s and 1970s; excellent management-union relationships; consistent dedication to research and development, with annual R & D expenditures usually 4-5 percent of sales; and large foreign investment of about DM 9.4 billion between 1952 and 1977. Nevertheless, the industry has also suffered a number of setbacks during the 1970s, including increased petroleum feedstock prices, increased labor costs, adverse exchange-rate movements, penetration of low-priced petrochemicals from Eastern Europe into the Western European market, and increased costs of environmental regulations.

Despite these problems, the German Big Three have maintained their prominence. They have cooperated in an informal rationalization strategy not unlike the oligopolistic behavior common to German chemical companies in the early part of the century. They have divested themselves of unprofitable operations, reduced employment, and retreated to historic company strengths. Internal competition and duplication of facilities are thus mitigated. BASF, for example, is specializing in bulk and petrochemicals, slowly moving into specialty chemicals, and is strengthening its foreign direct investment activity.

Japan

Unlike some other Japanese industries, petrochemicals were groomed to serve the Japanese domestic market. On a strong petrochemical base, the Japanese have developed a modern chemical industry. Japan rose from a very minor producer in the 1930s to a position behind only the United States in production capacity.[4] The rise in oil prices, coupled with a decline in domestic demand, have stimulated a strategy of exporting and foreign direct investment. The Japanese industry, although enhanced by state support and domestic market protection, experienced a decline in world export shares between 1974-77 from 7.4 percent to 4.8 percent.

Mitsubishi Corporation is Japan's largest chemical company. Petrochemicals accounted for approximately 45 percent of sales in 1980. Like many other Japanese firms, Mitsubishi has begun to emphasize diversification and internationalization and has embarked on various major projects in the United States, Australia, and the Middle East. A balance of petrochemicals and fine chemicals is manufactured by another Japanese major, Sumitomo Chemical Company, which is also pursuing a course of aggressive expansion into other countries. One of the company's major projects is a massive petrochemical complex at Singapore, the intent being to locate primary processing plants closer to the oil fields, decrease costs with available cheap local labor, and take particular advantage of the Pacific Rim petrochemical market. However, other Japanese firms are following much the same approach, which may lead to cutthroat competition.

Mitsui & Co., Ltd. is Japan's oldest and largest trading company, coordinating the domestic and foreign operations of various subsidiaries and affiliates. Mitsui Petrochemical Industries, Ltd. is the group's petrochemical specialist, with production facilities worldwide. As of June 1980 organic chemical products represented 66 percent of the company's sales. Mitsui attempted to build a major plant in Iran but was stymied by political upheaval. The company is currently diversifying, especially into electronics.

United States

The U.S. chemical industry grew slowly, handicapped by a lack of experienced chemists and financing difficulties. World War II provided the industry with a major stimulus, including government funding for construction of a large synthetic rubber plant. This endeavor became the foundation of the postwar petrochemical industry, and U.S. companies grew rapidly in the 1950s and expanded abroad in the 1960s through exports as well as foreign direct investment. The U.S. domestic market continues to be relatively dynamic, attracting the investments of many European firms.

The U.S. chemical industry is fiercely competitive, fueled by the oil companies' decision to move downstream into petrochemicals during the 1970s. They have a strong presence in petrochemicals, and it appears that they will retain it for some time. The U.S. growth rate for petrochemicals is projected to be only 4 percent during the 1980s, and the oil companies are forcing traditional industry leaders to develop higher value-added products. One of the principal advantages of U.S. petrochemical suppliers over their European competitors is the use of natural gas rather than naphtha as a raw material. Naphtha, a derivative of crude oil, has increased dramatically in price, for example, from $140 to $300 per ton during the first eight months of 1979.

The Du Pont Company is the largest U.S. chemical firm. Since 1919, the company has expanded internationally particularly in joint ventures and subsidiaries. Eighty percent of the parent company's products are dependent on hydrocarbon feedstocks. Almost all are purchased on a fixed contract basis from domestic refineries. Du Pont has thus been dependent on outsiders for feedstocks, and in order to circumvent this dependence, the company and Continental Oil Company (Conoco) formed a partnership in 1979 for oil and natural gas exploration in Texas. Conoco was the major partner, with a 66 percent ownership. In 1980 a second partnership was formed for oil and gas exploration in the Southwest. In 1981, Du Pont merged with Conoco, giving the company internal access to feedstocks and energy assets for the first time. Additionally, Conoco has coal reserves, the second largest in the nation. Some forecasters project that by 1990 coal will be utilized as a major feedstock, and Du Pont has significantly invested in research and development in this area. Du Pont has perhaps been more susceptible to pressure from European entrants into the U.S. market than others, with considerable overlap in downstream products. In the future, the company will focus on industries that are not as energy intensive.

The principal business of the Exxon Corporation is energy. Main lines of business include the exploration and production of crude oil and natural gas, the manufacture of petrochemicals, and the transportation and sale of these products. About 10 percent of company revenue is derived from its Exxon Chemical division, a major manufacturer and marketer of petrochemicals. Basically a cracker of heavy liquids, Exxon Chemical has product lines that include olefins, aromatics, and other intermediates. Some of this output is sold, but much is utilized internally for downstream products. In 1979 the company's petrochemical sector accounted for 40 percent of sales. Foreign earnings doubled in 1979, particularly in Europe and Canada, because of feedstock shortages and strong demand. However, in 1980 and 1981 chemical revenues and earnings declined very substantially.

The parent company does not subsidize any Exxon Chemical operations. A transfer price system is in effect involving feed streams from refineries, and Exxon Chemical periodically faces adjustments for changes in crude oil prices. Exxon expects involvement in petrochemicals to continue and to expand. The company expects to maintain its current 8.5 percent share of U.S. ethylene production over the next ten years.

Dow Chemical Company is well known for superior research, aggressive expansion, strong overseas market presence, and efforts to secure natural resource supplies for the future. These characteristics have helped assure the company's position as the seventh largest in the world and second in the United States in terms of sales. The petrochemical product line has evidenced the most rapid growth. The hydrocarbon sector not only produces intermediates but encompasses a subsidiary that trades and markets petroleum products and another division that is active in oil and gas exploration. Through backward integration, the company has accumulated large amounts of reserves, including over 300 billion cubic feet of natural gas deposits, which may provide a low-cost future ethylene capability. The firm purchases other necessary commodity petrochemicals on long-term contracts or as they become available in the spot market. In the 1970s, the company's powerful international presence helped to shield it against national-economic problems. With abundant research and development capabilities, Dow is also investing in the future and is experimenting with technology that uses coal as the primary source of petrochemical feedstocks.

U.S. petrochemical companies — including other major contenders such as Union Carbide, Monsanto, American Cyanamid, Hercules, and Celanese as well as oil companies like Mobil, Phillips, and Gulf, not to mention conglomerates like General Electric — are currently following a policy of rationalization. Firms are selling unprofitable operations, seeking greater downstream specialization, and limiting diversification. They are committing sizeable funds to long- and medium-term technology especially in energy alternatives. In the aggregate, the U.S. industry has remained strong, given a large, integrated domestic market that contrasts with a larger but more fragmented European market prone to political intervention. The diversity of the industry and the relatively low start-up costs for certain products permit a sizeable number of small firms to operate effectively at a profit. One major threat is growing government regulation of hazardous chemicals.

Table 5-3 ranks the top dozen chemical firms, in terms of sales and net income, and compares these rankings for 1959 and 1981 — excluding petroleum and pharmaceutical firms.

Patterns of World Production

Although the majority of world petroleum reserves are found in the Middle East (see Table 5-4), world petrochemical production is dominated by OECD nations, which have traditionally had the markets and technologies. From 1960 to 1973, petrochemical production showed extraordinary average annual growth of 10-17 percent, depending on the product — ethylene 17 percent, butadiene

TABLE 5-3
The 12 Largest Chemical Firms, 1959 and 1981

Net Income	Sales	1959 Company and Country		Ranking	1979 Company and Country		Sales	Net Income
(In $ Millions)							(In $ Millions)	
418.7	2,114.3	E.I. Du Pont	(U.S.)	1	Hoechst	(Germany)	16,480.6	251.6
171.6	1,531.3	Union Carbide	(U.S.)	2	Bayer	(Germany)	15,880.6	356.3
110.1	1,423.8	ICI	(U.K.)	3	BASF	(Germany)	15,277.3	197.6
50.0	719.6	Allied Chemical	(U.S.)	4	E.I. Du Pont	(U.S.)*	13,652.0	716.0
37.4	708.0	Olin Mathieson	(U.S.)	5	ICI	(U.K.)	13,290.0	(−46.5)
62.9	705.4	Dow Chemical	(U.S.)	6	Dow Chemical	(U.S.)	10,626.0	805.0
48.9	615.3	Monsanto	(U.S.)	7	Union Carbide	(U.S.)	9,994.0	890.0
25.1	585.5	Bayer	(Germany)	8	Veba Oel	(Germany)	9,645.7	35.9
52.3	583.6	American Cyanamid	(U.S.)	9	Montedison	(Italy)	9,103.8	(−524.2)
23.7	540.0	BASF	(Germany)	10	DSM	(Netherlands)	7,514.2	12.5
20.5	529.0	Hoechst	(Germany)	11	Rhône-Poulenc	(France)	7,155.0	(−461.3)
19.3	471.5	Montecatini	(Italy)	12	Ciba-Geigy	(Switzerland)	7,113.3	182.1

*These figures do not reflect Du Pont's acquisition of Conoco, which moves Du Pont to the number one position.

Source: Forbes and *Business Week* rankings.

TABLE 5-4
World Distribution of Oil and Gas Reserves
(as of January 1, 1980)

Region	Billions of Barrels of Crude Oil Equivalent
Worldwide total	642
North America	65
South America	25
Europe	24
Communist Countries	90
Asia/Pacific	22
Africa	30
Middle East	386

Note: A proved reserve consists of already located oil and gas known to be recoverable with existing facilities, present technology, and at current cost and price levels. This is calculated each year for each field. Proved reserves can be reduced by production, abandonment, poor performance, or price declines. If price increases or new technology is perfected, some of the oil once considered unrecoverable may be included in proved reserves.

Source: Compiled by the authors.

10 percent, benzene 13 percent, propylene 16.5 percent. During that same period industrial production grew by only 5.6 percent annually, and general chemical production grew by only 9 percent.[5]

Petrochemical growth was primarily due to the substantial growth of the chemical industry as a whole during the 1960s, a result in turn of generally strong demand growth and technological innovations. Research and development in petrochemicals and downstream products multiplied the possible nonfuel uses of hydrocarbons. New or substitute demand developed rapidly. The availability of relatively low-cost raw materials made it economically feasible for markets to be developed on such a large scale. And the low prices of petrochemicals fostered substitution of the synthetic products of organic chemistry for natural commodities.

Even before the oil crisis of 1973 there were signs that this situation was changing. Petrochemical product markets were becoming saturated. The substitution of synthetic products for natural materials such as paper, wood, and wool was declining. Economies of scale were running out, and it was becoming clear that few additional benefits could be achieved by increasing the size of basic petrochemical production units. The energy crisis, compounded by the general economic recession, exacerbated these problems, and in 1974-75 petrochemical production growth considerably slowed. By 1975 the production of benzene and butadiene was barely above the level achieved five years earlier. Benzene output declined by 29.5 percent and butadiene by 21.8 percent in 1975. Though less spectacular, ethylene and propylene demand also receded by 18.6 percent and 18.2 percent respectively.[6] In 1976 after the recession and oil supply interruption eased, production of propylene and butadiene regained their 1974 levels, while ethylene and benzene production remained considerably below the highest levels previously attained.

The outlook for future growth is very different from the experience of the 1960s. Changes have occurred both upstream and downstream. The price of feedstocks has risen dramatically. In general, the OECD countries' control over oil and natural gas supplies has diminished. Downstream output of petrochemical products has lagged in accordance with slow growth in demand. Perhaps most dramatically, the lingering soft demand for petrochemicals and fibers in Europe is responsible for massive overcapacity and a rash of withdrawals by U.S. companies from the European markets. In 1976 U.S. overseas investment in petrochemicals was comparable to total chemical industry investment in Japan or Germany, with nearly half of the total in Western Europe where it accounted for about 12.5 percent of total petrochemical capacity. In July 1981, Gulf Oil Corporation canceled previously announced plans for a $200 million chemical expansion in Europe and sought buyers for its chemical plants in Holland and Britain. Also during 1981 Monsanto Company sold its Spanish plastics and chemical operations, and Du Pont withdrew from its European acrylic fibers production facility.

Such pullouts reflect an overcapacity in Europe of approximately 35 percent in fibers and basic plastics. Chemical producers have been faced with declining prices, and the appreciation of the U.S. dollar has increased the cost of Europe's oil imports by up to 20 percent. Additional concern is focused on the oil exporting nations' intent to develop their own base chemical operations and on growing imports from Eastern Europe. Other disengagements include: mothballing of 20 percent of its U.S. PVC capacity by Occidental Petroleum in 1982; a 21 percent cut in its European ethylene capacity and 15 percent in propylene by Royal Dutch Shell; closure of 25 percent of its U.S. ethylene and polypropylene capacity and 10 percent of its LDPE capacity by Exxon Chemical; and individual plant closings by Cities Service, Gulf Oil, British Petroleum, Elf-Aquitaine, and ENI. Japan's Ministry of International Trade and Industry expects to announce plans at the end of 1982 for substantial domestic cuts in petrochemical capacity.[7]

Developed countries dominate all aspects of petrochemicals production except for the extraction of raw materials, mainly located in developing nations. Recently, these countries have shown a desire to upgrade value-added by processing indigenous raw materials before export. The petroleum exporting countries accounted for only 2 percent of the world's ethylene capacity in 1979, yet these same countries account for almost 25 percent of new ethylene plants under or scheduled for construction (see Table 5-5). In light of existing overcapacity, the petrochemical industry is viewing the extension of non-OECD countries into petrochemical production with concern.

Petrochemicals have become a particularly high priority for members of the Organization of Arab Petroleum Exporting Countries (OAPEC). By 1979 Middle East refining capacity increased by almost 50 percent compared with 1970. By 1985, it is expected to increase by another 60 percent. The largest portion of projected growth is scheduled in Saudi Arabia, where a number of joint ventures have been announced. OAPEC nations continue to view such ventures as the most effective means of capacity expansion but recognize that incentives in terms of concessionary feedstock prices, crude oil entitlements, tax relief and concessionary financing are needed to be competitive in world markets. Nevertheless, the OAPEC countries seem to have a clear comparative advantage in this sector based on cheap feedstocks, in many cases natural gas that was previously flared.

It makes sense to use this comparative advantage for increased domestic value added, import substitution, export enhancement and diversification, industrial linkage effects, and absorption of net investable financial resources.

Tables 5-6 and 5-7 present demand and supply forecasts that reflect the changing competitive relationships in the world petrochemical industry. Despite current developments, it remains difficult to project the future evolution of the OAPEC nations' production

TABLE 5-5
New Ethylene Plants under Construction or Planned, 1980

Region and Country	Number of Plants	Region and Country	Number of Plants
North America		Middle East/Africa	
United States	4	Iran	1
Canada	1	Iraq	1
Total	5	Kuwait	1
		Libya	1
Latin America		Qatar	1
Argentina	2	Saudi Arabia	4
Bolivia	1	South Africa	1
Brazil	2	Total	10
Colombia	1		
Mexico	2		
Total	8	World Total	53
Western Europe			
France	1		
West Germany	2		
Greece	1		
Italy	5		
Spain	2		
United Kingdom	2		
Total	13		
Asia/Pacific			
Australia	2		
China (Taiwan)	1		
China	4		
India	1		
Indonesia	1		
Japan	5		
Pakistan	1		
Philippines	1		
Singapore	1		
Total	17		

Note: These figures do not include Eastern Europe and the Soviet Union.

Source: *Oil and Gas Journal*, September 1, 1980.

TABLE 5-6
Demand for Petrochemical Products Forecast for 1987
(In Thousands of Metric Tons)

Product	Western Europe	North America	Japan	Middle East and Africa	Asia	Latin America
Ethylene and derivatives						
Ethylene	15,700	20,030	6,225	2,452	2,230	2,890
LD polyethylene	4,865	5,780	1,515	1,154	1,121	1,320
HD polyethylene	2,240	3,470	710	595	596	430
Vinyl chloride mon.	6,165	4,595	1,880	970	1,285	1,090
Polyvinyl chloride	5,300	4,270	1,550	1,194	1,332	1,130
Monoethylene glycol	1,045	2,535	600	261	473	372
Synthesis gas derivatives						
Ammonia	15,220	19,410	2,680	6,460	10,070	4,150
Urea	2,975	5,610	580	1,490	8,840	1,650
Methanol	4,860	5,670	1,510	135	657	462
Aromatics and derivatives						
Benzene	6,240	8,625	2,675	557	782	1,495
Orthoxylene	1,035	700	285	56	144	250
Paraxylene	1,030	2,475	885	155	420	420
Dimethyl terephthalic/ teraphthalic acid	1,310	4,010	960	392	1,270	810
Styrene	3,695	4,865	1,600	255	431	860
Polystyrene	2,260	3,030	905	190	490	540

Source: Gulf Organization for Industrial Consulting, *Petrochemical Marketing Strategies for the Arab Gulf States in the 1980's* (Doha, Qatar, 1979), pp. 43, 53, 62, 69, 70, 80, 87, 95, 101, 108, 113, 117, 118, 127, 128.

capacity, given a number of factors that could impede growth: high plant construction costs, which may be at least twice those of similar plant constructions in the OECD area because of skilled labor shortages, existing infrastructure inadequacies, and the necessity to adapt technology to a hostile environment; lack of skilled labor and managerial staff to run plants; small size of regional markets; high transportation costs, gloomy prospects for demand growth in the main consumer nations; and possible future trade barriers.

Meanwhile, the chemical industry in Eastern Europe has been rapidly expanding. The centrally planned economies are largely dependent on the Soviet Union for petroleum and natural gas. Only

Romania has important oil and gas resources of its own. During the past 15 years, the Soviet Union has placed top priority on the development of the chemical industry and now has the largest chemical sector in Europe and the second largest in the world. Entrance into the petrochemical sector began fairly late in comparison with other countries. By 1977, however, the Soviet Union was the second largest producer of methanol after the United States, the third largest producer of benzene.

Eastern Europe accounted for 25 percent of the world's chemical production in 1976, and it is projected that this will increase to 28 percent by 1985. Much of the Eastern European production will be

TABLE 5-7

Surplus (+) or Deficit (−) of Petrochemical Products Forecast for 1987 (In Thousands of Metric Tons)

Product	Western Europe	North America	Japan	Middle East and Africa	Asia	Latin America
Ethylene and derivatives						
Ethylene	+1,910	+1,045	0	+823	−220	+1,694
LD polyethylene	+535	−10	−100	+64	−366	+225
HD polyethylene	+495	+195	−25	−307	−219	+63
Vinyl chloride mon.	+115	+345	−90	−305	−320	+142
Polyvinyl chloride	+520	+85	−20	−197	−171	−53
Monoethylene glycol	+220	+385	0	+194	−128	+58
Synthesis gas derivatives						
Ammonia		+250 −2,210	+30	+1,345	+1,660	+540
Urea	+605	−1,670	+320	+1,925	−210	+225
Methanol	−1,355	−840	−250	+2,985	+197	+760
Aromatics and derivatives						
Benzene	+905	−195	0	+53	−2	−74
Orthoxylene	+30	+75	0	+96	−11	+2
Paraxylene	+90	+555	−150	−25	+6	+169
Dimethyl terephthalic/ teraphthalic acid	+395	+45	+105	−209	−610	+19
Styrene	−285	+235	−40	+440	−190	−11
Polystyrene	+450	+105	−10	−8	−78	−15

Source: Gulf Organization for Industrial Consulting, *Petrochemical Marketing Strategies for the Arab Gulf States in the 1980's* (Doha, Qatar, 1979), pp. 45, 54, 63, 71, 73, 82, 89, 96, 102, 110, 114, 120, 122, 129, 131.

sent to OECD nations under buy-back agreements involving deliveries of chemical plant and equipment from the West to be paid for by the export of Eastern chemical products. Even small increases in Eastern European petrochemical exports to Western Europe may present difficulties for European markets if they are low priced and threaten established price levels. West Germany's Big Three producers have protested imports from Comecon and blamed them for overcapacity of about 50 percent in some plastics and for a consequent collapse in prices. The imports are allegedly priced 40 percent lower than those produced domestically. However, because of buy-back agreements between East European producers and such companies as Montedison, ICI, and Rhône-Poulenc, these imports will have to be maintained.

Patterns of World Trade

In terms of production, consumption, and trade the developed countries dominate the world petrochemical market. Approximately 10 percent of OECD total countries' trade is in chemicals. The bulk of member countries' trade is not only intra-OECD (only 8 percent of member countries' imports of chemical originate in nonmember countries) but intra-EC trade alone amounts to 30-50 percent of the total across all chemical products. This is partly because imports from non-EC countries like Japan and the United States face relatively stiff tariff protection.

In the petrochemical industry, trade can occur at any of several production stages — in feedstocks, between processing steps (intra-industry trade), or in the end product. The end product may even be subject to further processing, but not within a petrochemical framework. For example, the processing of polyester into materials for garments will not necessarily be done in a chemical facility.

West Germany is the largest chemical exporter followed by the United States, France, the United Kingdom, and the Netherlands. The OECD as a whole has a positive trade balance in chemicals, although the majority of individual members have chemicals imports that are in excess of exports (see Figure 5-2). Petrochemicals dominate the trade profile, accounting for 50 percent of activity.

As noted earlier, many developing nations are expanding their own petrochemical capabilities, which will influence future trade

FIGURE 5-2A
Chemical Product Trade: 1979
($ Millions)
EXPORTS

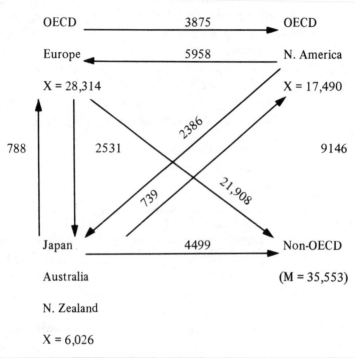

Exporting Country	OECD Europe	OECD North America	Japan Australia New Zealand	Non-OECD	Net Exports	Total Exports
OECD Europe	52,186	3,875	2,531	21,908	28,314	80,500
OECD North America	5,958	3,894	2,386	9,146	17,490	21,384
Japan Australia New Zealand	788	739	373	4,499	6,026	6,399

FIGURE 5-2B
Chemical Product Trade: 1979
($ Millions)
IMPORTS

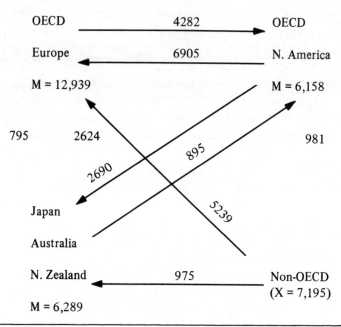

Exporting Country	OECD Europe	OECD North America	Japan Australia New Zealand	Non-OECD	Net Imports	Total Imports
OECD Europe	52,455	6,905	795	5,239	12,939	65,394
OECD North America	4,282	4,818	895	981	6,158	10,976
Japan Australia New Zealand	2,624	2,690	252	975	6,289	6,541

patterns. In the Middle East, countries have a very limited capacity for downstream utilization of petrochemical products, and their aim is clearly to enter the export markets, resulting in import pressures on the markets especially of Western European countries. The affected producers' primary concern is that the petroleum exporting nations, given the relative low opportunity cost of natural gas, will export cheap ethylene to Europe. This, in turn, could alter the relative prices of feedstocks and disrupt the European market both for feedstocks and for intermediate petrochemical products. The Middle East countries are well aware of the economies of scale already existing in European plants as formidable barriers that might impede their export capabilities. Vertical integration and own production of intermediates and feedstocks, such as ethylene, could severely limit their markets.

Some developing nations are expanding their petrochemical production mainly to satisfy internal consumption that is increasing with industrialization. This nevertheless affects the trade of developed nations, as exports from OECD countries stagnate or lose market share in the high-growth developing countries. Increases in Asian production will certainly affect Japan's trade and its petrochemical industry. South Korea and Taiwan account for about 20 percent of Japan's total chemical exports. Both of these countries have plans to develop their own petrochemical industries and have made significant progress. Japan will have difficulty in maintaining its market share in these two countries and in the Pacific Basin as a whole. Latin American countries, especially Mexico, Brazil, and Argentina, are also pursuing petrochemical development. However, these markets have never accounted for a large share of the exports of the established suppliers.

Most East-West petrochemical industry trade is not in actual petrochemical products. Rather, Eastern Europe is a substantial net importer of chemical plant and equipment from the West. In Poland, for example, the OECD countries account for more than 90 percent of total imports of chemical industry equipment. Plant and equipment from the West have greatly augmented the development and modernization of the Soviet chemical industry. Between 1961 and 1975 these imports totalled $5 billion, with Italy the primary OECD supplier. In order to avoid hard-currency payments for imports of technology, the East European countries have arranged compensatory buy-back contracts with suppliers of plant and equipment. This provides them with the opportunity to pay part of the cost of equipment with products rather than with foreign currency. Western Europe's concern, as noted above, is that the Eastern European countries will be able to adopt a stronger export policy because of the Western technology and buy-back agreements. European markets have been significantly penetrated in synthetic rubber, methanol, and ammonia. It is estimated that these imports will account for 10-20 percent of Western Europe's consumption in the 1980s.

Policy Aspects

Public policies affecting world production and trade in petrochemicals essentially focus on feedstock policies, protection of markets, and environmental measures.

Feedstock Policies

Several different feedstocks can be utilized for the production of certain petrochemicals. However, each plant is designed for optimum production using a specific feedstock. Use of an alternate feedstock will result in either a reduction of plant capacity or an increase in operating costs. New plants are being designed to permit some flexibility, but this generally requires substantially increased investments per unit of plant capacity. In this respect, the petrochemical industry developed quite differently in various countries as feedstock requirements and availabilities differed.

During the 1930s the United States developed a highly refined gas distribution and oil processing industry. The four basic petrochemicals could be produced from adequate supplies of the suitable feedstocks with a minimum of processing and invested capital. Plentiful natural gas was available, and a very large automobile fuel demand mandated that the United States produce a much higher proportion of light petroleum fractions than other countries. Hence, *new* ethylene production capacity for which natural gas condensate feedstock is not available will have to use relatively high proportions of heavy naphtha rather than the light naphtha fractions.

The U.S. refining capability for benzene will continue to provide a more than adequate supply of "high aromatic" feedstocks from which benzene can be economically extracted as demand increases. In the past there has been some concern that lead reduction in gasoline would result in a considerable increase in aromatic feedstocks required for high octanes, reducing benzene's potential availability for petrochemicals. This has not occurred because of the declining growth rates in both petrochemicals and gasoline consumption. Recently, a greater requirement for unleaded gasoline has been indicated. This may lead to a supply problem in the future. Following the oil crisis of 1973, U.S. policymakers refused to permit the domestic price of oil and gas to rise to world levels, resulting in *de facto* concessionary feedstock prices to U.S. producers. This was gradually phased out in the late 1970s and early 1980s with oil and gas decontrol (see Table 5-8).

Western Europe's first large-scale ethylene crackers were based on the low-octane light naphtha, a product of the primary distillation of crude oil. By the late 1960s, forecasts indicated that light naphtha requirements would be approaching the maximum from crude oil refining. Refinery cracking of heavier fractions generally produced high-value output that was expensive to use as petrochemical feedstocks. Therefore, the industry began to design new plants that would use the heavier middle distillate fractions up to and including gas oil. Most of the plants under construction will have the ability to use up to 50 percent of this raw material. In addition, gas condensates suitable for ethylene production are becoming increasingly

TABLE 5-8
Wholesale Prices

(Per Gallon)

Year	Jet Fuel Naphtha-type	All Petrochemical Feedstocks
1976	$ .315	$ .464
1977	.350	.477
1978	.375	.495
1979	.523	.852
1980	.882	1.019
1981	1.059	1.122

Source: "1981 Annual Report to Congress," *Energy Statistics, May 1982*, vol. 2 (Washington, D.C.: U.S. Department of Energy).

available from North Sea sources. In the future, projects utilizing this feedstock will probably be built. During the 1980s, European refineries are expected to experience a higher demand growth for naphtha and gasoline than the heavier oil fractions. So it seems likely that these heavier fractions will become more economical feedstocks for ethylene production.

The feedstock for Japan's ethylene production has developed similarly to that of Western Europe. Because of declining export growth for petrochemical derivatives, new Japanese ethylene capacity is relatively small. It imports a large part of its petroleum as refined products, particularly naphtha. In 1976, such imports were equivalent to about 40 percent of the naphtha feedstock needed by Japan's ethylene plants. These imports may continue through the 1980s, but, given the cost of naphtha, new Japanese ethylene crackers may be encouraged to utilize gas oil.

In Canada new ethylene production is being based entirely on crude oil, ethane, and gas condensate. These natural materials are being supplied indigenously from the Alberta oil and gas fields at very competitive prices.

Eastern European countries are, as noted, supplied by raw materials from the Soviet Union. Since the early 1970s, however, the Soviet Union has announced that it would eventually limit oil deliveries. The Soviet government has suggested that future investments in energy-intensive chemicals be concentrated in the Soviet Union. Instead of supplying feedstocks, the Soviet Union would supply chemical intermediates and finished products such as ammonia, methanol, and PVC. This attempt at rationalization has been opposed by various other Eastern European nations; their view is that this policy will discourage their own industries' development and promote an unbalanced structure of production. They also feel that this specialization may curtail the possibility of earning hard currency through exports.

Protection and Competitive Structure

Tariff structures in the petrochemicals sector, both in the developed and developing countries, have traditionally yielded high levels of effective protection. Tariff rates on basic feedstocks are usually quite low, averaging 4 percent. However, as processing steps continue the tariff rates increase. On intermediates the average rate is 8 percent, increasing to 10 percent on end products (see Table 5-9).

In the case of the EC, the effective level of protection is 12 percent for basic feedstocks, increasing to 25 percent for intermediates and, finally, declining to 15 percent for end products despite their own high tariff rates. This is due to the fact that the 10 percent duties on intermediates penalize European end-product manufacturers (see Table 5-9). In Japan, tariff rates escalate rapidly on downstream production — 4.4 percent for feedstocks, 6 percent for intermediates, and 9 percent for end products, yielding high levels of effective protection. The U.S. tariff pattern resembles that of the EC, except that end products enjoy high levels of effective protection. U.S. duties on feedstocks are generally zero while tariffs on intermediates average 34.5 percent. The lower tariffs on many end products are probably due to the abundance of natural gas in the United States, requiring less tariff protection to remain competitive in the domestic market.

Another aspect of tariff protection is the Generalized System of Preferences (GSP). Under the GSP, the EC, Japan, and the United States allow products from certain beneficiary developing nations to be imported duty-free. The GSP may be of some benefit to developing country exporters of petrochemical products by eliminating the high protective effect provided by tariff escalation. However, GSP treatment is subject to a number of rules and regulations — "rules of origin" that restrict GSP treatment to trade flows in which the exporting developing country has contributed significant value-added. This poses serious problems for the petrochemical industry because input requirements leave limited room for value-added. For example, over 80 percent of the cost of producing styrene is the value of the intermediate ethylbenzene. A developing country could not import this intermediate to produce styrene and export it under GSP treatment.[8] Additionally, if a developing country becomes a significant exporter, GSP treatment is likely to be limited by the ceiling systems of the EC and Japan or be withdrawn entirely under the "competitive need" formula embodied in the U.S. scheme.

Multilateral negotiating rounds under GATT auspices have resulted in a general lowering of tariffs on petrochemicals and the "binding" of negotiated rates. This has generally reduced rates of protection of petrochemical suppliers. However, other barriers to trade have emerged, such as import licensing schemes and customs valuation practices. Second, governments have resorted to various nontariff techniques to protect vulnerable industries that could not cope with declining tariff protection. These nontariff barriers include trigger-price mechanisms and special fees on imports. Nevertheless, such barriers do not appear to be a serious obstacle to petrochemical exports to the United States (after the elimination of the American Selling Price (ASP) procedure of customer valuation), the EC, or Japan. The reason for this may be the very high protective effect of the existing tariff structures in these major markets.

However, a number of problems are emerging concerning trade among the developed nations. Capacity utilization in most countries has declined, significantly increasing unit costs. Raw material costs have risen, and demand has declined, both seriously eroding the profitability of many petrochemical firms. Governments may well respond by imposing increased nontariff barriers. An example is the aforementioned two-tier oil pricing system of the United States. As a result, U.S. firms have enjoyed access to raw materials at prices below their European and/or Japanese competitors. The EC has alleged that imports from the United States are effectively being dumped on European markets, and, in 1981, the EC introduced a provisional duty of 14.7 percent on imports of paraxylene from the United States.

A number of other constraints limit trade in petrochemicals, independent of governmental measures. These include the characteristics of the production process, transportation costs of intermediates, marketing channels, and the like. In the petrochemical industry, such obstacles range from technological and economic constraints that limit the opportunities for entry to a dominant firm's ability to restrain competition. The petrochemical markets are significantly controlled by large, vertically integrated companies. Many share productive capacity through joint ventures. One joint-venture partner could integrate forward to capture a market for one of its products while the other partner integrates backward to assure itself supplies of petrochemical inputs. Useful extensions of each company's operations occur.

Long-term contracts also contribute to international market control. Most contracts between Western companies are three years long. East-West trade agreements are usually for longer periods. Producers and suppliers are tied-in, limiting outside participation. Technological constraints exist as well. For example, the physical

TABLE 5-9
**Tariffs, Effective Protection, and Imports of Selected Petrochemical Products
(1979 in U.S.$ Million)**

| Product[a] | Tariff[b] (%) | Eff. Prot.[c] (%) | | Imports From | | | | |
		Actual Prices	Full Cost Prices	OECD[d]	DC/oil[e]	DC/non-oil	Other[f]	Intra-EC
EC								
1. Packaging								
Ethylene	6.3*	26	20	5	8	0	0	725
Polyethylene	12.5*	25	23	377	0	3	33	2,166
2. Packaging								
Propylene	6.3*	7	7	62	0	0	8	337
Polypropylene	12.5*	18	18	97	0	2	2	493
3. Disinfectant								
Methanol	13.0*	22	19	16	45	2	11	99
Formaldehyde	7.6*	NA	0[g]	43	0	1	4	86
4. Fertilizer								
Ammonia	11.0*	19	15	24	28	5	50	114
Urea	11.0*	11	11	13	1	0	10	73
5. Antifreeze								
Ethylene	6.3*	26	20	5	8	0	0	725
Ethylene oxide	12.0*	30	23	0	0	0	1	91
Ethylene glycol	13.0*	33	18	4	0	3	0	149

268

6. Packaging							
Benzene	F	0	0	109	0	12	52	404
Ethylene	6.3*	26	20	5	8	0	0	725
Ethylbenzene	6.4*	27	47	3	0	0	0	239
Styrene	6.0*	6	6	88	0	0	0	417
Polystyrene	12.5*	27	30	97	0	4	4	1,340
7. Pipe, conduit, flooring							
Chlorine	11.0*	12	12	8	0	0	6	24
Ethylene	6.3*	26	20	5	8	0	0	725
Vinyl chloride	12.0*	27	20	1	0	0	10	311
Polyvinyl chloride (PVC)	12.5*	14	13	217	0	26	40	1,691
8. Tires							
Benzene	F	0	0	109	0	12	52	404
Ethylene	6.3*	26	20	5	8	0	0	725
Ethylbenzene	6.4*	27	47	3	0	0	0	239
Styrene	6.0*	6	6	88	0	0	0	417
Butadiene	6.3*	NA	NA	21	0	0	0	151
Styrene-butadiene Rubber (SBR)	3.2*	−1.2	−0.2	42	0	9	38	234
9. Polyester fabrics, etc.							
Methanol	13.0*	22	19	16	45	2	11	99
Paraxylene	F	0	0	144	0	10	16	248
Dimethyl terephthalate	10.0*	40	18	0	0	0	0	117
Ethylene glycol[n]	13.0*	33	18	4	0	3	0	149
Polyester fibers	8.0*	5	3	84	0	1	14	213
Polyester yarns	8.0*	8	8	148	0	5	5	512

Continued

TABLE 5-9, continued

Product[a]	Tariff[b] (%)	Eff. Prot.[c] (%) Actual Prices	Eff. Prot.[c] (%) Full Cost Prices	Imports From OECD[d]	Imports From DC/oil[e]	Imports From DC/non-oil	Imports From Other[f]
JAPAN							
1. Packaging							
Ethylene	6*	6	6	0	0	1	0
Polyethylene	11*	24	21	14	0	5	0
2. Packaging							
Propylene	6*	6	6	0	0	0	0
Polypropylene	22*	37	42	10	0	2	0
3. Disinfectant							
Methanol	5*	6	8	13	7	36	1
Formaldehyde	5*	NA	5g	12	0	0	0
4. Fertilizer							
Ammonia	4*	5	4	0	0	0	0
Urea	F	−8	−14	0	0	0	0
5. Antifreeze							
Ethylene	6*	6	6	0	0	1	0
Ethylene oxide	6*	6	6	0	0	0	0
Ethylene glycol	12*	98	49	23	0	2	7

6. Packaging							
Benzene	4*	NA	NA	0	0	1	1
Ethylene	6*	6	6	0	0	1	0
Ethylbenzene	2*	NA	−30	6	0	0	0
Styrene	8*	33	37	39	0	17	0
Polystyrene	14*	45	36	21	0	12	1
7. Pipe, conduit, flooring							
Chlorine	4*	4	5	0	0	0	0
Ethylene	6*	6	6	0	0	1	0
Vinyl chloride	6*	6	6	2	0	0	0
Polyvinyl chloride (PVC)	6*	8	6	23	0	22	1
8. Tires							
Benzene	4	NA	NA	0	0	1	1
Ethylene	6*	6	6	0	0	1	0
Ethylbenzene	2*	NA	−30	6	0	0	0
Styrene	8*	33	37	39	0	17	0
Butadiene	6*	NA	NA	27	0	0	0
Styrene-butadiene Rubber (SBR)	F	−1	−1	14	0	8	1
9. Polyester fabrics, etc.							
Methanol	5*	6	8	13	7	36	1
Paraxylene	2	3	3	50	0	5	1
Dimethyl terephthalate	8*	20	15	0	0	0	0
Ethylene glycol[n]	12*	98	49	23	0	2	7
Polyester fibers	10*	12	13	1	0	14	0
Polyester yarns	10*	10	10	2	0	17	0

Continued

TABLE 5-9, continued

| | | Eff. Prot.[c] (%) | | Imports From | | | |
Product[a]	Tariff[b] (%)	Actual Prices	Full Cost Prices	OECD[d]	DC/oil[e]	DC/non-oil	Other[f]
UNITED STATES							
1. Packaging							
Ethylene	F	0	0	14	0	0	0
Polyethylene	12.5*	27	29	58	0	2	0
2. Packaging							
Propylene	F	0	0	41	0	0	0
Polypropylene	12.5*	22	24	23	0	0	0
3. Disinfectant							
Methanol	18*	30	28	16	14	22	0
Formaldehyde	0.2*	NA	-25g	24	0	0	0
4. Fertilizer							
Ammonia	3*	7	4	58	28	36	69
Urea	F	-4	-5	145	0	6	0
5. Antifreeze							
Ethylene	F	0	0	14	0	0	0
Ethylene oxide	9*	22	22	0	0	0	0
Ethylene glycol	12*	23	26	1	0	2	0

272

6. Packaging							
Benzene	F	0	0	100	0	7	0
Ethylene	F	0	0	14	0	0	0
Ethylbenzene	14	60	150	0	0	0	0
Styrene	7.4*	−21	−14	9	0	0	0
Polystyrene	F	−29	−20	10	0	0	0
7. Pipe, conduit, flooring							
Chlorine	F	0	0	15	0	0	0
Ethylene	F	0	0	14	0	0	0
Vinyl chloride	12*	42	29	0	0	0	0
Polyvinyl chloride (PVC)	10*	6	8	81	1	39	0
8. Tires							
Benzene	F	0	0	100	0	7	0
Ethylene	F	0	0	14	0	0	0
Ethylbenzene	13.5	60	150	0	0	0	0
Styrene	7.4*	−21	−14	9	0	0	0
Butadiene	F	0	0	130	3	0	0
Styrene-butadiene Rubber (SBR)	F	−4	−2	28	0	0	0
9. Polyester fabrics, etc.							
Methanol	18	30	28	16	14	2	0
Paraxylene	F	0	0	66	2	4	3
Dimethyl terephthalate	13	33	22	0	0	0	0
Ethylene glycol[h]	12*	23	26	1	0	2	0
Polyester fibers	5	−21	−10	1	0	1	0
Polyester yarns	9	NA	NA	0	0	0	0

Continued

273

Table 5-9, continued

NA = Not available.

[a]Products are organized by end-use products and increasing stages of processing starting with the basic feedstock, for example, products. Successive stages of processing are indicated by indentations; polyethylene is produced from ethylene (in product 1). And joint inputs are flush left, for example, benzene and ethylene are combined to produce ethylbenzene (in product 6).

[b]Specific duties have been converted into ad valorem equivalents using 1977 trade weights. "F" implies duty free. All tariffs are post MTN rates, which will apply after the eight-year phase-in period. An asterisk (*) denotes that the product qualifies for duty-free treatment under the GSP, subject to the "competitive need formula" under the U.S. GSP and/or ceiling-type limits under the GSP programs of the EC and Japan.

[c]Effective rates of protection are calculated for each stage of processing.

[d]Excluding intra-EC trade.

[e]Developing countries with oil include OPEC countries and oil-exporting countries that do not belong to OPEC, such as Mexico, but do not include oil-producing countries that also import oil, such as Argentina or Colombia.

[f]Mainly socialist countries of Eastern Europe and Asia.

[g]Production coefficients are taken from A. V. Hahn, *The Petrochemical Industry: Market and Economics* (New York: McGraw-Hill, 1970).

[h]Ethylene glycol is produced from ethylene oxide, which in turn is produced from ethylene; see product 5 for intermediate stage effective protection and imports.

Source: Tracy Murray, *International Trade in Petrochemical Products*, report to UNCTAD and UNIDO (mimeo.), October 1981. UNCTAD secretariat calculations; production coefficients used to calculate effective protection were obtained with the assistance of the UNIDO secretariat.

characteristics of ethylene make transportation extremely difficult and costly. It is usually transported via pipeline, which may require the producer and the user to be vertically integrated. Such constraints are clearly nongovernmental, yet they do limit the opportunities for emerging suppliers to enter the petrochemical market and influence competitive structures.

Health, Safety, and Pollution Issues

Large increases in feedstock costs since 1973, combined with more modern technologies, have made it possible to design new (greenfield) plants or expand existing ones, to augment efficiency in respect of feedstock utilization, energy use, and environmental impact. The overall improvement in plant efficiency reduces unwanted by-products that must be disposed of.

Particularly in the chemical-process industries, governments have attempted to regulate environmental, health, and safety matters by direct intervention. A study conducted by the Water Management Group of OECD concludes that measures required to reduce environmental pollution by a petrochemical complex accounts for 10-12 percent of capital costs, plus operating costs equaling 2 percent of the value of output. At this time, it is estimated that about 11 percent of all capital expenditures in the German chemical industry are made to meet environmental regulations. In the United States, the Environmental Protection Agency is applying a new approach, "degree of hazard," to the disposal of chemical wastes. It is also pushing to expand the use of "bubble" regulation and controlled trading in emission permits and to adapt these concepts to water pollution control — in the past, these approaches have been primarily used in air pollution control — thereby allowing industrial expansion without a great degree of environmental degradation. Because petrochemical plants contribute to both water and air pollution, an increased use of these innovative approaches would be welcomed by the industry.[9]

The modern petrochemical industry is capital- rather than labor-intensive. Less militant, well-paid, white collar workers have increasingly come to dominate the labor force. The number of workers employed in the petrochemical industry has stabilized or declined — over 400 million are employed in OECD chemicals sector alone.

One reason the workers have become less militant is the response by industry and government to occupational health and safety concerns. In the past, the industry worked hard to address these issues and minimize government involvement. However, because of concern with long-term health effects, especially cancer, government has interceded by direct regulation. This has made the industry redefine its strategy for dealing with the government. An arm's-length relationship has developed in West Germany and the United States while low-visibility, informal relationships have evolved in France, Britain, and Japan. It is possible that both worker health/safety costs and pollution control costs will be lower in the newly emerging petrochemical complexes in the Middle East and in other developing countries than in the older, established areas.

Evaluating Global Competitive Structures

The OAPEC countries have become increasingly aware of the value of their natural resources. Many of them argue that hydrocarbon production should be limited to maximize unit revenues and to stretch the life of oil and gas reserves whose value, they believe, will increase more rapidly than the financial assets they can acquire with excess revenues. Additionally, they feel that reduced production will spur developed nations to find alternative energy resources and decrease their oil and gas dependence for fuel use. It has been forecast that by 1985 the Middle Eastern countries will have an ethylene capacity of approximately 2.3 million tons. About 50 percent of this will be located in Saudi Arabia. As projected, the Western European market will be outlet for roughly 70 percent of the downstream products manufactured in this region. Previously, it was believed that the Middle East would account for only 7-8 percent of European ethylene consumption during the 1980s. However, the development of this capacity has been slower than past forecasts indicated. Many projects have been postponed or canceled and the full impact of this development on the traditional petrochemical suppliers will not be felt until the latter part of this decade. As noted, supply will also be augmented by the chemical buy-back agreements with Eastern Europe. Most of these petrochemicals are scheduled to reach the West during the 1980s and into the 1990s, and almost 90 percent will originate in the Soviet Union. Petrochemicals such as methanol figure heavily in these agreements.

Despite the lack of hard data on Soviet petroleum resources and projected oil production, it appears that Eastern Europe may soon shift to a net importer position from its traditional role as a net exporter of oil. Therefore, the Soviet Union may be competing with the OECD nations both upstream and downstream in petrochemical production.

In the last half of the 1970s, the major chemical companies looked for overseas growth through foreign direct investment and exports. The United States, for example, registered a 16.3 percent average annual growth in chemical trade during 1975-80. However, in the 1980s it is forecast that such trade growth will experience a marked slowdown; in 1981 U.S. export volume grew by only 2 percent. The strong dollar, decontrol of gas and oil, and increased feedstock prices are making it more difficult to sell in European and Third World markets. This is compounded by weakened foreign economies. The most vulnerable sector is petrochemicals, which accounts for 50 percent of trade.

Prospective moderate demand growth will most likely be the result of the combined effect of the slowdown in overall economic growth and the decline in the elasticity of petrochemical consumption with respect to GDP. Utilization rates of production facilities are estimated at only 80 percent to the end of the decade, because of changes in demand and supply patterns. These effects will probably be most severely felt in Europe. Although growth will be slower, it is projected that the chemical industry will still easily outperform manufacturing in most developed and developing nations. The main reason is the industry's uniqueness. As long as technology advances, such superior growth performance will continue. Approximately 50 percent of current chemical sales are for products not invented 25 years ago. This is especially true in the petrochemical sector. Years ago natural gas was being flared almost everywhere as waste; now it is increasingly utilized as a valuable petrochemical feedstock. It is anticipated that the next 25 years will see a phaseout of high-cost raw materials generally and an extension of the industry into new products and ventures.

Hallmarks of the future evolution of the petrochemical industry are likely to include continued heavy R & D investment in product and process innovation; new forms of doing business, including management contracts and fee-based services; new petrochemical possibilities for alternative raw materials, especially coal; intensified efforts by established petrochemical firms to move downstream into high-technology, specialized businesses; continued efforts at upstream integration to secure sources of raw-material supply; and growing redeployment toward the most competitive raw-materials exporting areas, particularly the Middle East but also such countries as Malaysia, Indonesia, Canada, Venezuela, and Mexico.

DATA BASE AND CASE ANALYSIS

Given the structure and evolution of the world petrochemical industry, what is the probable role of investment incentives and performance requirements in determining its current and prospective future structure? At issue is the influence of such measures on project economics, location decisions, foreign direct investment, and patterns of international trade in petrochemicals and petrochemical products. A data base of case studies was assembled from interviews with major international chemical firms in several countries, backed up by published studies on the complex of investment incentives and performance requirements in host countries and media reports on the projects concerned.

The Data Base

Data on 15 projects are summarized in Table 5-10. Each investment decision was analyzed in terms of four areas that are identified by letters A through D and that relate to the effectiveness of incentives and requirements on: (A) the decision to make the actual investment; (B) the choice of host country; (C) the location within the chosen host country; and (D) whether the project was an expansion of previous capacity or a new venture.[10] Clearly, some projects can combine the decision to expand D with the A decision or the C decision.

In the summary table, the projects are rank-ordered in terms of the "level" of the petrochemical products supplied (except for case 15, which concerns a second-level product). As noted in the first section, the petrochemical industry can be considered in stages of levels according to the number of chemical transformations involved. Primary products are basic petrochemicals; second-level products are usually (but not inevitably) intermediate transformations of primary petrochemicals that must be further transformed into third-level products before they can be sold for use as inputs in other industries (level 3A) or applied directly as in the case of pesticides and fungicides (level 3B). By categorizing the projects in this way, any characteristics that are variable with the level of production may be expected to stand out.

Analysis

A priori, it is to be expected that petrochemical installations tend to be less footloose than those of many other industries. First-level output necessarily has to be located near a point to which the feedstock (petroleum derivatives or natural gas) can be delivered. As a general rule, the primary petrochemical is both easier and cheaper to transport than the feedstock, and therefore primary petrochemical installations are drawn toward the point at which natural resources are extracted from the earth or undergo primary refining. Third-level petrochemicals tend to be oriented toward the market — especially when the market is protected from import competition, as it is in most developing countries. Third-level projects are footloose only within relatively well-integrated (and usually national) market areas, although in regional trading blocs this mobility may indeed be international. Finally, second-level projects tend to be located close to either first-level or third-level projects so that they have a very constrained degree of mobility. Moreover, in the case of many products the economies of vertical integration reinforce the inherent bias in the choice of production site quite strongly either toward the primary-product unit or toward the third-level production site. The mobility of second-level production may thus be more apparent than real.

In any analysis involving investment incentives (IIs) and performance requirements (PRs), there appears to be a problem in determining which IIs and PRs are made to counter an existing comparative disadvantage characteristic of a particular production site, and which ones are attempting to create a preference among sites that are

TABLE 5-10
Summary of Investment Incentives and Performance Requirements Relating to 15 Sample Projects

Case Number	1				2				3				4				5				6			
Host Country	N. Amer.				Mideast				Mideast				Brazil				S. Korea				W. Ger.			
Product Level	I				I				I & II				II				II				II & III			
Capitalization ($000)	290,000				500,000				1,000,000				80,000				150,000				425,000			
Decision Criteria	A	B	C	D	A	B	C	D	A	B	C	D	A	B	C	D	A	B	C	D	A	B	C	D
Capital-Related:																								
Tax exempt R & D (+)									2*	0	1	0	2	1	3	0	3	2	2	0				
Tax holidays (+)					1	0	0	0					2*	1	3	0	3	2	2	0				
Accelerated depreciation (+)																	3	2	2	0				
Investment tax credit (+)																	3	1	1	0				
Development area (+)																								
Key industry (+)													2	1	3	0								
Excess profits tax (+)																	4*	2	3	0				
Cash grants (+)																					1*	1	2	0
Direct subsidies (+)																					1*	1	2	0
Concessionary financing (+)					5*	5	1	0	4*	0	1	0												
Loan guarantees (+)																	3*	1	1	0				
Access to capital markets (+)/(-)													1	-1	1	0	3*	-1	1	0				
Protection against devaluation (+)																								
Ownership limits (-)					2/0	2	0	0	2	0	1	0	2*	1	1	0	3*	2	1	5				
Merger limits (-)																	4	3	1	5				
Remittance limits (-)									2	0	1	0	3	2	1	0								
Trade Related:																								
Tariff exempt R & D (+)									2	0	1	0	2*	1	1	0	2*	1	1	0				
Tariff exempt exports (+)																								
Export tax credits (+)													3*	2	1	0								
Export financing (+)													3*	2	1	0	1	1	1	0				
Export guarantees (+)													3*	2	1	0								

280

Criterion	1	2	3	4	5
Export tax allowance (+)				3* 2 1 0	
Tariff protection (+)	1 0 0 0		1* 0 1 0	4 3 1 0	5 4 1 0
Export requirement (+)				2 1 1 0	
Input-Related:					
Feedstock subsidy (+)********	3/0 3 0 0	5* 0 1 0			3* 2 1 0
Energy subsidy (+)		3* 0 1 0			
Wage subsidy (+)		2* 0 1 0			
Curtailed strikes (+)					1* 1 1 0
High quality, low cost labor (+)	1 1 0 0			1* 1 1 0	
Wage controls (+)					
Tax exempt expatriates (+)					2 1 1 0
Job creation (+)					2 1 1 0
Input tax deduction (+)					2 1 1 0
Local labor requirement (-)	1 0 0 0	1* 1 0 0	2 0 1 0		2 1 1 0
Local content requirement (-)			1 0 1 0		2 1 1 0
Miscellaneous:					
Management control (+)/(-)	1 +1 1 0	1* -1 0 0			3* -2 1 5
Oil entitlements (+)/(-)		1* 1 0 0	4* 0 1 0		2 1 1 0
R & D (+)	1* 1 0 0		1* 0 1 0		4 2 1 0
No government competition (+)					
Restricted markets (+)					
Environmental tolerance (+)					
Price controls (-)				3 2 1 3	3 2 1 3
Profit formulae (-)				3 2 1 3	3 2 1 3
Plant site restrictions (-)				2 2 4 0	2 2 4 0
Closed industries (-)					
Summary criteria:					
Net effect: IRR	1 1 1 0	2 2 0 0	4 0 1 0	3 2 2 0	5 4 3 5
Net effect: Rental cost of capital	0 0 0 0	3 3 0 0	3 0 1 0	2 1 1 0	2 1 1 0
Net effect: Cost of labor	0 0 0 0	1 1 0 0	1 0 1 0	1 1 1 0	1 1 1 0
Total net impact	1	4	4	3	5

Table 5-10, continued

Decision Criteria	7 Mexico III N/A				8 Mexico III 56,550				9 Belgium III N/A				10 Singapore III 30,000				11 Colombia III 20,000				12 Sri Lanka III 2,170			
	A	B	C	D	A	B	C	D	A	B	C	D	A	B	C	D	A	B	C	D	A	B	C	D
Capital-Related:																								
Tax exempt R & D (+)													3*	3	1	3								
Tax holidays (+)													3*	3	1	3					3	1	1	0
Accelerated depreciation (+)	1	1	4	4					2	2	2		2*	2	1	2								
Investment tax credit (+)					1	1	4	4																
Development area (+)																	2*	2	2	2	4*	1	1	0
Key industry (+)																	2*	2	2	2				
Excess profits tax (+)									2	2	2													
Cash grants (+)																								
Direct subsidies (+)																								
Concessionary financing (+)													2*	1	1	2	0*	0	0	0				
Loan guarantees (+)																								
Access to capital markets (+)/(-)																								
Protection against devaluation (+)																								
Ownership limits (-)	1	1	1	1	1	1	1	1									3	3	1	3	4	3	1	0
Merger limits (-)																								
Remittance limits (-)	1	1	1	1	1	1	1	1									3	3	1	3	3	1	1	0
Trade-Related:																								
Tariff exempt R & D (+)													2	1	1	2	2	2	1	2	3*	1	1	0
Tariff exempt exports (+)													2	1	1	2	2	2	1	2				
Export tax credits (+)																	2	2	1	2				
Export financing (+)													1	1	1	1	1	1	1	1				
Export guarantees (+)													1	1	1	1	1	1	1	1				

282

Export tax allowance (+)	2 1 1 2
Tariff protection (+)	5 5 5 5 5 5 5 5 3 3 1 3
Export requirement (+)	1 1 1 1 1 1 4 4
Input-Related:	
Feedstock subsidy (+)********	1 1 1 1 1 1 5 5 1 1 4 4
Energy subsidy (+)	1 1 1 1 1 1 4 4 1 1 4 4
Wage subsidy (+)	1 1 1 1 1 1 4 4
Curtailed strikes (+)	1 1 1 1 1* 1 0
High quality, low cost labor (+)	2 1 1 0
Wage controls (+)	
Tax exempt expatriates (+)	
Job creation (+)	
Input tax deduction (+)	
Local labor requirement (-)	2 1 1 0
Local content requirement (-)	
Miscellaneous:	
Management control (+)/(-)	3 -1 1 0 3 -3 1 3
Oil entitlements (+)/(-)	
R & D (+)	
No government competition (+)	
Restricted markets (+)	?* ? ? 2 3 1 3
Environmental tolerance (+)	
Price controls (-)	
Profit formulae (-)	
Plant site restrictions (-)	
Closed industries (-)	0 0 0 0
Summary criteria:	
Net effect: IRR	5 5 2 2 2 2 2 2 1 2 2 1 2 2 1 1 0
Net effect: Rental cost of capital	3 3 1 1 3 1 2 2 1 2 1 1 1 2 1 1 0
Net effect: Cost of labor	1 1 0 0 0 0 0 0 0 1 1 1 1 1 1 1 0
Total net impact	5 5 2 2 2

Continued

283

Table 5-10, continued

Decision Criteria	Case Number 13 Mexico III N/A A	B	C	D	Case Number 14 Pakistan IV 89,700 A	B	C	D	Case Number 15 Brazil II N/A A	B	C	D
Capital-Related:												
Tax exempt R & D (+)									2*	0	3	0
Tax holidays (+)					3	2	1	2				
Accelerated depreciation (+)					2	2	1	3				
Investment tax credit (+)												
Development area (+)												
Key industry (+)												
Excess profits tax (+)					4	3	1	5				
Cash grants (+)												
Direct subsidies (+)												
Concessionary financing (+)									2*	0	3	0
Loan guarantees (+)												
Access to capital markets (+)/(-)												
Protection against devaluation (+)					3	2	1	5				
Ownership limits (-)									2	0	2	0
Merger limits (-)												
Remittance limits (-)	2	2	1	1					3	0	5	0
Trade Related:												
Tariff exempt R & D (+)					2	2	1	2	2	0	3	0
Tariff exempt exports (+)												
Export tax credits (+)												
Export financing (+)									2	0	3	0
Export guarantees (+)												

Key to symbols:

(*)   Indicates discretionary, otherwise statutory

Decision criteria:
- (A) Whether to invest
- (B) Invest in country of first choice or alternative
- (C) Where to locate within country
- (D) Whether to expand

Impact on decisions:
- (0) Not applicable
- (1) Unimportant
- (2) Negligibly important
- (3) Moderately important
- (4) Very important
- (5) Crucial

Criterion			
Export tax allowance (+)			
Tariff protection (+)	5 5 1 5	4* 4 1 4	3 0 3 0
Export requirement (+)			
Input-Related:			
Feedstock subsidy (+)********		3* 2 1 4	2 0 2 0
Energy subsidy (+)			
Wage subsidy (+)			
Curtailed strikes (+)			
High quality, low cost labor (+)	2 2 4 1		
Wage controls (+)			
Tax exempt expatriates (+)			
Job creation (+)			
Input tax deduction (+)			
Local labor requirement (-)			
Local content requirement (-)			2 0 2 0
Miscellaneous:			
Management control (+)/(-)	1 -1 1 1		
Oil entitlements (+)/(-)			
R & D (+)			
No government competition (+)			
Restricted markets (+)			
Environmental tolerance (+)			
Price controls (-)	5* 2 1 5	5 2 1 5	
Profit formulae (-)	5* 2 1 5		
Plant site restrictions (-)			
Closed industries (-)			3 0 3 0
Summary criteria:			
Net effect: IRR	1 1 1 1	5 2 1 5	4 0 5 0
Net effect: Rental cost of capital	1 1 1 1	2 1 1 2	3 0 3 0
Net effect: Cost of labor	1 1 1 1	1 1 1 1	2 0 2 0
Total net impact	1	5	5

intrinsically equal. In either case there may result a bias in the international location of production and the pattern of international trade in petrochemicals, but the efficiency costs can differ substantially. The data includes all incentives and performance requirements that were operative; we have attempted in the analytic sections to distinguish among three possibilities.

First, a country can offer a package of incentives and performance requirements or disincentives that constitute a net-incentive package in the hope of attracting projects within its borders. Any consequent misallocation of resources (in comparison with some Smithian world) depends upon the degree to which the site actually chosen is inferior (and the inferiority offset by the (net) incentives). There may also be income-distributional repercussions. If a host country is prepared to accept a lower set of direct benefits from the MNC in order to have the project located within its borders and to achieve such positive externalities as may exist, distributional problems do not arise. However, if countries compete with each other in order to have the project located within their borders, then the income-distributional effects can be identified as existing between MNCs as a group and host countries in general. When packages of incentives are offered on intranational, regional grounds, they do not strictly fall within the terms of the study that emphasizes internationality. However, the terms of the study can embrace incentive packages within a regional customs area or common market, where competition for a project takes place among national members of the bloc.

Second, a package of (net) disincentives or performance requirements can indicate that a country has a natural advantage as a host for petrochemical investments of a particular kind and is using PRs to ensure that the gains from its advantages accrue to it rather than the MNC. Performance requirements and disincentives serve to extract the rent for the host country. Such packages will ordinarily not affect the international location of the investment unless a host country accidentally sets the net cost of the package too high. If the package is designed merely to ensure that economic rents remain with the host country, they will not affect the international location although they may be seen as doing so. This strategy usually relates to countries with locally available natural resources.

Third, a country may offer a complex package of investment incentives *and* disincentives or performance requirements that are effectively almost neutral in their overall impact on the project's expected rate of return. Such packages are, presumably, designed to ensure that the host country actually receives certain perceived benefits from the project that it deems to be particularly important, and the host is willing to pay for that assurance in terms of offsetting investment incentives. Because it is impossible to develop standard packages of this kind that are neutral with respect to all individual projects, their existence may very well influence the international location of productive capacity. This tripartite distinction can be used to examine the individual groups of projects separated by the level of the product.

Primary Petrochemicals

Three such projects were examined, cases 1, 2, and 3. One of these is located in North America, where only one minor performance requirement was involved and where the effects of IIs and PRs appear to be negligible. The decision to invest there was made in a competition between four alternative sites and was decided by commercial criteria. If other sites did in fact offer any incentives, they were completely inadequate to offset the natural resource cost advantages that characterize the North American site. In this decision the choice of site in terms of the corporation's existing capacity and the markets in which fast demand growth was anticipated were very important.

Cases 2 and 3 refer to very large installations in one country in the Middle East. Case 2 is solely a primary petrochemical project, and case 3 involves second-level and third-level (3A) products as well. Total capital expenditures in project 3 are $1 billion compared to $500 million in case 2. Because it is government policy to establish a standard set of investment incentives and performance requirements, the two can be considered together. The government objective is to utilize indigenous natural resources and to develop downstream industries in addition to primary product capacity. The company involved in case 2 is already considering a joint venture involving a second-level product using its first-level capacity as an input. The country offers a particular and complex mix of natural advantages, as well as some severe disadvantages. The package of investment incentives and performance requirements, while favorable on balance, is a complex mixture of incentives but with a large dose of performance requirements introduced to ensure that the total project profile conforms to long-run development goals.

The package of IIs must overcome the very large capital costs involved, including the provision of much infrastructure. As a yardstick, a factor of two can be used to estimate the capital requirements involved in the Middle Eastern country petrochemical projects as compared with those in North America. Cases 1 and 2 involve a virtually identical plant, and yet double the capital outlays are involved in case 2. The II package must also overcome the fact that virtually all of the product must be exported (local markets are likely to be insignificant) and that transportation costs of output will be substantial. There is also a tacit acknowledgement of additional costs and political risk deriving from the strict observance of Islamic codes of behavior and the potentially unstable conditions in the region.

The local advantages involved the very low cost of feedstock (case 2 calculates this to be one-seventh of the comparable price in case 1) — a *natural* advantage rather than a subsidy. At present, gas is largely being flared, and it is this gas that will constitute the petrochemical feedstock. Because the gas (in case 2) is not transportable, it has no alternative commercial outlet, and its opportunity cost is effectively zero. The price of gas charged to the petrochemical complex represents a fair return on the costs of collection, processing, and delivery to the plant. Against this background of natural advantage and disadvantages, the II/PR package sets its sights on local development. It emphasizes heavily the natural advantage in feedstock and the tactical advantage of locating capacity there — the question is not only, "On what terms?" but also, "Will my corporation be excluded if I fail to invest now?"

The incentive package emphasizes subsidized loans to the new venture. In case 2, half of the total capital outlay is provided at a nominal rate of interest. This loan has to be paid off quickly out of profits, but the foreign partners have their exposure and their degree of commitment significantly reduced. The arithmetic suggests that the loan subsidy is simply "paying for" the infrastructure.

In addition, the joint-venture conditions require that a government corporation own 50 percent of the equity. This means that the foreign investors can be rewarded by relatively high rates of return on equity capital because the host country will share equally in such profits. There is, thus, no need to supply feedstocks at more than cost.

The incentive package also effectively acknowledges the local disadvantages in technology, management skills, and marketing channels. The role of the foreign partners is to provide these resources and, more importantly, to develop local abilities in these areas. In case 2, the contract calls for complete indigenization of employment within five years, and the government corporation is expected to take over the marketing responsibilities within seven years.

The package of incentives and performance requirements contains one unusual dimension. In both cases 2 and 3, the foreign partners were offered an entitlement to buy a certain volume of oil at the posted (official) price. Because the host country is the low-price supplier within the cartel, the entitlements might be expected to have significant monetary value if the spot crude oil price exceeds the posted price. However, the entitlement program has proved to be a two-edged sword. The terms of the entitlement require that the oil be purchased steadily (at the entitlement rate) and that the entitlement will lapse if these purchases are not made. During much of 1981 and 1982, the posted price (while the lowest in the cartel) was substantially above the price in the depressed spot market, so the entitlement has proved a blessing to the government and a large net cost to the foreign partners. The uncertainty involved also presented the foreign partners with a difficult technical problem concerning how the entitlement should be factored into calculations of the project's internal rate of return.[11]

In cases 2 and 3, the II/PR package was clearly very important, and its main impact was to offset the inherent disadvantages of building capacity in the Middle East. The package "clears the way" for the natural competitive advantage of feedstock availability to exert itself. In effect, the government is trading off some of their pure rent in feedstock availability in order to avail themselves of the necessary technology. If the trade-off were exact and the natural resources still earned an economic rent, then the incentives may be said to have had a positive effect on world welfare.

Four of the projects examined (cases 4 through 6 and case 15) involve production of second-level petrochemicals (intermediates). Each of these projects has a vertical-integration dimension that will have affected the investment. In cases 4 and 15 in the same Latin American country, second-level petrochemical plants were located in a backward region: one of these was tied into third-level plants in another region that take a significant proportion of its output. In case 5 (in Asia) the investing corporation has 100 percent equity in a caustic soda (nonpetrochemical) with plant location severely circumscribed by the need to integrate the facility with surplus ethylene production from Great Britain.

In cases 4, 5, and 15, one incentive was prerequisite to investments being made. This incentive consists of assured, high level of effective protection of the plant's output from import competition. The relatively small-scale plants designed for national markets cannot generally endure competition from world-scale plants.

In cases 4 and 15, the only other incentives provided are conditional: incentives on exports and financial incentives for the second-level plants in the underdeveloped region of the country. As an offset to the protection of the home market, a list of disincentives or PRs is imposed. One disincentive that may be unintentional is the cost of continuous negotiation with the government bureaucracy on price controls and matters under the jurisdiction of the planning commission and other national authorities.

Whatever the costs of government regulation and compliance in the Latin American country, they pale into insignificance compared with the costs of joint ventureship with the public sector in case 5. Here the problems have proven sufficiently intractable since the confrontation stage has been reached. The battery of incentives (including home-market protection) is fairly standard for the country, but they have not been sufficient to prevent the investing corporation from incurring sizeable operating losses (figured at $60 million over the most recent two years). This investment has proved to be costly indeed — it demonstrates the dangers of underestimating the disincentives inherent in governmental participation that may indeed not be neutral with respect to foreign companies.[12]

In case 6, the investment incentives were strictly local and affected the international location decisions only in the sense that localities from different member-states of the EC were in competition with one another.

Cases 7 through 14 involve third-level products. These have been subdivided into those products that form inputs into another industry and require a manufacturing process before they are usable (3A) and those petrochemical products that are directly usable (3B). Cases 7, 8, 9, and 10 are type 3A investments. All are market oriented.

Cases 7 and 8 in another Latin American country rely on the effective protection of the local market for the viability of the plants located there. In both cases, the U.S. manufacturing companies had existing joint-venture partners with whom relations were better than satisfactory, so the diluted ownership was of no consequence. Tax-credit incentives were tied to the location of the production unit in a backward area or chemical-industry development zone. For such locations, the incentives were generous and included a subsidy of electric power and feedstock costs dependent upon meeting a performance requirement that 25 percent of output would be exported for three years. Both companies decided to take advantage of the regional incentives offered. It is fair to say that the feedstock and energy subsidies were important contributors to the decision. Because of the country's membership in a Latin American regional trade association and the subsidies, the export requirement was not seen as burdensome. In addition, both corporations had global marketing organizations and, *in extremis*, could have used these linkages to dispose profitably of the relatively small volume of exports to which they had committed themselves. The incentive package itself was not an international influence on location, but it does have implications for the pattern of international trade.

Project 9 is located in the European Community. The plant is a small-scale multiproduct factory and is designed to provide an onshore supply base for European customers. This was deemed necessary if market share was to be enhanced significantly. This same view was also expressed in reference to case 6 — that a local source of supply was necessary if the firm was to be anything other than a third or fourth supplier. The incentives obtained in case 9 were "backward-area incentives." They included cash grants, accelerated depreciation, and a labor-training grant. There were no performance requirements. The labor training grant was seen as bringing the local labor supply up to the required standard and was not entered in the computation of the internal rate of return. This particular investment is strategic, in the sense that its computed IRR was barely acceptable. Although the IRR computation was unduly conservative in terms of sales forecasts, the corporation was most directly concerned with establishing itself onshore in Europe. The incentive package was available for serveral sites and with only minor differences — from among these subsidized sites in different countries, the choice was made on commercial grounds. The incentives, thus, seem to have no extraregional effect and may merely have affected the location decision within the EC.

Project 10 is also market oriented toward a region (ASEAN) and generally Asian-Pacific. This project is interesting because it was undertaken by a corporation whose planners are not permitted to take tax or other incentives into account in evaluating prospective investments. The incentives that were given are standard for the country, but of little apparent influence in the decision. The product is usually custom developed for users and has a high R & D (and value-added) content. The project was located in the Asian country because the Pacific Rim countries were seen as having high growth potential, and it is the only plant of its kind in ASEAN. Very important to the location of this facility — which does not conduct chemical transformations but rather uses inputs from refineries and petrochemical plants in the area and in the United States — is the freedom to import inputs at low or zero duty.

Projects 11 through 14 involve type 3B products, that is, petrochemical products that are generally used directly. All of these are market oriented. Projects 12, 13, and 14 are directed at a national market and Project 11 at a regional market.

Project 11 is located in an Andean country and, therefore, has export potential throughout ANCOM on a preferential basis as well as being able to fit into its parent's worldwide sales network. The product is a propriety version of a standard fungicide. It has undergone some pressure in the world market recently because of concern with its environmental impact as well as from the development of new, more powerful fungicides. The location of the plant was made after active consideration of other sites (including one in Asia). The decision was based largely on the speed with which the new capacity could be added and the preexistence of an active plant in Colombia with adjacent land available. Both the old and the new plants are 100 percent owned, the second plant falling under ANCOM rules and requiring an 80 percent export commitment to warrant 100 percent ownership. The Colombian authorities have been satisfied with a best-efforts performance and have not interpreted the 80 percent rule literally. The role of incentives in this decision was not of great importance. The preexistence of a twin plant and the implications of that arrangement for the firm's ability to bring the new capacity on-stream quickly were probably crucial. The 80 percent export commitment could be met — particularly because it was not necessary for the original plant (which predated ANCOM) to export in order to retain 100 percent ownership. An important incentive was the choice between export tax credits and a duty exemption on imported raw materials used for reexport. This incentive is standard and serves, effectively, to underscore the other conditions that encourage exports. The performance requirements that affect this project are standard ANCOM conditions. Limits on the remittance of funds is probably the most important single disincentive.

Cases 12, 13, and 14 are all oriented toward the host-country market. Case 12 is a proposed, strictly local operation in a small Asian country. A presence in the country is desired by the firm for purposes of corporate strategy — mainly to reestablish itself in South Asia. The operation also has the benefit of being able to serve as a downstream customer for the firm's refineries in Singapore and the Arabian Gulf. The incentives are secondary to the strategic considerations, but the venture (if successfully negotiated) should provide a satisfactory rate of return. The incentives are essentially duty-free imports of capital equipment and raw materials. These incentives are ensured by the presence of a government corporation as the joint-venture partner. Disincentives include the required use of local managers and the bureaucratic complexity of doing business in that country. The dangers of a repetition of the experience encountered in case 5 are quite possible, except that this venture is considerably smaller and less complex and that the drift of the local political and economic scene seems to be away from socialism — if it is changing at all. Note that this venture has a potential three- to four-year payback of invested capital, and earnings remittances are ensured under a bilateral agreement.

Case 13 is the cousin of case 7. It is a third-level petrochemical plant located in the same Latin American country and is completely dependent upon the protection of the market from imported competitive goods. This case is different in that it was located *away from* the backward areas and, therefore, actively renounced the associated incentive package. The product has a higher value-added than case 7 and requires more skilled labor. Because of these aspects, the incentive package was less attractive, and the questionable quality of the labor in the backward area was a strong disincentive against locating there. The plant also had the advantage of being built adjacent to an existing plant and, in this way, significantly reducing the capital cost of plant construction. Both cases 7 and 14 were decisions made by the same joint-venture partnership, and both were *expansions* of existing production capacity.

Case 14 is located in South Asia. This project is not a strong commercial success by virtue of government fixing of output and raw material prices, with lags in the adjustment of the former — the project is caught in a tight profits squeeze. Additional problems relate to the valuation of capital with a depreciating local currency and the impossibility of adding retained earnings to the capital base for purposes of profit calculation. Because the government wants the project to double its capacity, and because new equity would be needed for such an expansion, these questions are coming to a head. The disincentives to expansion are significant. Among these the problem of lagged adjustment under a set maximum return on equity for the plant, reinforced by price controls on the input and the output, is of primary importance. Moreover, the government has not honored the incentives allowed at the original time of development.

Incentive Analysis

We now need to isolate those investments described in the previous section in which different sets of incentives might have affected the decision to make the investment (decision A on the summary project data sheet) or to make the investment in the ultimate host country (decision B). It follows from the relative lack of freedom in plant location in the petrochemical industry that incentives are likely to have to induce rather large changes in project economies if they are to dominate commercial considerations.

In Group I (primary petrochemicals), the decision to invest in the Middle Eastern country could have been negated had no incentives been offered. The cost of infrastructure and the political risk were probably both high enough that the supply of feedstock at cost would not have been a sufficient magnet. Because no international chemical firm or consortium would build a primary petrochemical plant smaller than world scale, the projects would probably have lapsed had the government not generated a very astute package of incentives and requirements. Nor would these projects likely have been made in other countries at this time — particularly in view of overcapacity in commodity (primary) petrochemicals.

In Group II (petrochemical intermediates), the failure of the governments in cases 4, 5, and 15 to offer effective protection against imports would have negated the projects. The markets would have been supplied with products from world-scale facilities in other parts of the world. It is possible that strict packages of performance requirements could have resulted in a decision *not* to invest, but it is difficult to determine the critical margin. In case 15, it seems unlikely that the investment would have been made without the depressed-area incentive package. In case 5, the firm's difficulties with host government and its representatives are such that the decision to invest probably would not have been made had the corporation known the level of disincentives it was eventually to face. Because the firm has made the confrontation public — and, indeed, has withdrawn from the country — other MNCs considering investing in the country may be discouraged or at least try to exact a countervailing group of additional incentives and/or assurances. In other words, the true disincentives in this case were not revealed (the cost of joint ownership depends heavily on the harmony of the working relationship), and general recognition of the host government's attitude toward foreign investment may well stifle future capital inflows. Scale was not a variable in this case insofar as incentives were concerned. Project 6 would have been unaffected by any change in investment incentives.

Changes in incentives for projects in Group 3A (cases 7-10) — short of withdrawing the effectively blockaded protection against imports in Mexico for cases 7 and 8 — would not have affected any of the four projects. Cases 7 and 8 were completely market oriented. Case 9 was also completely market oriented (although the location of the facility within the EC could have been changed), and the firm in case 10 did not include incentives in its computation of the project's ROI. However, the omission of duty-free imports of raw materials from the incentive package could not be eliminated from the computation of ROI, so the decision could have been affected by an adverse change in the package.

Finally, Group III B (final petrochemical products), with the exception of case 11, are all market oriented. A reduction in incentives would have had an effect only if it had covered the degree of protection of the host-country market. Note that in case 14, the ROI was effectively prearranged, and, therefore, incentives had little effect on the desirability of the investment unless the rules of the game were changed or unless they affect capacity utilization. This did in fact turn out to be a problem. In case 11, the requirement for fast development of the additional capacity dominated the decision, but that could have been reversed by the elimination of the 100 percent ownership for export-oriented enterprises and possibly the export tax credits.

On the question of whether a more favorable package of incentives offered by other countries would have swayed petrochemical plant-siting decision in their favor, the evidence is necessarily vague. A failure to carry out a commitment in any one country may be expected to lead to an investment somewhere else, though this relationship may not apply to the two investments in the Middle East. Whether or not the replacement expenditures would have been in the same product or segment of the industry is not easy to determine because of the market orientation of many of the investments — in the absence of the investments described here, the host-country markets would have been supplied by exports from other plants where the needed capacity may well have been readily available. Only the investments designed to serve regional blocs would be subject to relocation internationally as a result of improved incentive packages offered by other countries.

The general conclusion must be that the petrochemical industry is so oriented toward feedstock availability, vertical integration, and market outlets that the decisions to invest (decision A) may be sensitive to incentive packages but that international location (decision B) is not sensitive to relative incentive packages except in regional blocs.

Performance Requirement Analysis

Separate analysis of the role of performance requirements on decisions A and B is difficult in the sense that, as indicated above, the tripartite distinction considers the net II/PR package to be the crucial issue in investment decisions in the industry. Partial analysis can, therefore, be misleading and must be conducted on the assumption that no offsetting incentive is introduced (or eliminated) when a performance requirement is strengthened (or eased).

Cases 2 and 3 certainly required net incentive packages as did those requiring high effective rates of protection. Additional performance requirements would have, almost of necessity, required the introduction of offsetting incentives. Any market-oriented investment can be negated by more severe performance requirements, particularly if they are seen as having a substantial negative impact on profits or profit repatriation. Investments aimed at regional markets could have been relocated among the member countries in response to more severe performance requirements imposed by individual countries or completely negated by an escalation of regional performance requirements. Like nontariff barriers, the complexity and subtlety of performance requirements are limited only by the imagination of politicians, bureaucrats, and economists.

Experience with IIs and PRs in the Petrochemical Industry

The experience with governments and governmental agencies is best examined in terms of the cases where nonstandardized packages were (or are being) negotiated or where IIs or PRs were effectively changed during the life of the investment. There can be no doubt that host countries are becoming more sophisticated in negotiations with multinationals and recognize the mutuality of needs and returns. Bargaining *ex ante* is now conducted on a higher level of complexity — see case 12 where a requirement that all managers be local caused one major firm to withdraw from consideration.

Experience in some countries has shown that governments can raise performance requirements or disincentives after the investment has been made. Cases in point are case 5, case 4, and case 14. If these increases in PRs are deliberate, then they and the bureaucratic burden that may fall equally on foreign subsidiaries and on host-country concerns become incidental intensifications of investment disincentives.

In contrast, the government in case 11 has shown a degree of flexibility in interpreting the ANCOM requirement that 80 percent of output be devoted to exports for 100 percent foreign ownership to be maintained. The worldwide recession/depression in petrochemical products coupled with the problems facing the product in question argue that such flexibility is warranted.

The Implications of Investment Incentives and Performance Requirements for the Pattern of International Trade in Petrochemicals

There can be little doubt that the IIs and PRs encountered in the 15 cases reported here do indeed affect the pattern of world trade in and production of petrochemicals and that much of any distortion in these patterns that has been generated can be traced to the influence of net investment incentives incorporated in each II/PR package. But because, with the possible exception of case 9, instances in which investment incentives have influenced the pattern of international trade involve developing nations, and because developing countries are often accorded special and differential treatment in matters pertaining to commercial policies, any distortion to world trade patterns must be assessed against the different standards that are currently applied to developing countries, rather than against some abstract perfectly competitive world. In this connection, it is useful in an analysis of trade patterns to consider regions (for example, customs unions) as single "countries."

Clearly the most important single incentive affecting the location of productive capacity is the blockading of the home market from imports produced in world-scale plants. This incentive alone accounts for the role of IIs and PRs in the establishment of plants in eight cases (4, 5, 7, 8, 11, 13, 14, and 15). In addition to the effective blocking of host-country market, access to imports and export incentives and/or requirements are applicable in cases 7, 8, and 11.

Developing nations are accorded special and differential treatment under (and outside) the GATT, and even though the establishment of infant industries behind tariff walls may not be explicitly condoned by the international trading rules, it is something that is tacitly accepted. It may well be that because of the foreign involvement in infant industries, the level of protection is the more likely to be reduced when competitive conditions permit the local production facility to be viable in the face of international competition. It might, of course, be argued that the increase in local demand over production capabilities of a minimum-size plant will result in a locally owned plant being erected and that protection will continue. In either event, it is doubtful that the incentive package will have done much more than accelerate the establishment of a protected plant in the individual developing countries. Moreover, because the incentive package may have expedited the transfer of technology, there is an argument to be made that its overall welfare effect (in a second-best context) is favorable.

The creation of export subsidies (cases 7, 8, and 11) as a part of the incentive package does not seem to contravene the spirit of the Tokyo Round.[13] In the subsidies code of the Tokyo Round, developing countries are exempted from the general ban on export subsidies, provided that they agree to "reduce or eliminate export subsidies" when they are no longer necessary. Further, developing countries must agree that their export subsidies will not be used in a manner that results in adverse effects on the trade or production of another signatory country. None of the three examples of export subsidization is likely to contravene this set of circumstances – in one Latin American country export requirements in return for the feedstock subsidy are only of short duration, and the Andean market country is not big enough to bring about serious trade disruption outside ANCOM.

The impact of the petrochemical production in the Middle East country on world trade patterns cannot be shown to be detrimental to world welfare provided that the feedstock is, in fact, charged for at collection costs (including a fair rate of return to capital) and provided that the subsidized loan is merely an offset to inclusion of large infrastructural requirements in project capitalization. In fact, if the opportunity use of the feedstock is simply flaring, then world welfare is improved by harnessing this resource. If the gas would otherwise be reticulated, the benefits are simply brought forward in time. That the transportation of the natural gas is exceedingly costly relative to the cost of transporting the primary petrochemical suggests that the two ventures are simply extreme examples of what has been called "modified free trade."[14]

Case 9 involves the creation of a subsidiary within the EC in order to improve the firm's share of the market. On purely commercial grounds, the investment would be marginal (at least) without the backward-area incentive package. The project will displace exports from the United States, and, if scale or natural endowment advantages afford a comparative advantage to the United States in these products, the incentives might be thought to have had some distorting effect on world trade patterns. There is certainly a *prima facie* argument to this effect. That argument could be countered by the allegation that the increased share of European markets that may be acquired as a result of the creation of local capacity could actually increase imports from the United States because the production of the European subsidiary will be augmented where necessary from the United States. Another counterargument might impugn the validity of static welfare criteria operating in a certain world for this case because its role is to reduce the uncertainties inherent in international trade conducted in accord with comparative advantage.

The use of net investment incentive packages (that is, including performance requirements) does not seriously distort the pattern of world trade in petrochemicals from that which might be generated by a free-trade regime — approximately modified by concerns for resources wasted because of the impracticalities of transportation and by a concern with special and differential treatment for developing nations as far as infant-industry tariffs and minor export subsidies are concerned.

CONCLUSIONS

The study appears to indicate that the petrochemical industry is not indifferent to investment incentives and performance requirements, but that, with one important exception, investment plans are to an overwhelming degree dominated by other factors. The one incentive that seems always to be necessary for investments where small-scale plants are required to service relatively limited markets is that the market be effectively protected from import competition and that the firm be assured that such protection will continue. The importance of this incentive may be attributed in large measure to the scope for economies of large-scale production and international differences in raw-material costs that is characteristic of the petrochemical industry. The importance of this particular investment incentive having been acknowledged, the behavior of investment planners in the industry appears to be dominated by three factors: accepted long-run corporate strategy; feedstock availability and cost for first-level investments; and the market orientation that preoccupies planners with third-level investments.

Corporate Strategy

This consideration seems to be a major force in international investment planning in the industry. Particularly for first-level investments, undertakings generally involve very large commitments of capital and personnel, and, for this reason alone, the investments must be analyzed in terms of the long-run global strategy of the firm. Moreover, the petrochemical industry is one that achieves much of its success through the incorporation of economies of vertical integration and production sharing. Perhaps more than in most other industries, firms must concern themselves with the linkage between existing capacity and additions to capacity in both a product-mix dimension and a geographic dimension.

Cases 1 and 2 indicate the importance of the product-leadership dimension of strategy for major, primary-level petrochemical investment decisions. The first (case 1) was undertaken in response to a perceived need of additional capacity and to "fill a window" in the firm's supply logistics in ethylene. The corporation considers itself a world leader in the production and marketing of this particular primary petrochemical, and, in the investment reported in case 1, the preservation of market position was an important consideration. Once the decision had been made, the location of the additional capacity was based on straightforward economic considerations; the influence of investment incentives and performance requirements was negligible. In case 2, the importance of maintaining the firm's market position was a very influential factor in the decision. It seemed clear that the host country planned to make use of its natural gas and that there was an active drive toward downstream value-added. Therefore, a world-scale plant producing the primary petrochemical involved was virtually certain to be created — a plant that would represent a significant addition to world capacity. The corporation could not easily envisage itself being excluded from a project of this importance simply because a failure to take part in the creation of the additional, highly competitive capacity would inevitably weaken the corporation's position in the world market. Investment incentives and performance requirements were indeed taken into account in the computation of the project's assessed profitability. Indeed, in case 2 the data show that there was a limit to the potential capital commitment on the part of the firm, and the investment incentives did bring the venture comfortably within that

limit. Nonetheless, it is a fair assessment to consider strategic considerations as being the primary factor in both the case 1 and case 2
investments.

The importance of geographic-mix factors is demonstrated in
cases 6 and 12. In case 12, the decision was based almost completely
on a long-run strategy involving reestablishing presence in a particular
regional market. The project is commercially feasible in its own right,
and all incentives that were available were accepted yet were not
decisive. This project was also influenced by the fact that it provided
an outlet for an upstream plant affiliated with the firm and located
in the same region.

Case 6 exhibits even more strongly the role of corporate strategy.
Here the company was implementing a "grand design" embarked
upon 16 years earlier and already implemented to the extent that
three other sites had been acquired and put into production — a
fourth site had been acquired to serve as a regional administrative
headquarters. This particular decision is similar to case 1 in the sense
that the expansion of capacity was decided upon first. The location
decision was subsequently made on the basis of normal commercial
criteria, including any performance requirements and investment
incentives that might be involved. But the limits of the location of
the plant were fixed (and fixed irrevocably) *ex ante* and completely
independently of any consideration of incentives or performance
requirements. Fundamental to this decision was the grand design,
together with the need to integrate the new plant with excess capacity of a first-level petrochemical facility in the home country. This
integration of plants and the economics of such integration set the
locational limits on the new investment.

A third aspect of corporate strategy is evident in case 4, where
four production units are located in the same country. These investments are deliberately designed to facilitate vertical integration.
The corporation stated explicitly that it views the operations in
the country as a "country commitment" rather than a "project
commitment."

The economies of vertical integration (Coase-type economies)
are of more than usual importance in the petrochemical industry
and play an important strategic role in investment planning. Two
factors contributing to the greater importance of this effect for
petrochemical firms merit explicit mention. First, the importance of
economies of scale in the industry implies a need for very large-scale

production units. The sheer size of these units and sector-specific capital imply a vulnerability to demand recession. Vertical integration in downstream operations offers a potential degree of stability in product demand that can reduce variability of revenues. Second, there is the product specificity of some firms' proprietary technology. Frequently a major corporation with a special concern for a group of petrochemical products will apply a large proportion of its research and development budget to the creation of products and processes involving the use of members of the product group. These products and processes may involve the development of new chemicals with quite individualistic qualities or the need for particular forms of quality control in upstream processes.

Feedstock Availability

The availability and cost of feedstocks are extremely important, particularly so in primary petrochemicals. As a rule of thumb in the industry, the value-added increases with the level of product. Obviously, the sensitivity of investment decisions to incentives in the form of feedstock subsidies decreases as the level of product increases. This is confirmed in cases 7 and 13, where parallel combinations of incentives and performance requirements — and background conditions within the investing firm — resulted in acceptance of the package for one project and its disregard in the companion project. This was a clear example of the relative importance of the cost of subsidized inputs in final product cost, although other factors did have some bearing on the decision.

It is not easy to distinguish between the relative importance of an assured supply of feedstock and a subsidized price of feedstock. Promises of subsidy are usually granted *sine die*, but that does not mean forever. To quote one executive: "What the government giveth, the government can take away." It is reasonable to assume that the assured supply is more reliable than any price incentive and, therefore, potentially more important in first-level projects in particular. A nation is virtually always in need of customers for its supply of natural resources, but the need to subsidize may depend upon market conditions. The higher the extent of effective subsidization, the greater the firm's exposure to substantial risk, and this too needs to be factored into investment decisions.

A related problem is the difficulty of determining whether a subsidy is actually in force even when the price of feedstock supplied to the project is low. In cases 7 and 14, the feedstock was subsidized because the price was quoted as a percentage of the arm's-length price. In case 2, the question is moot. The key here is the difference between the opportunity outlet for the resource and the price charged to the project. The investing firm estimated that the opportunity outlet of the resource was zero — the gas would be flared — and that the price charged to the project is effectively the cost of harnessing the resource and delivering it. Assuming that the price charged to the project is indeed a cost figure inclusive of a fair or market rate of return on invested capital, no subsidy of the feedstock exists. The host government gains from its mandated half-share in the equity of the project. Moreover, the venture's commercial viability is dependent upon feedstock being available at the quoted price as one factor offsetting the much higher costs for certain aspects of the project that would have been encountered in other locations. The crucial datum here is, of course, the internal rate of return that was adequate but not excitingly intramarginal — the IRR in case 2 was about equal to that in case 1, where virtually no incentives were obtained. Case 3 exhibits all the characteristics of case 2.

In the light of this availability of low-cost feedstocks in certain countries, the markets for such substantial additions to world capacity become important. The package put together in cases 2 and 3 involves the acquisition by the local government corporation of existing marketing networks as well as marketing know-how. In the short term, the plan is to use the marketing networks of developed-country partners to distribute the products of local corporations. The longer-term strategy is to develop downstream industries in the country near the primary plants in order to increase the value-added locally as well as to ensure markets for the primary facilities.

Market Orientation

Assured market access proved to be an important factor in the investment decision in all 12 second-level and third-level projects (cases 4 through 15). It is useful to distinguish three separate kinds of market orientation: markets in developing countries; markets in high-growth developing countries (for example, Brazil and Mexico);

and regional markets. Regional markets in turn have two distinguishing features: they are large enough to support plants of optimum size or plants of sizes with very limited economies of scale and they involve either a free-trade area or a common market.

Protection from important competition constitutes a vital investment incentive in the developing-country markets. Exclusionary effective protection of the import-competing industry in the host country for a significant but not necessarily explicitly defined period is apparently a prerequisite to investment in productive capacity in these countries. Once this criterion has been met, other incentives and/or performance requirements are relatively insignificant, although, as in all cases, incentives are sought and performance requirements accepted unwillingly or matched with counteracting incentives.

Four projects are located in developing countries other than Brazil and Mexico, and in each case there was no fear of competition from foreign sources. In two of these cases, cases 5 and 14, the package of incentives and performance requirements involved price controls, and these have proved to be very damaging to the success of the project from the standpoint of the foreign companies involved. It may well be that, for them, the existence of price controls will prove, in the future, an unsurmountable disincentive — although price controls hardly constitute a performance requirement in the sense that they are trade-distorting. Case 11 does have a commitment to export 80 percent of output, but this was incurred voluntarily as a price paid to achieve 100 percent ownership under ANCOM rules. The current weakness of the market for the fungicide supplied by this particular plant has prevented the company from meeting the 80 percent export commitment, but the authorities seem to accept that a "best effort" is being made. The plant in question is a small unit in a worldwide market and was deemed to have good export potential because of its location in ANCOM. Case 12 is not yet in full operation. All four cases support the hypothesis that once the local market is safeguarded, investment incentives and performance requirements are not decisive — with the exception of the issue of price controls, whose damaging features were discovered *ex post*.

In Mexico and Brazil, continued petrochemical growth is anticipated. There is, then, a natural infant-industry argument for the establishment of small-scale plants in these countries to ensure a solid base in a market with excellent long-run potential. The five cases of investment in these two countries are all relatively small plants. Most are designed to be able to produce a variety of related petro-chemical products.

In a free-trade world, none of these plants would exist. The effective blockading of the domestic market is standard host-country procedure. In some instances, the protection was put in place when the facility was built, and in other cases protection was already in place. The bargaining leverage afforded the host country by the prospects of a protected market means that it need not offer any other incentives and can impose a set of performance requirements on the operation of the subsidiary.

The location of the plants *within* countries did prove sensitive to available packages designed to develop backward regions in some, but not all, instances. Such packages represent a standardized set of inducements intended to offset higher operating and/or capital costs in the laggard regions. The desirability of such a package to the foreign firm depends on the individual characteristics of the facility and its product. Cases 7 and 13 offer a clear example of the individuality of the decision-making process.

In three cases (cases 6, 9, and 11), the decision to invest was made on the basis of the ability of the local market to absorb the output of an optimum-size production unit, and no investment incentives were needed for the project to be undertaken. Projected demand growth was deemed adequate. The lack of need for protection or other incentives generally could be traced directly to the ability of the proposed unit to serve a market large enough to support a plant that achieves maximum economies of scale. For third-level products (cases 9 and 11), this does not necessarily involve a major commitment of capital, although in case 6 the commitment was large and the plant was world-scale.

In all three instances, the production unit was to serve a regional market with some form of preferential tariff treatment within the region. Projects 6 and 9 were located within the European Economic Community, and project 11, in ASEAN. These preferential arrangements do not represent investment incentives, because the protection offered against outside sources is quite conventional and not subject to negotiation on a project-specific basis. The economic views that prevail in the host countries are such that the imposition of performance requirements is not considered.

The character of the petrochemical industry places great emphasis on location-specific aspects. The emphasis on feedstock (and energy) availability in primary-level production and on markets in third-level production drastically inhibits the ability of incentives or of packages of incentives and performance requirements to affect the international location of plants. The location-specific qualities are such that related commercial factors will dominate any feasible package of incentives and requirements that a host country might offer — apart from the importance of an effectively protected market in developing countries. Competition among countries to attract investments in petrochemicals can, in practice, take place only among members of the same regional bloc for second- and third-level production units — because members of regional blocs all offer the same access to a given market — and among different sources of feedstocks.

Case 1 is an interesting example of the dominance of commercial factors in the location of a primary-petrochemical plant. The need for additional capacity having been decided, several sites were considered, including such disparate places as Trinidad, Tierra del Fuego, Edmonton, and Indonesia. The location decision was made on a wide range of factors that included such considerations as the anticipated size and growth of markets and the transportation of the products to those markets that were anticipated to experience the fastest growth. A secondary factor was the degree to which a new plant would permit a general reorientation of sourcing patterns among the company's production units and markets. These considerations supplemented such normal factors as costs, the availability of complementary inputs, political stability, or other positive features. There is no evidence of any significant competition in the form of investment incentives by individual countries within the group. Transportation costs and various other cost factors could have dominated differences in feedstock prices in case 1. One possible alternative investment site that was considered and examined in considerable depth concluded that the price of feedstock would have to be negative if the project, as outlined, was to be attractive in terms of the firm's normal rate-of-return criteria.

Countries within the EC do compete with each other for new projects, but only through regional incentive packages. The EC defines permissible packages of incentives and requires that any areas designated as backward and therefore authorized to offer such packages, be approved in Brussels. In addition, regional governments have some latitude to embellish the standard package of incentives, and, of course, the incentive offered in case 6 could not be precluded by any practical set of regulations. In the strict sense, then, countries within the EC do not systematically compete, but different potential sites in different countries can be weighed in a competitive sense. These distinctions are in any case not likely to be decisive on any international basis because, normally, each member country will have backward regions.

SUMMARY

This chapter has attempted to outline the role of investment incentives and performance requirements in investment decisions and consequently in production patterns with respect to the petrochemical industry. The first section of the chapter traced the development of the industry from its origins to its present state, focusing on its essential characteristics and its dimensions in a number of the major supplier countries. Different levels of petrochemical manufacturing activity were identified, each of which was presumed to have a set of optimum plant-location requirements. Manufacture of bulk or commodity petrochemicals, for example, was indicated as being drawn to the sources of feedstocks — either petroleum refineries or sources of natural gas — whereas manufacture of petrochemical products (whether or not for direct use) was indicated as being drawn to the sources of final demand. Given the capital intensity and scale requirements of much of today's petrochemical manufacturing activity, therefore, one would expect IIs and PRs to have relatively little to do with plant siting decisions except in instances where they are directly related to feedstock availability or assured access to markets. This was indeed found to be the case.

Table 5-10 summarizes the results of the 15 case studies evaluated here. Inspection of the table reveals the ways in which IIs and PRs appear to have had an influence on global production-location decisions in the petrochemicals sector. On the feedstocks side, incentive prices and concessionary financing were generally found merely to make possible the realization of a country's global comparative advantage and to offset elements that might otherwise thwart conversion into market performance. In some cases (for example, oil entitlements) the incentive proved to be of doubtful value because of market developments, even though it may have greatly enhanced the core attractiveness of the project as originally negotiated. On the market-access side, the key incentive is a high, assured level of effective protection against competitive imports from world-scale plants abroad, perhaps coupled to implicit guaranties against domestic competition that might erode profitability. There is little doubt that significant distortions of trade and production patterns result here — the outcome of traditional commercial policy considerations (effective protection) coupled to foreign direct investment flows that enable the country to get started in the industry concerned.

Beyond these two investment incentives — subsidized inputs and effective protection — a wide variety of IIs, both automatic and discretionary, was found in every project examined. In each case the firm involved was more than willing to capture the benefits and sometimes negotiated hard for the best possible terms. But in no case did these measures appear to be determining in *international* location decisions, although *interregional* decisions did appear to be affected, for example, Brazil, EC, Mexico, and South Korea. Indeed, a number of firms were rather strong in their insistence that investment incentives are permitted to play no substantive role in project decisions and associated assessments of project viability. Unless a project makes sense on its fundamentals, it is not undertaken. The assurance of a protected domestic market was rarely viewed as an investment incentive in this context, even though the resulting profitability profile of a project is just as artificial and could also be subject to policy change as in the case of other types of investment incentives. It remains unclear why this difference in perceptions exists.

With the exception of statutory performance requirements such as earnings remittance limits, local hiring targets, and ownership restrictions, no PRs of major significance appear to influence trade and investment patterns in the industry. Nevertheless, a number of cases involving export targets were encountered, the results of which probably had an effect on trade flows in the industry. In a number of cases such exports might not have materialized because of production cost levels not particularly competitive with those at alternative sites. However, the general impression is that the overall influence of such PRs is relatively minor. Much more important is a variety of disincentives (price controls, profit ceilings, bureaucratic red tape, corruption) that are of a general nature and may affect foreign investors in any industry with reference to the countries concerned.

In sum, if one were asked from the evidence available here to evaluate the influence of investment incentives and performance requirements on world trade and investment flows and production patterns in the industry, the basic results of the study could be captured in Table 5-11. The top half of the table indicates the projects for which the dominant influence affecting the investment decision is global, national, and regional markets, derived from a natural comparative advantage, firm-specific advantages, or strategic considerations. The bottom half of the table indicates those investments in which any net incentive (or disincentive) influenced (a) the project's approval, (b) its country location, or (c) its regional location within a nation (or customs union).

Once again, the importance of market protection and, to a lesser extent, feedstock concessions in decision (b) is evident. At the same time, both commodity and factor incentives played a role in decision (c). In no case was decision (a) affected by net incentive packages.

The study of the petrochemical industry did not uncover any evidence of competition among countries in other regional blocs competing for given projects, although it seems inevitable that interdependence must be recognized in the formulation of standard packages. ASEAN might be an interesting area in which to make such a comparison.

NOTES

1. OECD, *The Petrochemical Industry: Trends in Production and Investment to 1985* (Paris: OECD, 1979).

2. Most notably Shell, British Petroleum, and Exxon.

3. The company has recently been reregistered as a public limited company and will now be known as Imperial Chemical Industries, PLC.

4. In 1977 production shares were United States, 27.9 percent; Germany, 9.2 percent; France, 5.2 percent; United Kingdom, 5.9 percent; and Japan, 11.5 percent.

5. OECD, *The Petrochemical Industry*, p. 7.

6. OECD, *The Petrochemical Industry*, pp. 12-15.

7. The *Economist*, July 3, 1982.

8. Tracy Murray, *International Trade in Petrochemical Products*, report to UNCTAD and UNIDO (mimeo.), October 1981.

TABLE 5-11
Summary of Influence of Incentives and Performance Requirements

	Decisions by Cases		
Short-Run Profit	International Unified Market	Country	Subnational Region
I. Economic			
A. General: Natural comparative advantage	none	1, 10, 12	1
B. Firm-specific: (economies of transportation)	11	11, 15	13
II. Strategic (long-run)			
A. Corporate	6, 9	none	none
B. Government	none	none	none
III. Net Incentive			
A. Commodity			
1. Inputs	none	2, 3	4, 7, 8
2. Market protection	none	4, 5, 7, 8, 13, 14, 15	none
B. Factor			
1. Incentive offered	none	15	2, 3, 6, 15
2. In absence of factor incentives	none	6, 9	9
Not Relevant	1, 2, 3, 4, 5, 7, 8, 10, 12, 13, 14, 15	none	5, 10, 11, 12, 14

9. In New Jersey, the second largest petrochemical state, it was estimated that 63,075 tons of pollutants entered the atmosphere in 1978.

10. In this context a new venture can mean a new product only. It does not necessarily mean that the firm is establishing itself in the host country for the first time or that a new joint-venture partner was involved.

11. Note that the company withdrew from the project in late 1982, citing worldwide overcapacity in ethylene.

12. In the course of interviews conducted, the dissatisfaction with the local government partners was repeated with much the same sentiment. The firm in question no longer considers the country to be a potential investment location. Indeed, as of the end of 1982 it had sold all its holdings and withdrawn from the country — the company had been the country's largest single foreign investor.

13. See Robert E. Baldwin, *The Multilateral Trade Negotiations: Towards Greater Liberalization* (Washington: American Enterprise Institute, 1979), esp. pp. 20-21.

14. James E. Meade, *Trade and Welfare* (London: Oxford University Press, 1955).

6

Summary and Conclusions

Stephen E. Guisinger

This study addressed three broad questions regarding foreign investment:

1. Do countries compete for foreign investment?
2. Are host-country incentives effective in attracting foreign investment?
3. Do performance requirements imposed by host countries alter either investment or operational decisions of foreign investors?

The study was conducted by a team of consultants who interviewed government officials of ten countries, both developed and developing, and representatives of more than 30 multinational companies. The team selected 74 investment projects in four industries — automobiles, computers, food products, and petrochemicals — for intensive review.

In brief, the study team found that competition does exist and that incentives are effective. The team also found that performance requirements do affect investment and operational decisions of foreign investors, although the influence of performance requirements appears uneven across industries and countries.

This study of incentives and disincentives differs from others chiefly in that it uses a comparative framework across countries, rather than a longitudinal or descriptive study of individual countries. The importance of competition cannot be directly inferred from studies that examine each country in isolation. The comparative

313

framework permits assessment of the common elements of strategies, but at a cost of the rich detail and historical perspective that individual studies provide. Hence this study should be viewed as a complement to existing research.

COMPETITION FOR FOREIGN INVESTMENT

The study team found that countries compete for foreign investment in much the same way that manufacturers compete for market shares. Using the parallel between markets for products and the "market" for foreign investment, the team found that countries compete in three separate "markets": one for investments oriented toward the domestic market of a single host country; one for investments oriented toward a common market; and one for investments to produce for the worldwide export market. Countries — the "sellers" — supply investment sites and price these sites through a variety of incentives, formulating different strategies for each of the three markets because the competition varies in each. The most intense competition was found among member countries of a common market; the least intense competition was found for investment in production to serve a single host-country market.

The degree of competition for foreign investment a country faces shapes its strategies to attract and control foreign investment. For example, the study team found that the greater the competition, the less able were countries to impose performance requirements. Figure 6-1 depicts the factors that shape foreign investment strategies: intensity of competition, combined with national constraints, influences choices of strategic elements. These choices constitute a foreign investment strategy. If a country competes in more than one of the three "markets," it may adopt different strategies in each.

The combinations possible among the external factors and the market orientation of the foreign investment strategy produce a far greater number of strategies than can be summarized in this report. Still, a few examples help to illustrate the effects of the forces represented in the diagram. A small, experienced, industrialized country active in an intensely competitive market for common market investments is likely to display a strategy composed of the following elements:

1. Exclusive reliance on factor instruments of protection, such as cash grants
2. Relatively high levels of incentives
3. Reliance on explicit policies
4. Few explicit performance requirements and, therefore, little linking of incentives with disincentives
5. A great variety of incentive instruments
6. High selectivity among industries in terms of incentive levels
7. A high degree of discrimination among firms
8. Very active promotion
9. Concentration on provision of services
10. High degree of centralized control over promotion and incentive-granting activities

By contrast, a large, advanced, and experienced country actively seeking foreign investments in the same market will tend toward the following set of choices among these same elements. In general, the greater the intensity of competition, the more closely will large countries approximate small-country strategies with the exception of elements 3 and 4 in this list, for which the differences will be accentuated:

1. Principally factor protection but some use of implicit commodity protection
2. Relatively high levels of incentives
3. Mixture of implicit and explicit policies
4. Some performance requirements directly linked to incentives
5. Moderate to great variety in incentive instruments
6. Moderate selectivity among industries
7. Moderate discrimination among firms
8. Limited promotion
9. Limited provision of services
10. Decentralized administrative control

In general, smaller countries have the advantage of centralized control over all aspects of foreign investment policy; as a result small countries are capable of much finer tuning and faster response to new opportunities, often adopting new instruments and new methods of promotion that larger countries subsequently emulate to some degree. But larger countries have the advantage of bargaining

FIGURE 6-1
Determinants of a Country's Strategies to Attract and Control Foreign Investors

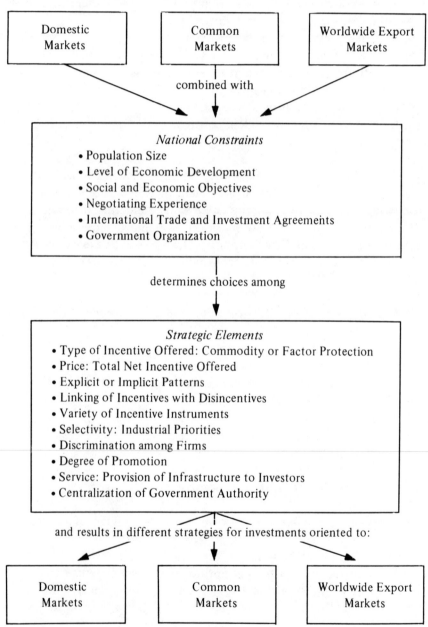

Intensity of Competition for Investments Oriented to:

| Domestic Markets | Common Markets | Worldwide Export Markets |

combined with

National Constraints
- Population Size
- Level of Economic Development
- Social and Economic Objectives
- Negotiating Experience
- International Trade and Investment Agreements
- Government Organization

determines choices among

Strategic Elements
- Type of Incentive Offered: Commodity or Factor Protection
- Price: Total Net Incentive Offered
- Explicit or Implicit Patterns
- Linking of Incentives with Disincentives
- Variety of Incentive Instruments
- Selectivity: Industrial Priorities
- Discrimination among Firms
- Degree of Promotion
- Service: Provision of Infrastructure to Investors
- Centralization of Government Authority

and results in different strategies for investments oriented to:

| Domestic Markets | Common Markets | Worldwide Export Markets |

power, especially in the case of foreign investments oriented toward domestic import substitution. Control of commodity protection and access of investors to the domestic market permit larger countries to make greater use of linkages between performance requirements and incentives, cross-subsidizing exports from rents generated by protection to import-substituting investments.

Competition among countries for foreign investment, especially among developed countries, has often been almost exclusively associated with higher levels of incentives. Although it is undoubtedly true that the "price" paid for foreign investments through incentives is a principal instrument of competitive strategy, this study has emphasized that it is not the only one. Besides raising incentive levels, competition has spawned an array of diverse incentive instruments. This diversity has permitted governments to differentiate their "product" by differentiating their price. Diversity has also served to obscure overall levels of incentives from competitor governments and even — unintentionally — from the intended beneficiaries themselves. In addition, competition has led to greater discrimination among firms, as governments seek to provide only the minimum incentive necessary to induce foreign firms to invest.

In sum, competition has had multiple effects on competitive strategies. Collective attempts to limit incentives without addressing the other elements of competitive strategy may not contain competitive forces. Moreover, some elements of strategy, most notably promotion and provision of services, may have few of the self-defeating aspects of the other elements. It stands to reason that competitive strategies designed around these elements will generate less friction among competing countries and less obvious welfare loss than some of the other elements.

EFFECTIVENESS OF INCENTIVES

The study found that in each of the three "markets" for foreign investment, incentives were effective in altering the location decisions of foreign investors. In two-thirds of the 74 cases surveyed, the choice of country was influenced by host government policy. For investments oriented toward domestic markets, incentives take the form of commodity protection. For common market investments, incentives are granted through instruments of factor protection, although on occasion implicit commodity protection — the potential exercise of a government's procurements powers or trade-disrupting actions directed specifically to the firm — affected the firm's location decision. In the market for investments to produce for worldwide export, the influence of policy measures in intercountry choices was less powerful, but still important.

The standard of comparison used in determining effectiveness points out an important asymmetry in the effectiveness of policy measures to influence investment location. Effectiveness was determined by comparing a country's attractiveness to investors under current incentive (and disincentive) policies with the hypothetical conditions that would prevail if a country removed all incentive policies as before. It is more realistic to assume that the policies of other countries will remain constant if a country lowers, rather than raises, its net incentive to foreign investment. If a country raises its incentives, it is likely to provoke a similar increase in the incentives offered by its competitors, nullifying the relative advantage the country was attempting to secure. This asymmetry is characteristic of the so-called prisoner's dilemma, a stalemate in which independent action produces far less satisfactory results than binding collective action.

Because there are so many kinds of incentives and because governments tailor incentives to each firm, the measurement of incentive levels between countries or over time has become an exacting task, requiring vast amounts of information. Furthermore, obtaining this information is complicated by the confidential nature of some of the investment agreements. In international forums, this measurability is often referred to as *transparency*. Not only is transparency a subjective concept, but also, almost by definition, degrees of transparency are difficult to evaluate. The study team found no indication of any substantial movement toward greater transparency of incentive policies in the countries surveyed; indeed, the reverse appeared to be true. Analysis of the ways that competitive forces operate on country strategies supports this observation. The more intense the competition, the greater the movement of country incentive policies away from transparency. Especially within the European Common Market, where over the past 25 years a relatively small number of instruments of commodity protection have been replaced by a broad array of factor protection instruments, transparency seems to be losing, rather than gaining, ground.

EFFECTIVENESS OF PERFORMANCE REQUIREMENTS

Performance requirements — such as minimum value of exports or a minimum amount of domestic content — were instrumental in altering the location of four of the 74 cases surveyed in the study. In two of these cases, multinational companies had been manufacturing in the host country before the performance requirements were adopted; in the other two cases, a market presence had been established through exports. In these four cases, the governments required the firms to increase exports from or to reduce imports into the host countries if they wished to maintain their access to these markets. The linking of trade-related performance requirements to continued enjoyment of domestic protection creates an implicit subsidy to exports and import substitution, while lowering the firm's overall protection.

A large number of the investments included in the sample — 38 of the 74 — were subject to explicit requirements regarding minimum domestic content or exports. Of the remaining cases, some were subject to indirect performance requirements because the incentives granted were made in proportion to the net trade balance implicit in the original project proposal. The influence of these performance requirements varied across industries and regions. In the automobile industry, nine of the 12 projects studied were subject to performance requirements. It is evident that performance requirements increased exports and reduced imports of automobile products and parts in the host countries that have imposed performance requirements. The automobile investments most subject to performance requirements were those oriented toward the home market of large countries. By contrast, computer investments in common market countries have been subject to very few performance requirements. Thus, for some industries in some regions, performance requirements have affected trade flows.

COMPARISONS BETWEEN DEVELOPED
AND DEVELOPING COUNTRIES

Differences in the propensities of countries to grant incentives and impose performance requirements can be explained by underlying factors such as country size and variations in the intensity of competition in the markets for foreign investment in which countries operate, depicted in Figure 6-1. Differences in the experiences of developed and developing countries with regard to performance requirements can be traced to variations in these factors. Thus, a greater degree of competition was observed among developed countries because countries in this category are more likely to be members of a common market. Very little direct competition was observed between developed and developing countries for proposed foreign investment ventures. Indirect competition between developed and developing countries did occur when developing countries used trade barriers to initiate local production of goods previously exported from developed countries.

Differences between developed and developing countries also can be observed in incentives and performance requirements. Factor protection was more commonly employed by the developed countries primarily because the ability to provide commodity protection was proscribed by the rules of the EC to which the developed countries in the sample belonged. Performance requirements were more frequent in the developing countries of the sample because the requirements for successful application of performance requirements — a large, protected internal market — were more often found among the group of developing than among developed countries surveyed by the study team. However, it bears repeating that developed countries achieve much the same results using implicit performance requirements imposed through selective incentive granting that developing countries achieve with explicit performance requirements. Thus, the study team could not determine whether the trade-distorting effects of government interventions to increase exports and reduce imports were more pronounced in developed or developing countries.

Index

Africa, 68, 74
ANCOM, 292-93, 297, 299, 305. (*See also* South America)
Andean Compact Group, 82, 165
Argentina, 262
ASEAN, 148, 292, 306, 310. (*See also* Asia)
Asia, 43, 63, 67, 68, 74, 91, 150, 178, 218, 245, 290, 292-94; and existing markets, 164; Japanese competition in, 183; market access, 164
automobile industry, 27, 29, 41-42, 48, 52-53, 72, 96-167; aspects of, 146-50; and Austria, 113; balance of payments, 166; capital conservation, 98, 108; and changing patterns, 96-98; employment, 97; entry timing, 165; environmental standards, 42, 108, 114; exports/imports, 148, 165; f.o.b. and cif values, 132; greenfield sites, 113; import restrictions, 164; incentive packages, 142, 108-14, [absence or removal of, 150-57; influence of, 125-35; linking, 163]; infrastructure, 42; investment costs, 125; Japanese firms, 41, 43; labor cost differentials, 107; land, 125; local sales, 106; local suppliers, 42, 43, 139-41; market access, 142, 162, 163, 165; mechanization/labor costs, 146; mobility of production facilities, 42; multinational enterprises (MNE), 97-98, 101, 124, 125, 142, 158-61; production cycle, 101; profitability, 107, 149-50; ranking of factors, 142-46; renegotiation and counterproposal, 155-56; R & D, 102; site location, 165; status of prestige, 42; supplier problems, 134; types of products, 165; U.S. and Japan, 97; world car concept, 98
Australia, 68, 80, 248

Badisch (BASF), 247
Bayer, A. G., 247
Belgium, 68, 81
Big Three, 142
Brazil, 62, 80, 82, 84, 178, 185, 188, 196, 201-02, 205-06, 262, 309; coffee exports, 73; and economies of scale, 206; export/import restrictions, 205-06; export

incentives, 87, 201-02; operational restrictions, 205; petrochemical market orientation, 304-05; R & D, 206; rules and national security, 201; transfer of technology, 206, 218. (*See also* related industries)
British Petroleum, 255
Business and Industry Advisory Committee (BIAC), 50
Buy America Act, 158

capacity utilization, 16, 40, 296
cash grants, 19, 24-26, 34, 42, 125. (*See also* related industries)
CEDI tax rebates (*see* Mexico, Decrees)
Chile, 93
Chrysler, 162
"circuit board stuffing," 183
Cities Service, 255
COBRA, 201
Common Market, 221. (*See also* Economic Communities)
competition, 162; exit barriers, 17; for foreign investment, 11-19; intensity determinants, 12-19; lack of differentiation, 17; prisoner's dilemma, 38, 318; switching costs, 17
computer industry, 24, 27, 29, 41, 43-45, 51, 53, 168-236; after-sale activities, 218; balance of payments, 221-22; components, 171, 172, 208, 213; cost reduction, 43; decisions, 190-91; defined, 168-69; duplicate investments, 178; EC, 192, 223; equipment, 173; expatriates and locals, 179; global strategies, 170; governmental policies, 169-70, 177-89, 193, 209; implied obligations, 208; integrated circuits, 171, 172; investment influence, lack of, 228; Japanese firms, 43-45, 187; leasing, 215; loans, 213; local markets, 196; local suppliers, 180, 181-82, 200, 219; local workforce, 197; low labor costs, 196; manufacturing, 178, 190, 216, 222; market access, 178, 180, 202, 204; overextension, 219; peripherals, 173, 183, 219; procurements, 181, 203-04; psychology of new firms, 222-23; R & D, 196; reduction of labor costs,

321

About the Authors

Stephen E. Guisinger, Ph.D., Professor and Program Director, International Management Studies, The University of Texas at Dallas, Richardson, Texas.

R. Hal Mason, Professor of International Business and Business Policy, Graduate School of Management, University of California, Los Angeles.

Neil Hood, Professor of Business Policy, University of Strathclyde.

Stephen Young, Senior Lecturer in International Business, University of Strathclyde.

Robert R. Miller, Professor, The Institute for International Business Analysis, College of Business Administration, The University of Houston, Houston, Texas.

H. Peter Gray, Professor of Economics, Rutgers University, New Brunswick, New Jersey.

Ingo Walter, Professor of Economics and Finance, Graduate School of Business Administration, New York University, New York, New York.